Try It This Way…

- An ordinary guy's guide to
extraordinary happiness.

J. Michael Curtis

authorHOUSE®

AuthorHouse™
1663 Liberty Drive
Bloomington, IN 47403
www.authorhouse.com
Phone: 1-800-839-8640

Published by AuthorHouse   9/11/2012

ISBN: 978-1-4772-5389-2 (sc)
ISBN: 978-1-4772-5388-5 (hc)
ISBN: 978-1-4772-5432-5 (e)

Library of Congress Control Number: 2012914019

*Any people depicted in stock imagery provided by Thinkstock are models,
and such images are being used for illustrative purposes only.
Certain stock imagery © Thinkstock.*

This book is printed on acid-free paper.

For Cole and Cade,

Two inspirational guys

Foreword

.

"I taught him everything he knows."
–Bev Curtis, April 2011

Preface and Introduction

One of my favourite Woody Allen quotes is "Life is full of misery, loneliness, and suffering - and it's all over much too soon." I'm not sure if that quote summarizes the human condition or not, but it has always made me wonder about it. I see the human condition as equal parts tragedy and heroism. Sometimes these days it's difficult to see life as a bowl of cherries. We have major issues at home and around the world. And as we get older, understanding life doesn't get any simpler. Although, in many ways, if you're willing to put in some effort in attempting to understand the human experience, it can become increasingly more fascinating.

That's a fairly sassy Foreword from Bev, isn't it? As you might imagine, I've had to be on my toes. In August 2011, Bev and I celebrated our fortieth wedding anniversary. We've raised two sons into healthy productive adulthood together. And we're helping guide two grandsons through early childhood. Actually, Bev *has* taught me a few things in the last forty years. And really, all modesty aside, in my 63 years I have learned a few things on my own too.

Ecclesiastes said there's nothing new under the sun. The greatest truths have been true for thousands of years. When you hear them and they fit for you, they seem like common sense. But sometimes just hearing them phrased in a new and different way brings them home to a depth of comprehension that sticks with you for the rest of your life. Some of the things I learned from Bev are in that category. They're a new way of expressing something you already know to be true, only now you know it in a new and fresher way. But some of the things I learned from Bev I had never considered before and hearing them from her for the first time profoundly changed my view.

I'm going to mention some of those lessons here and then expand on them a little during the book. Here are some of the most significant lessons I learned from Bev:

Everyone has a suggestion for someone else

Isn't this the truth? It's always easier to see someone else's shortcomings and quirks than it is to see our own. And aren't we generous with our advice and suggestions? And don't we mean well when we offer those helpful little hints for improvement? Haven't we all heard; "…maybe if you tried it a little more this way rather than that way, it would work better for you." Yes for sure everyone has a suggestion for someone else. We'll examine this principle in Part II of the book.

Distribute your money lovingly

This may seem counter-intuitive at first but when you realize the value and the truth in this principle, it can change your life and set you free. If your car needs repair, you need to spend that money anyway, so why begrudge it? Why not spend it as cheerfully as you can? What are you hanging onto when you grip your money so tight the Queen[1] cries for mercy?

Thoughts have power

Wow this is so true. We manifest into our lives what we think about and concentrate on, so watch what you say and watch what you think. If you concentrate on poverty, that's what you'll have. If you concentrate on abundance, that's what you'll have too. Another of Bev's mantras is "concentrate on what you want more of".

The material in this little book comes from a variety of sources. Most of the ideas expressed here are my own. Others come from great thinkers and writers both recent and ancient. When I express my thoughts about one of these ideas, whenever possible I cite the source. One of the benefits of writing a book of this type is that you don't need to conduct a lot of tedious time-consuming research. You can pretty much sit at your keyboard and

---

[1] I offer this explanation for our American friends. We have the Queen of England on some of our paper currency, e.g. the $20 bill.

hack away. How wonderful – a book about my own ideas and beliefs! Who's a better authority than I to write such an important book?

And maybe this statement ought to go without saying, but I endorse all the ideas, rules, and guidelines I have described in this book. If I don't agree with someone else's position, it doesn't appear here.

Before we get much further I want to tell you something about me that I believe is relevant to how and why I came to write this book. Shortly after my 14th birthday, my dad shot and killed himself. He had been battling alcoholism for years and near the end that battle wasn't going so well for him. He had become unemployable and chronically depressed. I guess he felt that he had no hope for the future and that we'd be better off without him.

His sudden and tragic death was traumatic enough but the cold and dysfunctional aftermath was at least as influential in forming my adolescent world-view and messing me up rather badly for many years. I have an older brother and an older sister. The two of them are close in age – less than two years difference – but a gap of 6 ½ years exists in age between my brother and me. At the time of my father's death, my sister was a newlywed and my brother a medical student. Both my siblings had busy, young adult lives at the time. When some families encounter tragedy, they are drawn closer in mutual support. But for us…nah, not so much. When my dad died, my nuclear family splintered in four different directions. My mom was still there, but after all that she had been through for so many years, she was in no condition to offer much in the way of emotional support to me. Being just 14 and alone, trying to cope with the tragedy left me vulnerable and scarred. I was just a kid who played outside on the street with my buddies. I had many lonely and painful nights staring at the ceiling in the dark, wondering what I had done wrong.

So there I was at age 14, left virtually alone to sort out this mess and to figure out adolescence on my own. What a joke. I cannot exaggerate how alone and unsupported I felt from that tragic day forward. I know now from having raised two sons, how important a father can be to a boy in adolescence, in providing counsel and support, and in demonstrating integrity and adherence to values. But that was not my dharma. Nope, none of that warm fuzzy supportive family stuff for me. Tough it out, dude.

The bright side of this complex of negative experience is that it helped turn me into a seeker. Since I had been so tossed around emotionally, I became interested in the human condition. When I matured, I decided to develop patience and compassion, to feel less anger and to become less judgemental. Many years after my father's sudden death, when I was in my 40s, as a result of my psychological work with a couple of counsellors, I pieced together a history of what had happened to him and why he turned out the way he did. As an adult, and as a result of investing in this hard work, I came to appreciate my father's experiences and the effects they had had on him. At this more mature stage of my understanding, my father was no longer an evil cartoon character; he became a warm-blooded man, with human frailties as well as some very positive attributes. Before he went to war, my father had been an energetic and optimistic young man, wanting a future in hotel management. He was a natural athlete and a natural musician. He could play any sport well and could play the piano by ear. He was bright; university educated[2], and had a great sense of humour. And I think the attribute that most contributed to his tragic downfall was that he was sensitive.

In the second decade of the 21st century, it's eminently cool for a man to be sensitive. But I'm not so sure it was that case in the 1930s and 1940s. So this bright, sensitive, athletic, and musical young man with a great future in front of him went off to fight for his country in World War II. I think the horrors of war were too much for my dad. He took up self-medicating with alcohol and came home from the war broken, disillusioned, and alcoholic. Then I came along as a baby-boomer in 1949. According to what I have pieced together, I was supposed to be the element that would bring my parents back together and restore happiness and harmony to our humble home. No pressure at all.

I tell this story so you'll have an inkling of where I come from and why I would choose to write a book like this. Because of these experiences I became keenly interested in human potential and in working hard to overcome emotional obstacles. The easy way is to shut down, give up, and blame external influences for your failures to reach potential. Any fool can become cynical and bitter; that's the path of least resistance. But I know that the human spirit has too much strength and resiliency for that sort of cop-out to life.

Most of the material in this book comes from my own long-term observation of the human condition. Like a lot of guys, when I was in my 30s most of my focus was on raising little kids, earning a living, and providing for my family. Bev and I raised two sons, Steven born in 1978

---

[2] Being university educated was unusual in those days, especially for a young man coming from a working class background in rural Manitoba.

and Robert born in 1981. When I was in my 30s and Steve and Rob were little, that was an exhausting but rewarding time. But anyone who has raised kids knows that you don't have a lot of quiet time for reflection when they're little. The upside is that you're packing away all kinds of rich experiences that you can draw on and learn from later.

And also like a lot of guys, when I was in my 40s my focus was on helping teenagers cope with all the complications, joys, and confounding difficulties of the teen years. That's also a time when many of us take on increasing responsibility and stress in the workplace. So during that decade many of us don't have a lot of quiet time for reflection either. But once more you're packing away all kinds of rich experiences that you can draw on and learn from later. Being in your 40s with teens is a very different time than being in your 30s with young kids.

In my own case, during my 40s I began to take a passionate interest in adult learning and personal development. I read books and listened during my commute to learning tapes from authors and thinkers like Stuart Wilde, Deepak Chopra, Stephen Covey, Joan Borysenko, Sonia Choquette, Wayne Dyer, Brian Tracey and others. I began teaching adults in the evenings and gained some credentials in training. I created a sole proprietorship dedicated to developing adult potential, through which I would lead seminars and workshops. I did this while working full time at a professional management job and helping guide my teenage sons. With input from a couple of professional counsellors, and on my own, I also began to examine some childhood and adolescent issues that were hampering my personal growth. It was an awakening time for me.

Like a lot of guys, when I was in my 50s I had young adult children and entered a period of increased responsibility and authority in the workplace. Now I did have more time for quiet reflection and contemplating the experiences I had had in past years. During my 50s, a lot of those experiences began to make sense to me and I began to distil them into lessons, rules and guidelines, i.e. what to do and what not to do if you want to have a good life and make good use of the time you have.

That's what this book is about.

When I turned 60 I began to think more seriously about retirement than I had before. For the last three years of my working full-time, I trained in guitar building, care, and repair under a local luthier. Currently I operate a small guitar and bass care and repair business from an in-home shop. I also work one day a week as a courtesy shuttle driver for a car rental company. And we have our two grandsons, who are a regular source of joy and amusement. But compared to the pace of life I used to have, now I have time to write this book.

In this book you'll find a mixture of practical, simple and sometimes funny suggestions as well as some more serious material. That's on purpose. While I believe what I say in this book, I want to keep it light most of the time, so when you come to the serious meaty stuff, you'll be in the mood to digest it. You may discern some metaphors and themes running through the book. If so, that's a good thing. It means I've been successful in conveying my own personality through the material. For example, when I recommend some good practices for caring for your motor vehicle, the attitudes and values behind those sorts of practices have broader value and application to other parts of your life as well. When I recommend that you change your oil regularly, keep your tank half full, and when you wash your vehicle, actually work at it rather than just spraying water at it, sure I am talking about motor vehicle maintenance. But I'm also talking about a general approach to life. Feel free to search for, discover, and interpret metaphorical passages for your own meaning.

I've been told all my life that I'm funny. I take that as a compliment. I believe a sense of humour is an important attribute for enjoying life and learning from it. Without a sense of humour you can become a grim individual. I've never wanted that.

So what gives me the right to write down and explain these recommendations? Like, where do I get the nerve? What wanton hubris is this[3]?

Well, that takes me to one of my rules, i.e. *power and authority are there for the taking*. Given reasonable assumptions, you realize and exercise what authority you can by how you behave (see Working for a Living). In this life, in the workplace or any other place, no supreme granter of authority will ever come up to you with a baton, touch you on the shoulder and say, "I hereby grant you the power and authority to write a book on guidelines and recommendations for living a good and purposeful life."

One spring evening in 2011, Bev and I were having dinner with our son Steve and his wife Jill. I expressed one of my opinions and Jill said, "You should write a book." Until then, writing a book hadn't occurred to me. But with that comment the seed was planted and started to think about it. Naturally I wondered whether I was qualified to write a book. Then I realized that this was one of those situations where I needed to

---

[3] That's a quote from Tommy Lee Jones in the movie "The Client" (1994). It's one of my favorite movie quotes, largely because I like the word "hubris".

step up and step out of my comfort zone. After some reflection, I granted myself the authority I needed and decided to write this little book. I don't claim to be any kind of sage or expert. But at the same time, I do know a thing or two about making good and bad decisions, and the consequences that result.

If I come across as judgemental in places, I don't mean to seem that way, well most of time anyway. It's pretty hard not to seem judgemental with subject matter like what I have chosen here. Mostly, I'm just providing my observations and basing my recommendations on what I have found to work. In some cases, like when I recommend you stay away from gambling I admit to being judgemental. In those cases, I hope you can forgive me.

I hope you like this book. I hope you find funny the parts I intended to be funny. And I hope you take seriously the parts I intended to be more serious. Please read the footnotes. They're more than just references. I intended them to be part of the book and I make some points in the footnotes. Above all, I hope you pay the bookseller for this book. If you're reading this in a bookstore, don't shop-lift my book; that would be wrong.

Part I:
Lighter Fare

Part I is a collection of practical recommendations. I picked these topics carefully because I thought they were fairly light and easy to relate to. They comprise a gentle and easy entry into the book. I also picked them because I figured they were good bases for metaphorical extrapolation. If you take care of your motor vehicle you might take care of other things and your relationships in general. If you enjoy camping and the great outdoors, you will likely be sensitive to the environment and how your behaviour and choices can impact it. And if you're sensitive to that, maybe you'll be sensitive to how your behaviour and choices affect the other people around you too. See what I mean?

Before we get into the material, I want to ask you an important question. Did you read the Introduction completely? Are you one of those readers who skip the preface and introduction because you want to get right into it? If you haven't read the Introduction, please do so now. Reading the Introduction will help you get the most value and enjoyment from this book.

Driving and Car Maintenance

Go ahead and accuse me of simplistic thinking if you like, but I think I can tell something about a person by the way they take care of their vehicle and the way they behave behind the wheel. Of course what I think doesn't matter. What matters is what's going on for you. Having said that, I suspect that how you care for your motor vehicle and how you drive might provide some clues to your inner state.

We spend a lot of time in our vehicles. Don't ruin that time by being angry at other drivers or impatient with traffic and red lights. Try to remember that the people in all those other cars and trucks are not there just to irritate you and obstruct your way. Actually, they're trying to get somewhere else just like you are. They breathe air and bleed red just like you do.

A guy I know had an epiphany experience on this topic. He used to be an uptight, angry driver and hated his commute. One day it hit him "… those other drivers are just like me. They're just trying to get where they're going. They don't mean me any harm. In fact, we're connected…" Since that epiphany, he's been a changed man in traffic…and in life.

I had a similar but less dramatic experience and it's changed me too. I recall years ago that a light would go red in front of me, my stomach would tighten, as would my grip on the wheel and I would fume until I would start again. Sometimes I would look at older drivers who seemed to be completely calm and at peace, patiently waiting for the light to change back to green. I would wonder to myself, "I wonder whether I will ever be that way when I'm older, retired, and with lots of time on my hands."

Now I can answer "yes", because that is precisely how it is for me now. Part of it is simply being "…older, retired, and with lots of time on my hands." Part of it was training for my Class 4 license, which I needed to drive passengers for pay, as I do now as a shuttle driver in one of my current part-time occupations. When I contemplated earning my Class 4 license, I realized that I may have established some bad habits since 1965, when I got my driver's license.

So I enrolled with a driving school and told the teacher I wanted to train for a Class 4 license[4]. What an experience that was, taking driver training again after 45 years. It changed the way I drive. Believe it or not, now I actually obey traffic signs, the rules of the road, and speed limits. I guess now I drive like an old guy (only more alert), and I don't think that's a bad thing. My priority has changed from getting there fast to getting there safely – and without a ticket. Now I get there almost as fast, and I'm no longer a resentful, uptight, nervous wreck behind the wheel. It's much better this way.

Let's switch from the philosophy of driving attitudes to some practical rules on maintenance. We need to be able to rely on our vehicles. Treat them carefully and respectfully. Remember how thrilled you were with your first car when you bought it?

Change your oil every 5,000 km

Changing your oil regularly is the simplest and most effective thing you can do to maintain the long term health of your engine. So be religious about your oil changes. The easiest way to remember when your car is due for a change is to get your next change on a 5,000 km point. Then from there it will be easy to remember the next change due. So if your baby has 82,426 km, change the oil when you get to the 85,000 km point. Next change will be 90,000 km and so forth.

Prefer a garage to a drive-through oil change. You will likely need to make an appointment, but so what? Do it. If you take your car or truck to a garage rather than a drive-through, the staff will eventually get to know you and your car. I believe that if they know you and know your car, they will be much more likely to act in your best interest. The guys that work in the drive-through places will remain strangers and will almost always try to up-sell you on something you may not need.

Most shops offer some sort of "21 point inspection" along with your

---

[4] In Alberta, a Class 4 license is the lowest level for professional drivers. The holder of a Class 4 license can operate a taxi, limo, ambulance, or small bus and get paid for it.

oil change. That's a good way for you to find out if something else needs attention. If your car is getting an oil change at a garage and something else does need attention, you'll be in the right place to get it done. At a drive-through, you have guys that know how to change oil quickly. At a garage you have mechanics, who know how to take care of whatever your car needs.

Develop a business relationship with your service advisor

If you get your oil changes done at a garage, find one you like and go to the same garage for all your service needs. That way you will develop a business relationship with your service writer. Once you find a garage and service writer that you trust, treat him like you trust him. Very likely, he will act in accordance with that trust.

I've been doing this for years and it has worked well for me. I go to the same garage every time. I call the service manager by name and make sure I remind him of my name when I book the appointment. Before long, he knows me and my vehicles and we trust each other.

Early on in the relationship, sometimes I put them to the test a little. For example, I may be quite sure that my brakes are working fine and don't need any rotor or disk work. But when I book an oil change, I ask them to check the brakes at the same time. After the oil change is done, when I get a report that the brakes are fine with a recommendation we check them again in 6 months, I check off a little box mentally. That's the beginning of trust.

If you relocate or the shop changes ownership, you'll need to start over again. It's still worth it. Be a good customer. That means you don't question their assessments and you don't groan and complain about something on your bill costing $10 more than you thought it would. A good business relationship is a two-way street. You want good service? Try being a good customer. The next time your car won't start and is towed into their shop without an appointment, they might fix it up for you the same day.

Of course the above rules pertain to off-warranty work. If your vehicle is new, you'll need to get your servicing done at the dealership where you bought the car or another dealership that sells the same brand. When that's the case, you shouldn't have much to worry about anyway. If your vehicle is new, it shouldn't need much in the way of expensive repairs. If it does, your warranty will pay for it.

Keep your tank half full – drive on the top half of your tank

Driving with your tank at least half full provides the advantage of reducing the amount of dirt and crud in your engine. In cold winter weather, you have a greatly reduced likelihood of experiencing the heartbreak of your car's not starting because its gas line is frozen. Should you get stopped or stuck on a cold winter's night, you don't want your tank at 1/8, because you'll need to run the engine to stay warm and avoid freezing to death. Perhaps most importantly, you will have the psychological comfort that comes from knowing that your tank is at least half full. You have a reasonable driving range and you won't run out of gas.

And, if you happen to tend toward being a redneck, the value of your pickup truck increases when you fill 'er up.

Buying gasoline

This topic is interesting to many people. Like a lot of people, sometimes I feel like I'm being hosed[5] at the gas pump. It seems to me the gasoline sellers raise their prices when they feel like it, out of all reference to external forces like the price of a barrel of crude[6], and coincidentally in time for long weekends when a lot of us like to travel. In 2007 when a barrel of oil was about $150, gas sold for around $1.20/litre. Now a barrel of oil is around $100 yet gas still sells for $1.10. The price of a barrel of crude has dropped by 33% while the price of gasoline has dropped 8%. So clearly the price of crude is not the only determining factor in the price of gas.

If only one supplier raised his prices while the others stood pat, I might believe that it's all a free market, like they claim. But when Esso, Petro Canada, Shell, Husky and all the off-brand sellers all raise their prices on the same day by the same amount, so that every supplier has the same price all the time, I kind of wonder if some sort of collusion isn't at play. Hmmm…think so?

And have you noticed that when prices go up, they shoot up by 9

---

[5] No pun intended…well maybe a little.
[6] Sometimes gas prices go up because the price of a barrel of crude goes up. The difference here is that the price goes up and stays up. I'm talking in this section about the other type of price fluctuation; i.e. the kind the oil companies impose to maximize their profits.

or 10 cents a litre? They stay steady for a few days or weeks, then begin to inch back down again a penny or two at a time. That pattern seems to repeat itself over and over. That factor also makes me suspect some monkey business. Around here at least, Wednesday or Thursday are the days when prices shoot up. Why not a Monday or Tuesday? Nope – got to be Wednesday or Thursday. What a racket.

Here's what I recommend, gentle reader. Keep your eye on the price of gas in your area and see if you can discern a pattern. When prices edge down, keep your tank full. When prices shoot up by 9 or 10 cents a litre, you'll have a full tank. Don't be in a hurry to fill up when prices are high, unless it's -20 deg C or colder. Chances are you may not need to buy again until prices start to drop.

I get a charge out of buying gas when prices are down. That may seem petty to you. If it does, ignore my recommendation. But I respond the way I do because I feel manipulated by the gas companies. When I buy low, I feel I'm maintaining some small shred of control. Pathetic.

In Part II in my chapter on Finances, I'm going to encourage you to distribute your money lovingly. What I'm saying here may seem to contradict that position. Not really. The corollary to distributing your money lovingly is not to give it to someone you don't want to animate with it. We all have to buy gasoline. We can buy less by driving conservatively in good vehicles that consume less gasoline. But in our culture, most of us have to buy gasoline. Watching the prices, discerning the pattern, and buying low whenever you can is the closest you can get to not animating the price-manipulating gasoline suppliers any more than you have to.

When things are broken or worn out, fix or replace them

If your windshield is cracked, replace it. Don't drive around with a cracked windshield. It's a safety hazard and it's bad for your self-esteem. When someone else gets into your car, they're going to think you don't value your personal environment enough to replace your cracked windshield. But more important than what someone else thinks is what do you think? What, a cracked windshield isn't worth replacing? You just look through a cracked windshield every day when you drive? Value yourself and value your driving environment. You wouldn't walk around with torn clothes. Don't drive around with a cracked windshield.

Similarly, if your wipers wear out, replace them. The garage where you get your oil changed will change the blades for you while they're doing the oil change. Where we live, with snow in the winter and rain in the summer, we need windshield wipers that are in perfect condition. Otherwise you get those irritating patterns on your windshield where the wipers don't contact properly.

Cheap wipers are around $20. The best ones are around $50. I suggest you buy the best ones. They're Teflon coated, work better, and last longer. If you can't bring yourself to spend $50 on a wiper blade then replace the $20 ones annually when you have your fall oil change.

When your tires are worn out, replace them. I don't need to spend much time on this topic because the value is clear and obvious. Worn tires are a safety hazard. Your car is much easier and responsive to drive when the tires are in good shape and properly inflated. All tires have a mileage rating. For example, when you buy them, the manufacturer will recommend that they're good for 80,000 km or something of that sort. Your odometer reading will be on the bill when you buy a new set of tires. Keeping track of the mileage on your tires just isn't that difficult. Also, you or your garage will be able to tell just by visual inspection when it's time for new tires.

I knew a guy who thought he couldn't afford new tires so he thought he'd wait until fall rather than buying them on sale in the spring. During summer, of course, he had a flat and had to wait two hours for a tow truck. Since he didn't have an AMA membership (too expensive) he was out two hours and had to pay for a tow and four tires at regular price. That was not a happy outcome for him.

And when your vehicle's body becomes dented or scratched, bite the bullet and get that damage fixed also.

I shake my head at folks who wait until they decide to sell their vehicle to have necessary little things like a broken windshield and worn wipers replaced. They pay the same price that they would have paid had they done the jobs when they needed to be done. They enjoy none of the benefits; those accrue to the new buyer. Something is wrong with that picture. Value yourself enough to take care of routine maintenance so you can reap the benefits yourself, rather than the person you sell to. Keep your vehicle in top shape. You're worth it.

But the cracked windshield, worn wiper blades and tires are just examples. I've mentioned wiper blades and windshields. These are examples of components that irritate you when they aren't right. But more seriously, your vehicle has key components that affect your safety on the road. This category of components included brakes, tires, and steering. I suggest you don't cut corners on you key components. The point here is that I am recommending the value of preventative maintenance. Not investing in keeping your vehicle in top operating condition is a false economy. If something's going to go, it's going to go anyway. It's going to cost you either way and it will likely cost more if you ignore a problem and something bad happens. You don't want a preventable failure causing an accident or emergency.

I remember an old TV ad where the mechanic looks into the camera and says, "You can pay me now...or you can pay me later." His meaning is clear. Keep your vehicle in top mechanical condition. You spend a lot of time in it. You want it to be safe and easy to operate. And preventative maintenance is economical when compared to the cost of repairs.

Take care of your vehicle. Its condition and appearance are a reflection of yourself. I have a 14 year-old Nissan Pathfinder. People often tell me that it looks like new. And it's true. It runs like new too. But that's not an accident and it's not luck. It's a direct result of how I have cared for it, with time, effort, and some money. The older it gets, the fonder of it I become. I like to think that the Pathfinder is like me – an oldie but a goody.

Stay calm and be a good driver

When another driver cuts you off or won't let you in when you want to change lanes, don't take it personally. This is the time to detach and keep your ego in check. I used to tell my sons when they were teens about mastering their inner selves, "don't let other people control your emotional state." Well, if I may say so, that's good advice for teens in school and pretty much for anyone any time. But it sure applies to all of us when we're driving.

You can't control how other people drive, but you can control how you respond. If you don't like the way another driver is driving, just let him in and bless him on his way. Suspend your judgement and concentrate on your own driving.

Don't follow too close. If you leave one extra car length's space in front of your vehicle, you'll arrive at your destination about one second later. Of course, if you leave extra space in front of you in traffic, you can expect that another driver will cut in front of you. That's like leaves falling in autumn; count on it. When this happens, resist the temptation to speed up to prevent the bozo from cutting in front of you. Just let him/her[7] in and then calmly restore the space you prefer between your vehicle and theirs. Chances are, you'll catch up to him at the next red light. And when you stop at a light, you should be able to see the tires on the vehicle in front of you touch the road. If you can't, you're too close.

When we lived in Montreal in the mid-80s, drivers there had a slightly different understanding from the rest of Canada about the meaning of the color of stop-lights. They used to say, "green means go, red means proceed with caution, and yellow means go like hell." Driving in that environment was exciting and great for developing skills. I can boast that, strange as it may seem, I was never in a traffic accident in Quebec, and I drove a lot.

Seriously, please don't drive like that. When the light goes yellow, hit the brake not the gas. I know someone who was almost killed in an intersection collision when she booted it after a light went yellow and the guy coming from the other direction kept speed, knowing his light was turning green. That meant two ruined cars, a near-death experience followed by years of painful recovery, and huge financial losses. Slow down. What are you hurrying for anyway?

Don't speed in the city, but know where the photo radar sets up

The 10% rule[8] for speed is pretty safe for highway driving. By "safe" I don't mean that driving that speed is necessarily safe; I mean if you drive 10% over the limit, you're unlikely to get a speeding ticket. But in the city, just don't speed. At the same time, it's only good common sense to know where those fun-loving and wacky photo radar rascals set up. They will frequently set up in spots with reduced speed limits, knowing they can nab unwary taxpayers who don't recognize them from behind and don't realize they're in a reduced speed area.

Some of the reduced speed areas defy common sense. So that's a good spot for a photo radar scoundrel to catch his limit. Close to our place we have a playground zone where the speed limit is reduced from 50 km/hr to 30 km/hr. No little kids ever cross the street there because: 1) the

_____
[7] Some of the most aggressive drivers these days are young women. Why, I don't know. That may be the topic of my next book.
[8] If the highway speed limit is 80 km/hr, you can likely drive at 88 km/hr and feel confident you won't get a ticket. Similarly, in a 100 km/hr zone, you can likely do 110 km/hr.

playground is completely fenced off, 2) there's no cross-walk, 3) it's a high traffic street. So everyone from our neighbourhood knows that the photo radar guy sets up there regularly from spring through fall. And he sets up on the side opposite the park. So people, who aren't from the neighbourhood, get expensive photo radar tickets from going by him at 40-50 km/hr, which, in my opinion, is perfectly safe for that stretch of road.

If you happen to agree with me that photo radar crooks are engaged in a dastardly, cowardly, and despicable business that's below contempt[9], then please join me in warning approaching drivers when you see one, with a neighbourly, kindly, and jaunty flip of your hi-beams.

Anyway, I advocate not speeding in the city and of course that includes slowing down for the reduced speed areas. But I also believe that it's prudent to know where the photo radar spots are. In my own case, since I got my Class 4 license, I don't exceed the speed limit in any area, city or highway. I just watch the speed limit signs and make sure I don't speed. Now that I'm used to the habit of not speeding, I enjoy having zero anxiety about getting a speeding ticket. I no longer have a fight-or-flight physiological stress response when I see a cop car. And I don't miss it a bit.

Easy on the gas; easy on the brakes

As for driving style, you won't be surprised that I recommend "Easy on the gas; easy on the brakes". If you step hard on the gas pedal when you leave a green light, then brake hard when you come up to a red light, all you'll accomplish is increased wear on your engine and brakes, increased gas consumption, increased environmental emission, and increased stress for you, your passengers, and other drivers. I can all but guarantee that if you drive like that, the more sensible drivers will pull in calmly behind you at the next red light. Always remember that the rate limiter[10] for city traffic is the stoplights not the speed you drive between them. By all means, when you're driving, take it easy.

I saw a public service bulletin on TV that was providing hints to help

---

[9] Gee, I hope that doesn't read too judgmental or opinionated. We wouldn't want that.

[10] Any chemist or chemical engineer will tell you that the kinetics of all chemical reactions and processes are controlled by a rate limiting factor. Changes in parameters other than the rate limiter will have minimal or negligible effect on the overall rate of the process. This principle applies to lots of other processes too, like city driving.

us improve gas mileage. The narrator suggested that when we drive, we ought to imagine an egg attached to our accelerator pedal and a full cup of coffee on the dashboard. We want to use the accelerator gently enough that we wouldn't break the egg. And in general, we want to drive in such a way that we wouldn't spill the coffee. I liked those images.

And please don't drive with your foot on the brakes. I've seen timid drivers doing that[11]. They're also wearing out their engines and brakes and wasting gas. I take pride in using my brakes as little as possible. I watch the traffic around me, especially ahead of me, and ease off the gas when I know I'm going to have to stop soon. Then I can brake gently or not brake at all. I don't pay for brake jobs as often as other people do.

When you have a merge lane, merge.

Don't come to a dead-stop in the right-turn lane leading to an open merge lane if you see traffic coming from your left. You don't need the merge lane plus an open lane or two to the left of the merge lane. All you need is the merge lane; that's what it's there for. Make your right turn and drive forward in the merge lane with your left turn-signal on. The people in the right lane on your left will expect you to merge. Go ahead and do it. When a space opens up, merge into traffic with a polite wave to the driver who created the space and let you in. People who stop in the right turn lane or in the merge lane get rear-ended by drivers who expect them to merge.

And on the other side of the coin: if you're driving along in the right lane and you see someone is about to merge into traffic from the merge lane ahead on your right, move over a lane to the left to let them in. If that's not possible, slow down a little to make a space for them to merge into traffic in front of you. Wave them in if possible. That's courteous driving. That way, everyone keeps moving. God bless.

Keep your car clean, inside and out from spring to fall

It's OK to let your standards slip when there's snow, ice, and slush on the road. It's impossible to keep your car clean then anyway. You'll make yourself a nervous wreck trying to do so. But for the other six months of

---

[11] This is no doubt a metaphor for life in the broadest sense. Don't go through life "with your foot on the brake". When you're pointed in the direction you want to go, go in that direction, and don't hold yourself back.

the year[12], keep your car clean. Driving around in a car that's dirty on the outside or inside is like walking around with dirty clothes. Imagine you're picking up your favourite movie star and taking her to dinner at a nice place. Would you show up in dirty clothes and a dirty car? No? Then why would you treat yourself with any less respect?

Don't use your car as rolling storage. I know people who leave all kinds of junk in their car (and I don't mean spare tire and jack) because they really don't know where they want to store it at home and can't get it together to dispose of it in some final decisive way. As Brian Tracy would say, "This is not for you." If you plan to donate two bags of old clothes to the Salvation Army bin, do it. If you plan on donating two bags of books to the library or second-hand bookstore, do it. But don't drive around with that stuff in your trunk or backseat for six months. That sort of sloppy practice says something about you, and it's not complimentary.

Washing your vehicle

If you value the finish on your vehicle, don't take it to an automatic car wash that has revolving brushes. That sort of car wash will get the dirt off but it will also scratch your paint. The modern "touchless" car washes are better but they don't really get your car very clean. And you don't become intimately familiar with every nick, scratch, and imperfection. You need to know where those scratches are so you can seal them with touch up paint.

I recommend you wash your vehicle by hand. In the winter, you'll need to go to a coin operated wand wash. Here are my tips: Stay away from the brush and don't be afraid of a little light work. The brush will scratch your paint, especially if the guy before you has left a lot of dirt and grit on the brush, which is likely. So here's how you get your vehicle clean with only two or three loonies[13]. Let's assume your vehicle is dirty, which is a good bet, since it's winter. Two or three loonies and you're out, unless you need to vacuum.

The first loonie goes to "Wash". You spray your vehicle all over with soapy water under pressure. Keep going around with the detergent until the spray stops, remembering to include the wheels. Now comes a little light

---

[12] Up here at Latitude 53, winter is 6 months and summer is two months of bad skiing
[13] For our American friends, we call our $1 coin a loonie because of the image of the loon on it. Similarly, our $2 coin is called a twonie (pronounced 2-knee).

work but it will make all the difference. You need to use two big sponges[14] or two wash mitts, one for each hand, and quickly go over the entire wet and soapy surface, physically breaking up the layer of dirt on the surface. Use a light and rapid motion. If you skip this step out of laziness or hurry, your car won't get clean and you'll just be wasting your time.

The next loonie goes to "Rinse". You spray your vehicle all over with clean water under pressure, working from the top down. Keep rinsing until the spray stops, remembering to include the wheels. Your third loonie goes to "Wax". You follow the same process, only with spray wax. After the spray wax is done comes the next bit of light work. You keep a couple of clean[15] towels in the trunk for this. Take one towel into each hand, folding it nicely, then go over the entire surface with the towels. Now you will have a clean, shiny car with a finish that will look good for years.

If your vehicle isn't that dirty to start with, you can combine the second and third loonies into one and finish the job with two loonies. The most important steps are the two when you need to work a little, i.e. the sponge or wash mitt step after the detergent cycle and the towelling off part at the end. I've seen people spraying loonie after loonie at their vehicles, doing nothing more than that, and then driving out without towelling off. Sorry, but that's a waste of time and money. If you're going to go to the car-wash, put in a little work and get your car clean. Standing there and spraying it just won't do the trick[16]. As soon as the water dries, that car will still be dirty and spotty.

If you know it's going to rain or snow in a day or two and that your vehicle is just going to get dirty again, you can skip the towelling off part at the end. But don't skip the sponge/wash mitt part. That way, the vehicle will be about 98% clean when you drive out wet. When it dries, it will be spotty but not dirty.

In the summer you can wash your vehicle in the driveway with a hose, carwash mitt and some soft towels, using similar techniques. You won't have detergent, but you'll have unlimited clean water and sunlight to see what you're doing. Wet an area with the hose, and then go over the area

---

[14] You need to make sure your sponges or wash mitts are clean, or you'll scratch the paint, just like you would with a brush.

[15] After three or four washes, you need to take your towels inside to run them through the washing machine. Since your vehicle is 98% clean by the time your towels come into use, they stay pretty clean.

[16] If we look really hard at this one, we might see a metaphor in this that applies to a general approach to life. Just saying.

again with the wash mitt, using a light touch. Then rinse again with the hose to wash away the dirt. Work from the top down. After finishing the wash in this fashion, towel off the vehicle. After that, you can go around the vehicle again, buffing an area at a time with some spray wax and a microfiber towel[17].

Mmmm...pretty car. Keep it clean and it will look good and last longer.

---

[17] Microfiber towels are easily available now from retailers everywhere. They're much better than regular towels for buffing a clean surface.

Camping and the Great Outdoors

I encourage you to get outside and feel the sun on your face and the wind in your hair. We evolved from primates that lived and worked outside, not inside in front of a computer terminal or TV. I feel that as a species, our soul is outdoors. We need to feel what it's like outside. Is it sunny or cloudy? Can you feel a breeze on your face? Is it dry or humid? What does it smell like? Can you hear birds or insects? We also need to sense how the leaves are progressing through the seasons, what time it gets dark, and what phase the moon is in. I believe that if you spend some time outdoors each day, you will be more grounded in general. Get out there and feel it.

I've enjoyed the outdoors since I was two years old. In fact, my earliest childhood memory is from when I was two at Laclu Ontario, in the Lake of the Woods area, just east of the Manitoba border. We lived in Winnipeg and my parents rented a rustic cabin at Laclu for a two or three week vacation during the summer. When I say rustic, I mean rustic. The cabins had no electricity or running water. My mom used to cook on a wood-burning stove. My dad had to chop the wood. The cabin had an outhouse behind it.

But what a treat for the senses! Every day we had beautiful sights of the lake with sunsets and sunrises, the sounds of loons and other birds, the smell of pine forest and wood smoke, the feel of sun and water on your face and back and the taste of fresh-cooked fish, pan-fried potatoes with onion, and homemade bread. And when it rained, we had a different set of sensory treats. At night, my mom would draw canvas curtains to separate the cabin into sleeping areas. Those canvas curtains had that faint pleasant canvas tent smell. Since I was youngest I'd go to bed (on a hard cot of course) before the others. The cabin would be illuminated by the soft yellow light of aromatic coal-oil lamps. I would drift off to a restful sleep to the sound of my parents and siblings talking quietly. It was magical. If I could go there now, I'd probably still find it magical. It's been more than 60 years since I was two but those sensory memories remain.

My first memory was standing inside a boathouse looking at a boat docked there. I thought to my little self something like, "I get it…a boathouse is like a garage for a car, only it's for a boat!" What a bright kid.

So anyway, I grew up loving the outdoors and that attachment has never gone away. We don't live in the lake country anymore but the Rocky Mountains are just hours away. When our sons were little, Bev and I used to take them camping in the mountains. We bought our first tent-trailer in the early 80s, when Robert was still a toddler.

Rob toilet-trained in Wabasso campground in Jasper National Park. He was born in 1981 so this must have been 1983. We'd wake up in the morning and find Rob's diaper to be dry. I would lift Rob up and Steve, Rob, and I would run off across the loop as fast as we could – the boys in their sleepers with feet and me in my sweatpants and Birkies[18] - to get to a urinal before Rob wet his diaper. Steve and Rob would be laughing and giggling because they had a sense of how funny the situation was. When Rob successfully urinated standing up into the urinal, Steve and I congratulated him enthusiastically. And that was that. We returned to the trailer in top spirits and found Bev waking up. Each morning we would repeat the adventure. When we returned home after that trip, Robert was trained.

One of my fondest memories of those early camping trips was the preparation Bev put in to make it fun and easy for the boys to dress themselves. Bev would collect a few brown paper lunch bags, one for each boy for each night we would be away. Into each bag she would pack a clean T-shirt, clean underwear, and clean socks. Then she would staple each bag shut and felt-pen label each one with a big S for Steve or a big B for Robert (we called him Bob in those days). Each morning the guys would open a bag and get dressed in clean clothes. I wonder if the guys remember those little paper bags like I remember the boathouse at Laclu. Is that a sweet memory, or what?

Once the kids grew to be teens, Bev proclaimed she had lost interest in camping. She doesn't go with us anymore. But Steve, Rob, and I still go. Steve has his own family and his own camping trailer now. Rob enjoys a

---

[18] Birkenstock sandals

trekking style of camping in Banff's eastern slopes. He goes out alone with his pack, mess-kit, tent, and compass. And whenever we can, at least once a year, we go camping together. I'll go with each one individually and when possible, the three of us go together.

So, with all those camping trips behind me, all those hours logged around the campfire, and all those bug bites scratched, I'm bound to have some helpful hints and preferences on how to make your camping trip more easy and enjoyable.

Water for your campsite

This rule goes back to an old boy-scout standard that "your campsite isn't complete until you have collected water and erected a clothesline." For water I use the collapsible semi-clear plastic containers that hold about 4 gallons. They're convenient and cheap at about $10 each. The containers have a spout to start and stop water flow and a loophole opposite the spout so you can hang the full container from a tree. When you hang the container the spout is down at the bottom, which of course is what you want. When you buy a new water container, you need to tie a small length of rope through the loophole into a loop about three inches in diameter, so that you can hang it.

In the last few years, I've found at least one tree on most campsites with a sturdy nail hammered into the trunk by some previous camper, just for holding one of these water containers. I keep a small pack of big nails for that purpose in my trailer. I like to hang two water containers, which offers greater convenience and an additional symmetry to the campsite than we would have hanging a single one.

But whether you hang one water container or two, the important thing is to hang it/them rather than trying to balance it on the picnic table. They take up space that way and often flop and fall down onto the ground. When you pick them back up, they'll be nasty and dirty. You don't want that. They're meant to hang.

Some campers use a hard plastic water container that is meant to sit on your picnic table. Since they're made of hard plastic with a flat bottom surface, they're much less likely to fall off the table than the ones that are meant to hang. The disadvantage of those hard plastic ones is that they don't collapse and therefore occupy more space when you're packing up.

No matter what kind of water container you use, you need to plan for how you will fill it. The opening on those containers is about 2 inches in diameter. It is distinctly uncool to have cold water spraying all over your boots or Birkies and pant legs while you fill your water container. One of the best innovations I've come up with for this purpose is a two foot length of garden hose, with a normal female screw connector at one end. Most campgrounds these days have water faucets rather than pumps. Most of these faucets have threads on the faucet for this application, just like in your backyard. I had been camping for many years filling my water container with a funnel before I realized that a length of hose would be easier, less messy, and eminently cooler. This innovation is so elegant that I suspect it may not be my original idea. No matter though – I did think of it on my own. Since it's a recent innovation for me, I actually enjoy filling my water containers this way.

For campgrounds that have hand-pumps, you'll need a nice big funnel to fill your water container. Otherwise, water will splash all over the place and only a small fraction will go into your container. I made myself a nifty funnel by cutting the bottom and half the sides off an empty and clean four litre plastic windshield washer bottle. I used that home-made funnel happily for about 30 years before I thought up the two-foot length of hose. The funnel works fine but you'll still get some water on your boots or Birkies, especially when using a pump. Keep both a funnel and length of hose in your trailer.

Clothesline

Now on to clotheslines. This is a topic I enjoy. I take a lot of ribbing and teasing from my sons and other camping buddies about my clotheslines. They say I put up too much clothesline. My camping buddy Walt has taken numerous photos of me putting up clothesline at the beginning of a trip while giggling and snorting. Here's my thinking: Yellow propylene rope is cheap, effective, and takes up very little space in your trailer or car trunk when you're packing up. I like to set aside at least 50 – 60 feet of yellow rope for clothesline. I tie one end around a tree trunk about 8 feet high and run it over to another tree trunk about 20 feet away. If the trees are appropriately spaced, I'll join three or four of them with yellow rope this way.

Employ a few old-fashioned wooden clothespins[19] and you're good to

---

[19] Don't buy the cheap plastic clothespins. The clothes and towels you hang on the line will end up on the ground.

go. Once I have used a towel (dishtowel, face towel, shower towel) I hang it on the clothesline to dry in the clean mountain air. Same goes for my water proof jacket, my fleece, or my vest after I've used them. I wear sweats (sweatpants and a hoody[20]) to sleep in because it gets cold overnight in the Rockies. In the morning after I'm dressed, my sleepwear goes up on the clothesline until the afternoon.

Before long, all kinds of clothes, towels and so forth are waving in the breeze from my clothesline. That keeps everything aired out and dry and reduces clutter inside the trailer or truck. The clothesline also creates a psychological and partially visible barrier, setting off our campsite from the adjoining ones.

A shipshape campsite includes a supply of fresh clean water and a good length of taut clothesline. Don't let anyone try to tell you otherwise.

Put your coffee together the night before

A practice that I started many years ago, when our kids were little, is to put the morning coffee together before going to bed the night before. I use a blue enamel coffee percolator. The previous evening, I put fresh water and ground coffee into the percolator. Then I put the coffee pot onto one of the elements of the propane stove inside the trailer, which is about 2 feet away from where I lay down my sleepy head for the night. The idea is when you wake in the morning and you intend to get up soon, you just roll over and spark-start the gas element under the coffee pot. Then you can roll back and doze until the beautiful and gentle sound of the coffee beginning to perk tells you it's time to reduce the flame, and get out of your nice warm sleeping bag. The coffee will be ready to go once you have the fire started.

Sipping my coffee around the morning campfire is one of the sweetest moments of the day for me when I'm camping.

Starting your campfire

Once I step out of the trailer my next step is a nice glass of orange juice. In the Rockies the overnight temperature falls to 5° C or less. That OJ is so cold it's very refreshing.

So with the morning coffee perking and working on a glass of cold

---

[20] "Bunnyhug" if you're from Saskatchewan

OJ, it's time to start your campfire. As I just said, it gets cold overnight in the Rockies and it's often still cold in the morning when you wake up. Sometimes we need that campfire to warm our hands and our souls. This is not a time for screwing around and experiencing any difficulty whatsoever getting that fire going. So here's my "one match method"...

Take two pieces of split firewood (that you split last night and kept for the morning, of course) about 1 – 2 feet long and 3 – 4 inches in diameter. Place the two pieces lengthwise and parallel in your fire pit, about 6 inches apart. Now take three pages of old newspaper that you keep in your trailer for starting campfires and rumple them up into balls. Take the three balls of newspaper and place them in a line between the two parallel pieces of firewood. Now pick up a handful or two of kindling and pile the kindling carefully over the balled up newspaper. For kindling, I like to use the chips that are always left behind on the ground from splitting firewood, or some dried up twigs. Now light the newspaper with a wooden match. As the kindling starts to catch, lay some small split pieces[21] of firewood across the top, perpendicular to the original two pieces that lay on the bottom on either side of the burning newspaper. As the fire starts to gain size and confidence, you can build it up by laying increasingly larger pieces in layers, two or three at a time, perpendicular to the layer below. Should you need to fan the flames, your cowboy hat will do the trick beautifully. A good cowboy hat should be part of any camper's clothing inventory. In addition to keeping your head warm in the morning and evening, it will keep rain off your head and face better than any other kind of hat. And as I said above, it's great for fanning your campfire.

This process should take about 5 minutes. The fire is hot enough to sit by. Now your OJ is done and the coffee is ready. Pour yourself a steaming hot cup of coffee and pull up a folding chair by the fire to enjoy it. As Homer Simpson would say, "Mmmmm...coffee...."

Enjoy oatmeal for breakfast

The fire is going and you've finished your first cup of fresh, hot, strong coffee. You may begin to have thoughts of breakfast. I like oatmeal when I'm camping. It's quick and easy to make, it's hot, and it's wholesome. I like the 3-minute kind, not the instant kind nor the long-cooking kind.

---

[21] You have carefully split these pieces to be bigger than the kindling but thinner than the original two pieces.

I have found that about 2/3 cup[22] is about right for me. So I just grab my 2/3 cup measure and scoop out the oatmeal into a cereal bowl. Then I measure 2/3 cup of water twice (i.e. the water to dry oatmeal ratio is 2/1) into a small pot and bring the pot to the boil. While the water is heating up, I add a dash of salt. When the water boils, I stir in the dried oatmeal, turn down the heat to low and a minute or two later, I stir in some raisins and brown sugar. After three minutes, I cut the heat and cover the pot for a minute or two while I pour another cup of coffee.

If you'd like to add some more substance to your breakfast, you can soft-boil an egg or two in a separate pot. The eggs will take more or less the same time as the oatmeal, so that works out well. And the flavours and textures go well together too. While the timing of the egg cooking is critical if you want your eggs just the way you like them, the timing of the oatmeal is not. You can serve up the oatmeal when the eggs are done and both will be fine, as long at the oatmeal has had its 3-5 minutes.

Bev brought home a wonderful gizmo a few years ago that takes all the guesswork out of soft-cooking an egg. It's not a timer; it's a product that uses internal temperature to create a color-change. I don't know what you call this thing but I sure recommend it. It looks like an acrylic egg only with a flat bottom. You put it into the cold water with your raw eggs then put the saucepan on high heat. Once the water starts to boil, you can cut the heat and look at your "indicator egg" for temperature change. To start, at room temperature, it's red. Once the eggs begin to cook, the red begins to turn dark purple from the outside-in. The indicator's face has markings for soft-medium-hard. Once you've done it once or twice, you'll know exactly when your eggs are done just as you like them.

The indicator egg thingy costs about $10 and can be used over and over again. No moving parts. Since it works on internal temperature, you don't need to fuss over the fact that water boils cooler at higher altitudes, hotter with added salt, or any of that physical-chemistry stuff. I keep one in my trailer all the time.

Dress for the weather

For goodness sake, don't be a tough guy when you go camping; dress for the weather and the conditions. If you're going camping in the Rockies, even if it's July or August, you ought to plan for cool to cold nights, hot

---

[22] I mean 2/3 cup of the dried staple before it's cooked.

days and sun, or rain showers. The temperature can vary 25 de C in one 24 hour period.

Here's a checklist of what I recommend you bring:

- Towels
- Vest
- Jeans
- T shirts
- Underwear
- Camping pants
- Camping shirt
- Birkies
- Fleece top
- Boots
- Gloves
- Camping hat, e.g. cowboy hat
- Warm sox and regular sox
- Hooded sweatshirt and sweat pants
- Water resistant jacket
- Books
- Toiletries

Don't waste firewood

I used to tell my kids this story when they were young and impressionable. It's a scene from The Lone Ranger or some other cowboy TV show or movie from the 50s. The Lone Ranger and his aboriginal[23] (they were called Indians in those days, which is incorrect because Indians come from India[24]) companion Tonto encounter an abandoned campfire. Tonto says

---

[23] I haven't met an aboriginal person yet who likes to be called "Indian". Any that I have asked about it would prefer to be called something else, anything else, if you need to refer to their race at all, which they're quite happy if you don't. The aboriginal people I've asked would prefer Native, First Nations, or Aboriginal, anything but Indian.
[24] Please don't say "East Indian" to differentiate between Indian and Native. When you say "East Indian" to mean Indian, that's pretty much implies that you

to the Lone Ranger, "*This – white man's fire. Indian make small fire, sit up close; white man make big fire, sit far back*".

Now that was back in the day before anyone talked about conservation. But now everyone is more aware of the finite nature of natural resources, both renewable and non-renewable. Renewable natural resources need to be treated with respect. Just because trees grow doesn't mean we should piggishly waste firewood. The fact is, most campground firewood comes from trees that are harvested just so campers can enjoy campfires. It's not just deadfall.

Once you appreciate that reality, it helps you change your attitude about how much firewood you use. When my kids were little, firewood was free. Now depending on what campground you visit, we either pay for a campfire permit or directly buy bundles of firewood. At first I was shocked and a little resentful when these fees were administered. Now I understand that it's a good thing. Paying for firewood reminds me of its finite nature and the financial and habitat cost of its harvest and distribution.

Everyone loves a campfire. When I go camping, I start one each morning as soon as I get up. Then I start another one when preparing the evening meal. We keep that one going through the evening until bedtime. We have some of our best discussions around the campfire. I use the campfire for some cooking and to heat water for dishwashing and face washing. I also use it as an incinerator to minimize the organic waste I need to throw out. And I use it to keep warm on cold mountain nights and mornings. But I don't build a "white man's fire" just to see how big I can make it. That would be wasteful and insulting to nature.

Be quiet

Like in the Robert Munsch book I used to read to my kids when they were little, "Mortimer! Be quiet!!" Please don't be a noisy camper. We've probably all experienced those mouth breathing yahoos on the campground who come out there to drink and howl. That behaviour gets old quickly. It's

---

think First Nations people are called "Indians". That's an insult to our aboriginal brothers and sisters. You don't mind being called "Canadian" do you? I have lots of Indian friends and I can assure you that they feel just as comfortable being called Indian as you do being called Canadian. Indians are not "East Indians" unless they come from Chennai. Even then, they're Indians, and North American Native people are Native, First Nations, Aboriginal, or best of all, just people.

so tiresome and so disappointing. This kind of behaviour is straight-out stupid and totally insensitive. If you want to be noisy, do it at home.

During the summer months in our neighbourhood, I hear someone's gas-powered lawnmowe[25], electric weed-whacker, or chainsaw about 16 hours/day, 7 days/week, unless it's raining. And of course, we have the cool dudes who ride by on their Harley's. That's a lot of noise.

When you're out camping in the beautiful great outdoors, you don't need your car stereo or portable stereo. Play those at home. And keep your voice down; you don't need to shout. We don't need to hear your loud drunken voice and overhear the uproariously funny conversation you're having that's causing everyone on your site to split a gut. When you're camping, there are a thousand little things to hear, just like things to see, taste, feel, and smell. But to hear them, we need quiet. Quiet is nurturing for the soul.

When you're camping, you're in nature's cathedral. Show some respect. Feel the magnificence. Be quiet.

Clean up after yourself and be respectful of habitat

When you're all packed up to go home, walk your campsite. Make sure you haven't left anything behind. Make sure that the site is in a condition that is at least as good if not better than it was when you arrived. This is not your backyard, but in another sense, it actually is your backyard. Respect it and care for it. Be gentle with it. You don't need to see bears every time to know that you're camping temporarily in an ecosystem. Be aware that even if you don't see bears, that you are surrounded by a complex system of birds, small mammals, insects and other invertebrates. And that's just the fauna – let's not forget all the green plants, fungi and other micro-organisms.

Let's be like a Jain[26], and leave a small footprint. Or better yet, leave no footprint at all.

---

[25] I use a self-propelled reel lawnmower. No gas, no oil, no noise, no vibration, no pull-start, no grass bag, no maintenance. Just a quiet and peaceful clickety-click-click. And it cuts beautifully.

[26] Jainism is an Indian religion that prescribes pacifism and a path of non-violence towards all living beings.

Your Social and Entertainment Life

In this chapter, I'm going to provide you with valuable insights into social etiquette that you won't get anywhere else. You may encounter some strong opinions. But rest assured, this is good stuff if you want to be socially successful this season.

Arrive on time

When you're meeting friends at a club or restaurant, or when you're showing up as an invited guest at their home, arrive on time. Showing up on time is respectful. Being late is disrespectful. When you're late, you're pretty much saying something like:

> *"My time is important. Your time is not, at least to me"* or
>
> *"Since I'm a bigger and more important and busier person than you are, my time is more important than yours"* or
>
> *"My showing up late demonstrates that I am higher in the social pecking order than you are."*

If you're horrified to think that your chronic tardiness might be sending that sort of message, then start showing up on time for your social engagements. If you think you might encounter traffic, then plan for that and leave earlier. If you suspect that cramming in one more task before you head out might put you in jeopardy for being on time, then don't perform that task.

If you arrive a few minutes early, would that be such a bad thing? I try to be on time. When I meet my good buddy Walt for lunch at 11:45,

I arrive at 11:44. When I walk in, Walt's always sitting there. Walt is punctual. I appreciate that. It's organized and respectful. Maybe once out of 20 times I arrive before Walt. When that happens, it's because I'm early not because Walt is late. When you're punctual, you send the message that you're steady and reliable.

Don't talk or cough at movies

This should go without saying. When you go to a movie or concert, don't talk or cough. And don't crinkle the cellophane wrappers on your snackies any more than you have to. Other people are trying to enjoy the show. If you've been ill and think you might cough, don't go to the movies at a theatre. Use Video On Demand instead and watch at home. And turn off your cell phone. I mean really off. We don't need to hear a Ping every time you receive one of those really important text messages.

Bev and I were at a Diana Reeves concert once, back when cell phones were not as ubiquitous as they are today. The performer was just preparing to soar into a number that required her complete concentration. Just at that magic moment, some joker's cell phone rang. The singer hitched and paused in her delivery and then stopped. She smiled graciously at the stupidity of the situation and the audience gave her a polite ripple of applause. I'm sure that person shut has off his/her cell phone in similar circumstances since that incident.

When you're with someone else, put away your smart phone

This section is going to rub some of my younger viewers the wrong way, maybe make them a little uncomfortable, but I believe you need to hear this or read this. Even though I know I'm fighting a losing battle on this one, I feel that in the interests of common civility, somehow this message must get through.

When you sit down with a friend or a loved one at a café or restaurant, please don't put your phone on the table-top, so you can send or receive texts, check e-mail or netsurf at any relatively quiet moment. Leave that phone in your pocket or purse. Give your full attention to the person you're with. Those highly important seven texts can wait a few minutes.

Similarly, when you step into a car with someone, you don't need to whip out your phone to send or receive texts as soon as you've done up your seatbelt. Just leave that phone where it is. Be a companion to the driver. Presumably you're together because you're pals or otherwise related. After you reach your destination, you can catch up with your backlog of text messages.

Don't put up with bad or dumb radio or TV

If you don't like what's on the tube or radio, turn it off and walk away. I can barely listen to the radio anymore. I can't listen to commercial radio because of the commercials. I find most radio commercials to be loud, aggressive, and basically semi-stupid. They're a vexation to my gentle spirit. But sometimes I like to listen to commercial radio for the music. We have a local station that plays 80s and 90s music. Sometimes I like that mix when I'm in the mood for it. But for some reason, they think we really need to be reminded after every song they play what station we have dialed in. As if they're going to sell more ads that way. I don't get it. At the end of every song, they put on this annoying little jingle, singing,

"♪Capital Eff-Emmm...♪"

Now I'm trained that when a song is nearing the end, I immediately change stations. Sometimes I play a game with myself and see how close I can get to the end of the song before the jingle starts and I change stations. But change I definitely do. I wish a marketer would ask me what I like and don't like about that radio station. Where's a marketer when you need one?

I used to enjoy listening to commercial free public radio, the good old CBC. But having suffered several serious budget cuts, the peoples' radio is now almost unlistenable. Naturally, the quality of their programming has shrunk along with their budget.

Take the drive-home show for example. For us that means Radio Active. The CBC website describes the show as *"An eclectic mix of politics, arts, storytelling and local comedy..."* I would call it, *"Mostly repetitive boilerplate"*. If you take any 30 minute section, it will pretty much follow a standard repetitive format. You have news at the top of the hour, followed by weather, sports, traffic update, what's coming up later in the show (mostly more boilerplate), what's coming up in the local news at the bottom of the hour, a few minutes of actual programming, some terrible music that would never be played anywhere except the CBC, a few more minutes of actual programming, then some more promos, another traffic update, and we're off with news at the bottom of the hour. We have two traffic updates and about 10 minutes of actual programming in every 30 minutes. The rest is boilerplate. We need two traffic updates every 30 minutes? That's four every hour. Way to kill time, guys. Nope - no can do.

And CBC daytime programming? Don't get me started. CBC used to be good at any time of day. Remember "Morningside"[27]? That was top-notch radio. Now we have "Q", with the silky smooth, self-promoting Jian Ghomeshi. Now, this guy is a good interviewer when he's actually interviewing someone. But Ghomeshi spends major minutes in each half-hour segment talking puerile inanity and promoting what's going to be on Q later this morning, later this week, and next week. When I tune in, I want to hear some real programming, not Ghomeshi gushing on enthusiastically about what's going to be on after 11 AM, who's going to there on Thursday morning or next week. I get so exasperated I change the station or switch to my own recorded music.

During the afternoon, CBC seems to select what they think will be the absolutely least interesting to their listeners and then they put that on. With important global news topics, rather than providing some facts-based analysis that goes beyond the superficial like they used to, they now dumb it down for us by finding some individual person in whatever country the story is breaking, and ask that person to express how the situation affects her/him personally – and usually it's how does it affect her/him emotionally. I used to love the CBC, but as Eric Clapton would say, now I love it less[28]. It's like the people's network is thumbing its nose passive/aggressively at the public and government for cutting its budget...

> *"You and your budget cuts!! See what crap and drivel you're forcing us to put on the air???"*

When it comes to television, control the media and your schedule by using your PVR capabilities. Television has gotten so bad that I can only watch pre-recorded or otherwise commercial-free TV. Please don't sit down, turn on the tube, let your lower jaw go slack, and just gaze at it. I must admit that I watch a show or two nearly every day, but I watch it

---

[27] In 1982, Peter Gzowski took over CBC's Morningside from Don Harron and hosted this excellent show for the next 15 years.
[28] "(When Things Go Wrong) It Hurts Me Too" from the album Crossroads (1988)

when I want and I zap through the commercials. I even pre-record sporting events. I let them get 30-60 minutes ahead then I start. When they go to commercials or the athletes start cursing each other and shoving each other around, zap goes the fast-forward. If you get into the habit of doing that, you won't be able to watch regular TV again. I don't feel at all guilty about not watching commercials, because I distribute my money lovingly. I don't need to be told what to buy and to do it now. And I don't need to be encouraged to eat a bacon double cheeseburger when watching the NHL.

Everyone is entitled to their own taste of course, but I suggest you give up any sort of "reality"[29] TV, including all talent competitions where judges criticize and dismiss contestants, any show where the audience screams[30], any game show, any awards show, any show where some poor hack interviews celebrities, or anything that has been produced by Oprah[31] or her new network. These shows will make your brain numb, your eyes cross, produce arthritis in your knees, bend your spine, and damage your digestion, so that you are bothered by irregularity and chronic flatulence.

If you don't like what's on TV and you don't have anything recorded that you want to see right now, turn it off and walk away. Pick up a book (maybe like this one). And if you don't like what's on radio when you're driving, listen to your CDs or your iPod. Or try driving in silence. I do that about half the time. I like driving in silence. It's quite pleasant. As Ari Gold would say[32], "Silence is golden."

---

[29] Reality TV makes up about half of what's on these days. I think these shows are less expensive to produce than scripted programs. And they're sufficiently low-brow that they attract a big segment of the commercial-watching public. I have never seen an episode of any kind of "Survivor", any kind of "Amazing Race", "American Idol" or anything with Donald Trump or Oprah in it.

[30] The shows where the audience screams hysterically are often the talent competitions where judges criticize and dismiss contestants.

[31] Many of us deep thinkers believe that Oprah has too much influence on gullible North Americans, even if she does give away cars. She's right up there with Dr. Phil, who to me is an Oprah with a mustache that doesn't give away cars.

[32] Ari Gold is Vincent Chase's agent in "Entourage". See: http://www.youtube.com/watch?v=6McLXorvIUM

Dress reasonably well – other people can see you

No sweatpants in public please. Jerry Seinfeld put it best when he confronted George Costanza for wearing sweatpants[33]: *"You know the message you're sending out to the world with these sweatpants? You're telling the world 'I give up! I can't compete in normal society. I'm miserable so I might as well be comfortable.'* Jerry nailed it nicely with that admonishment.

I'm not saying we need to dress up when we go out in public, but I think we may all agree that societal standards and expectations have slipped, say in the last 40 years. When I was in my 20s, people actually used to dress up a little when going to a movie or a restaurant, certainly when flying on an airplane. Now when we go out to the local mall to run an errand, it sure doesn't look like that. Almost everyone, except for some young women, looks pretty much the slob.

Guys, why not comb your hair, shower and shave when you go out? I see guys handling produce in the supermarket[34] that look like they've just gotten out of bed in the same sweats and stretched and stained T-shirt they wore the day before, scratched their crotches and bellies and gone straight to Sobeys to handle the fresh tomatoes. Ugh! Could you have a little self respect, please?

And middle-aged guys please…no shorts with dark shoes and dark socks. Those skinny white legs make an unattractive contrast to those dark socks and shoes. Some guys, when they reach a certain age in their 40s or 50s seem to think that now it's OK for them to go out that way. I'm not sure why. My intuition tells me that they feel that now that they've reached that age, shorts with dark socks and shoes make a strong masculine statement. Like, "I've earned it – now I'm going to show it off."

In that way, the shorts with dark shoes and socks is a different thing than the sweatpants. First, the sweatpants thing crosses gender lines. Both men and women do it, showing us their swollen, oversized butts love handles and butt-cracks. And the statement is different. Where the sweatpants say "I've totally given up and I just don't care anymore," the shorts with the dark shoes and socks say, "look at me! I'm a mature male and I've earned the right to wear this shocking combination."

---

[33] For this short clip, go to: "http://www.youtube.com/watch?v=dz7cw6jbwFY"
[34] To be clear, I mean customers not the guys who work in the store.

Eating and Drinking

In this final chapter of Part I, I'm going to provide you with some astute advice on mindful and smarter eating and sophisticated tasteful drinking. I'll provide some tips on what, how and when to enjoy your favorite beverages. Remember you are what you eat. So if you eat a cheeseburger, you can draw your own conclusions about that.

Know why you're eating

Some of these thoughts about mindful eating come from my yoga teacher Glenda. I've been practicing yoga for about 12 years now, the last 10 or so under Glenda's teaching. I like her as a teacher because she goes beyond the physical practices and also teaches us a little about yogic thought and philosophy. I've learned some good lessons from Glenda. Some of those lessons concern the yogic approach to diet and eating. I'm going to share some of that thought here.

At the outset, we need to know why we're eating and tell ourselves the truth about it. When you're sitting down with some chips and/or popcorn and a cold beer to watch a sporting event on TV, you're not eating to nourish your body, right? Glenda has confided to me that sometimes she eats popcorn while watching "Dancing with the Stars". But I'll bet she doesn't put any melted butter on it.

I can't imagine a guy saying to himself, "I think what my body really needs tonight is the healthy balanced nutrients I'll get from some Frito Lays, popcorn, and Kokanee!" Most likely that guy doesn't think about it all and just crams it in while watching the game.

And that's the point. I'm not going to tell you never to eat junk food.

But I will suggest that when you do so, that you are mindfully aware of what you are doing and why. That way, you'll be able to stop before you make yourself sick.

Many of us have heard about the raisin meditation, when you linger over one delicious raisin, savouring every nuance of flavour, aroma, and texture. The point of that exercise is to raise your mindfulness and present-moment consciousness. So if you're going to sit down with some junk food[35], know what you're doing and why, and for goodness sake, don't do it often, even if it's the Stanley Cup playoffs.

At the other end of the spectrum, when you sit down in the morning and savour that first sip of fresh orange or grape juice, be aware of what you're doing and why then also. And when you enjoy a nice bowl of hi-fibre low fat whole grain breakfast cereal with some fresh bright red raspberries on top, with a little yogurt and or low fat milk, you can say to yourself, "I'm doing this to nourish my body."

Eat mindfully – When you're eating, eat

As Glenda my yoga teacher has said, "Put it on a plate, sit down, and eat it." At the time she was teaching us a little about the yogic approach to eating, and part of that is eating mindfully. That means you don't read a book or a magazine or watch TV when you're eating. If you do that, you will be distracted from what you're doing. Instead of eating mindfully you'll be eating mindlessly, and that way you can't enjoy the sensual part of eating. And since you're distracted, you also run the risk of overeating. Since you're not tuned into your body you may not realize that you're full until you're overfull.

Of course the above applies when you're eating alone. But eating with a friend or loved-one is another story. Then you enjoy the food but you enjoy the other's company also. When you eat with someone else, put away your reading material, your laptop, and your cell phone or iPhone. Be present and concentrate on what you're doing.

One exception to this rule is having breakfast with your spouse. That's

---

[35] Some may argue that if you're mindfully aware of what you're eating, you wouldn't eat junk food at all. My favorite junk food is cheesies. I just love that fatty salty goodness. Because I have to watch my blood sugar, blood pressure, and weight, cheesies are just a memory for me. Same goes for chips. I may eat some popcorn once every 3 months.

a vulnerable and intimate time[36]. You're both a little rumpled and still waking up. That time of day calls for a gentle approach. It's OK to have your morning coffee and breakfast while reading the newspaper, even if the love of your life is across the table from you. Bev claims she is less extroverted than I am. She really doesn't like too much chatter first thing in the morning. But she does like to read the paper while she's having her toast and coffee. That's A-OK with me. I read the Sports and Comics; Bev reads neither. We never have to compete for parts of the paper. Conversation starts slowly for us in the morning, and that's just fine with me.

Table manners, please

Just like your parents taught you, don't talk with your mouth full. Deepak Chopra pointed out how common this bad habit is in Western culture. You see it all the time on TV – someone chomping away on a big mouthful and talking at the same time. Sometimes both participants in the conversation will talk with their mouths full and do so at the same time. That's not a visually or aurally pleasant practice. Dr. Chopra suggests in his modest manner that we take one bite of food, chew it carefully, fully aware of and enjoying what we're doing, swallow, maybe have a sip of water or wine, and then maybe contribute to the conversation. When you're chewing, you may be listening, but you definitely are not talking.

A close second in bad table manners to talking with your mouth full is putting your fingers into your food[37]. You have a knife and fork or spoon to handle your food. Keep your fingers out of there. If you want that last tasty morsel of food and you can't seem to pick it up with your fork, try using your knife to put it onto your fork. Using your thumb to do that is revolting. If you can't collect that last tasty morsel without sticking your fingers in your food, just leave it. We'll all appreciate that.

Many people believe that loud belching at the table is not in good

---

[36] When I was working full time as a Research & Development Business Unit Manager, I never took breakfast meetings. Some guys were just too busy to meet any other time. So I didn't meet with them. Breakfast is private time for me. I wasn't spending that vulnerable time with some aggressive dude in a suit and tie. Of course, that's no longer even a possibility for me since I'm retired . Heh heh.
[37] In 2003 Bev and I travelled to Bangalore, Karnataka, India for my nephew's wedding. At gatherings like this, Indian custom includes eating with no cutlery. It's all done with the left hand, while the right hand remains on your lap. That took a little getting used to.

form. In a group of dudes, most guys enjoy the spectacular sound of a loud belch. It demonstrates your gusto and appreciation for the food or beer. To be on the safe side, you may want to avoid loud belching in polite mixed company, unless you're female. A well groomed and made-up lady in fine clothes who emits a loud belch in polite mixed company will always please the gathering with her good spirited high-jinks[38].

But in any case, don't talk with your mouth full and don't stick your fingers in your food.

Eat until you're no longer hungry, then stop

This principle seems simple enough and fairly obvious. So how come it's so hard to stick to? Glenda has taught us that being full means having your stomach 2/3 full. And that 2/3 full is 2/3 food and 1/3 water. I believe in North America, we like to go around with our stomachs full all the time. If you have this habit and get used to it, you may start feeling hungry long before you need to. As soon as your stomach is no longer full you may start feeling hungry.

I believe this is especially true for young parents with young children, i.e. babies and toddlers. I see it all the time. These parents are always trying to get their kids to eat more[39].

> *"Eat more lunch. Want an afternoon snack? Eat more dinner. Just have two more bites. Finish your plate. Want a bedtime snack?"*

I don't know this to be true from empirical evidence[40], but I suspect sometimes that the little kid has the ability to know when she has had enough food. And the parents, in their earnest anxiety, teach their kids the habit of having a full stomach. What, these kids are going to starve? I don't think so. I reckon if they're hungry, they'll ask for food.

If you have this habit yourself, know that it's not good for you. Basically your stomach cannot do its job properly if it's too full all the time. You know that uncomfortable feeling you get if you eat too much at Christmas or Thanksgiving? It's not pleasant. You just want to lie on the floor. If you walk around that way, you're not digesting your food properly. It's not a healthy way to live.

---

[38] But I have yet to see this happen.

[39] I'm not preaching from a high and mighty platform here. We did this too. I don't understand it, but we certainly did this too.

[40] This is all nothing more than my conjecture – but I bet I'm right.

I have to watch this one myself. Bev has told me that I have big appetites. I know that's true. I don't overeat as much as I used to but I still have to watch it. And I like foods that pack on the bulk, like starchy pasta, rice, and creamy sauces. Mmmmm… But I don't eat fatty red meat much anymore. Anyway, at dinner, I'll be happily eating away and Bev will say to me, "Are you still hungry?"

Well there goes my gusto, but I know she's right. We're supposed to eat until we're no longer hungry, not until we are "full". If you feel full, you've eaten too much.

Glenda told us that one of her favourite teachers, Richard Miller, said at a workshop he was leading for yoga teachers, "A little hunger goes a long way." I wasn't at that workshop, but Glenda reported it to us at one of our classes. Dr. Miller had encouraged the workshop participants not to eat too much while at the workshop. Now we're talking about spiritual people here. I'm not suggesting that you walk around hungry. But I am suggesting that we eat mindfully and consider eating less. Many of us North Americans eat more than what's good for us.

Fast 12 hours every day

They don't call it "breakfast" for nothing. If you plan on having breakfast at 7 AM the next morning, finish dinner by 7 PM and don't eat again until breakfast. What, no bedtime snack? Exactly!

You don't need a bedtime snack. Actually a bedtime snack is not good for you. Not only is it fattening, but having just eaten before bed will interfere with your sleeping. If you're finished dinner by 7 PM and go to bed at 11 PM, your stomach will be in just the right condition for sleeping. Its work is mostly done for the day. If you eat at 10:30, your stomach will have work to do rather than being able to rest.

But, you say, you won't be able to sleep without a bedtime snack. Nonsense, that's just a habit you've formed and it's just your ego nattering at you[41]. Try it and you'll see. Try no food between dinner and breakfast and I predict you'll sleep much better.

---

[41] See Part II – Master your internal world – control your ego with discipline.

Acidic and alkaline foods[42]

Human blood pH should be slightly alkaline (7.35 - 7.45). A pH of 7.0 is neutral. A pH below 7.0 is acidic, while a pH above 7.0 is alkaline. If your system is below or above this range, that's not healthy. You will need to make some changes.

An acidic pH can occur from an acid forming diet, emotional stress, or any process that deprives the cells of oxygen and other nutrients[43]. The body will try to compensate for acidic pH by using up alkaline minerals stored in your body. If your diet does not contain enough minerals to compensate, your system will become acidic. If your system becomes acidic, your health will suffer.

When a person's body fluids are too acidic, that condition is called acidosis. One reason why acidosis is common in North America is diet. The typical North American diet is too high in acid producing animal products like meat, eggs and dairy, and too low in alkaline producing foods like fresh vegetables. To maintain health, the diet should consist of 60% alkaline forming foods and 40% acid forming foods. To restore health in the person with an acidic system, the diet should consist of 80% alkaline forming foods and 20% acid forming foods.

Generally, alkaline forming foods include most fruits, green vegetables, peas, beans, lentils, spices, herbs and seasonings, and seeds and nuts. Generally, acid forming foods include meat, fish, poultry, eggs, grains, and legumes.

So the bottom line is more broccoli, fewer cheeseburgers, and more aerobic exercise. But you already knew that, right?

No brown liquor between May Long Weekend and Labour Day.

Cold beer is the drink of choice for gentlemen during the glorious but brief warm and sunny months. If you must have distilled liquor during summer, go with vodka or gin. There's nothing like a fine 18 year-old scotch or nice cognac with a good book or a good friend in front of the

---

[42] See http://www.rense.com/1.mpicons/acidalka.htm
[43] Like a sedentary couch-potato lifestyle. Turn off the TV and take your dog for a brisk walk outside in the fresh air. Get those arms and legs moving, your heart pumping, and your lungs exchanging oxygen.

fireplace on a cold dark night in February. At a time like that, you wouldn't think of a brisk, ice-cold gin and tonic.

But when it's 28 deg C and sunny outside, that Gee and Tee with a twist of lime seems a lot more appealing, doesn't it? Or maybe a nice Caesar[44] with a fresh crisp celery stick. When mixing a Caesar, the ice goes in first, then the Tabasco and Worcestershire[45], then the vodka, the Clamato juice, and finally the celery stick, with which you can give the cocktail a little stir. Make sure you use plenty of ice in those summer cocktails.

And as I said above, cold beer is always in good taste in the summer. That's especially true after you've cut the grass and you're starting up the Bar-BQ. Most guys like to have a cold one when starting the Barbie and also when doing the actual cooking. You can keep those cold ones handy on the deck in a camping cooler with crushed ice or freezer packs. That way you don't need to go into the house to get one from the fridge every hour.

And please, no white wine in delicate stemware for guys on the deck. You can enjoy a nice chilled glass of Chardonnay with your dinner indoors. But when you're outdoors, leave the white wine in fine stemware to the ladies in their cotton sundresses. As Brian Tracey would say, "That is not for you". Guys, when you're chilling on the deck, stick to a cold brewski or maybe a Caesar.

Along the lines of brown liquor in winter and clear liquor in summer, you can prefer darker beer in winter and a clean fresh lager in summer. In my case that means Big Rock Traditional ale in fall and winter and Stella, Budweiser or Kokanee in spring and summer.

This "No brown liquor between May Long Weekend and Labour Day[46]" is more a guideline than a rule. For example, a rum and coke[47] is good anytime. Although anyone who has any breeding knows that you use dark or amber rum in winter and white or amber rum[48] in summer. Also,

---

[44] The Caesar is a Canadian invention. The delicious and nutritious Caesar was developed at the Keg Steakhouse in Calgary Alberta.

[45] Some bartenders add the tabasco and Worcestershire after the vodka and Clamato. I like to add it right over the ice because I can see what I`m adding and I think it's more stylish that way.

[46] I picked up this guideline from Brian the dog on "Family Guy", so it must be a good rule to follow. We all know how sophisticated and urbane Brian is.

[47] If you're on a sugar-restricted diet like I am, that rules out Coke. To me the taste of Coke is like the taste of cheesies, just a pleasant memory. You might try sugar-free Coke in your rum.

[48] Amber rum is the all-season radial of rums. Good any time of year.

fruity drinks with rum like orange juice or tropical blend cocktails are more suitable to summertime (or tropical winter vacations). And of course every guy knows that any fruity drink that sports a little paper umbrella is for the girls, regardless of season.

Another notable exception is tequila, which is in good taste in all seasons. Tequila shots are always a nice idea, on tropical winter vacations or at home, at any time of year. But tequila cocktails like margaritas with crushed ice are only for hot occasions. Only someone who didn't know better would ask for a margarita at Christmastime. Although a shot of tequila at Christmastime is an indication of urbane sophistication and good manners. See what I mean?

Or for a refreshing change you could try no alcohol at all – it's good discipline for the ego.

One final note for the guys. When you drink a beverage, whether it's coffee in a mug with a handle, a pint of beer with or without a handle, a glass of wine, or a highball, keep your four fingers on the glass (or mug). The last think you want to do is hold onto the beverage container with one or two fingers then wave your other two little fingers up into the air[49]. That looks hoity-toity and effeminate. You don't want to do that and I don't want to look at it.

---

[49] I picked up this tip from Jimmy Walker on "Good Times" back in the 70s. Jimmy was poking fun at snooty white folks who hold their drinks like that.

Don't buy or drink bottled water

Please don't sit back in your chair, sipping on bottled water and tell everyone how passionately concerned you are about protecting the environment. Bottled water has a huge environmental footprint. Think about all the fossil fuel derived energy and material that is used in producing the bottles, filling the bottles, transporting the product to its point of sale, then recycling or otherwise disposing of the empty bottles afterward.

And for what purpose when we have good quality drinking water available at the turn of a faucet? In many North American jurisdictions, the quality and purity of bottled water is entirely unregulated. You really don't know where the water in your bottle comes from and what's in it. This is ironic considering the quality of our tap water is monitored and regulated.

Here's one illustrative case that's close to home. In our town, we have a light industrial area in the Northwest corner. Just beyond the edge of town are a farmer's field and a natural slough. For years the farmer spread pig manure on his field in the fall. You could smell the rich aroma as you commuted back into town from the big city to the West. Most Western Canadians know just how good pig manure can smell. The farmer has discontinued that practice in recent years, likely due to an order from the County. At the North edge of that property lays the slough. It's a popular marshalling ground for hundreds of ducks and Canada geese in the fall. Several water fowl stay there during the summer. Any Canadian who has spent any time outside the city knows how much fecal matter these birds leave behind. That slough is a rich organic soup. It's a perfect environment to brew all sorts of protozoa and micro-organisms.

Now does that bucolic description sound like a good location to draw "pure natural spring water" (or other such marketing nonsense) for bottling? Right at the Western edge of our light industrial area and just adjacent to the farmer's field is a big private label water bottling plant. You can have your very own labelled brand of bottled water, just by entering into contract with this plant. Anyone drinking bottled water from this plant had better <u>hope</u> that they are bottling tap water. I wouldn't much want to drink the ground water from under that farmer's field and slough.

I heard a documentary of CBC a couple of years ago about the environmental impact of bottling and transporting water and handling/recycling the waste empty bottles. Leaving out all the details, the narrator ended with an image that has stayed with me ever since. She said that if we look at our typical bottle of drinking water, imagine it being ¼ full of oil.

That ¼ bottle represents the energy and materials consumed in bringing that bottle to you. Yikes! Yuck!

If you live in India or Mexico or parts of Eastern Europe, by all means drink bottled water. But if you live in an urban part of North America, doing so is unnecessary and borderline gross. Say no to bottled water.

Mike camping: Two of my favourite things-camping and my old guitar.

Bev - Bev enjoying the view on our Alaskan cruise.

Gracie: Gracie fetching a stick in Moab Lake, Jasper National Park

Part II:
Fare More Substantial and Chewy

I hope you enjoyed Part I. We covered some practical material there. Now we know the important principles of motor vehicle maintenance, how to set up your campsite and start a campfire and some valuable social etiquette, like not wearing your sweatpants out in public or drinking bottled water. I recognize that for some readers, some topics in Part I are going to be more interesting or palatable than other topics. Really, you don't need to fix your cracked windshield if you don't want to. I'm just recommending that you do. I think you'd be happier with a clear undamaged windshield, but that's your call.

One purpose of Part I was to prepare you for Part II, which is the heart of the book. The tone in Part II is going to be a little different than in Part I. Part II deals with some of the most important life-lessons I've learned. This is more serious stuff. In Part II I have attempted to present the order of chapters and topics cohesively and logically. Later material builds on earlier material – that sort of thing.

Most of us can picture the image of the presentation of "Pheasant Under Glass", the ultimate in upscale urban dining in the first half of the 20th century. The dish was served under a glass dome to help keep it moist and warm between the kitchen and the table. Each dish was carried out from the kitchen to the table by one white-coated waiter. The waiters would place one dish before each diner with the glass domes still in place. Then with a flourish, all the waiters would whip off the glass domes at the same time, releasing the rich aromas to the delight of the diners. It was a spectacular presentation.

Now that you have that image in mind, I humbly present you with Part II "Fare More Substantial and Chewy". Let me whip away that glass dome. Now tuck your napkin into your collar or place it on your lap and enjoy -- with some gusto.

Master your Internal World

To paraphrase Steven Covey[50], if you want satisfying, loving, and supportive interpersonal relationships, master your internal world first. That's easy to say. Maybe "master" is too high a goal for most of us. Maybe not, if we relax a little and understand that doing so is a life-long effort and discipline. I know that for myself, I've been working at it for about 20 years now, and while I've made a lot of progress, by no means would I say that I have "mastered" my internal world. One of my favourite teachers, Stuart Wilde, used the term "assaholic[51]" to represent the tendency of the human condition to make progress and then fall back. As Stuart said, "I'm so assaholic, it's grim." But I continue to work at it.

The cast of characters – The Ego and the Conscience

Let's start by examining just what the "internal world" is. We'll need to introduce the cast of characters. Most people's reality consist of their conscious thoughts, perceptions, sensations, and feelings, and everything else that's external, like the weather, the physical environment, cars and trucks going by, dogs and cats, and what other people say and do. The first part is the internal world and the second part is the external world.

Of course it's not that simple. Many of the best minds examining the nature of reality now believe that most (if not all) of what we perceive as

[50] The Seven Habits of Highly Effective People, first published in 1989, by Stephen Covey, has sold more than 15 million copies in 38 languages since first publication.
[51] Stuart only used the term to apply to himself. I gather that he considered himself to be in essence, an ass.

the external world is a projection of our thoughts and feelings. In fact, many believe that our thoughts and feelings have profound impact on our external worlds[52.] One of the major contributing scientists in this field is Dr. Candace Pert. The movie "What the Bleep Do We Know!?" features Candace Pert among several other top scientists and thinkers. Dr. Pert's thinking and scientific evidence is central to the theme of the film. In the film she describes how the "molecules of emotion" color our perception and hence our creation of reality[53].

This little book is not a scholarly work. I can't collect empirical data or write at the level of a top shelf academic intellectual like Candace Pert. For now, let's make an everyday distinction between the internal world and the external world. When you take a look inside to check out the internal world, who's there?

Sigmund Freud's[54] psychoanalytic model divided the psyche into three components, the ego, the id, and the superego. The ego is the conscious mind while the id and superego comprise the subconscious mind. That's what we all learned in Psych 101. The id is the combination of primal urges that we all experience, like hunger, sex, and aggression. The superego is the conscience. That's the part that provides us with the ability to make moral judgements of right and wrong based on a set of principles, values, and norms.

In the basic model, if you imagine a big iceberg, the ego (the conscious mind) is the part above water while the id and superego (the subconscious) is the part below water. The ego is the part that an external observer can see while the other parts an external observer cannot see, because they are below the surface. And also like an iceberg, the part below the surface is surprisingly big compared to the part above water.

You can see how we need all three components. A person who lacks a conscience is a psychopath, someone who has no sense of right and wrong. Psychopaths are not happy and fulfilled people. They make up a major proportion of the incarcerated populations in our prisons[55]. At the same

---

[52] What the Bleep Do We Know!? is a 2004 film that describes the spiritual connection between quantum physics and consciousness. See also http://www.whatthebleep.com/.

[53] These ideas are developed in Dr. Pert's first book "Molecules of Emotion: the Science Behind Mindbody Medicine" (Simon and Schuster, 1998).

[54] Freud is out of vogue these days, but the model is a good starting point in describing what the internal world is.

[55] As has been documented many times, many prison inmates believe they have done nothing wrong. They will insist that they're just misunderstood and

time, to be ruled by your superego without the influences of the other components would make you overly judgmental, inflexible and irrational. Folks who are ruled by an oppressive superego are not happy and fulfilled people either.

The ego is the rational part of our psyche. It's where we figure things out. It's the part that interprets the external world and makes up the major part of what most of us understand to be our personality. Gotta have it. Basic Psych 101 also says that the function of the ego is to satisfy the id's impulses, not offend the moralistic character of the superego, while still taking into consideration the reality of the situation. That's a tall order. No wonder we have problems with our egos; they're never at rest.

An unchecked and uncontrolled ego is the major challenge of mastering the internal world.

Control your ego with discipline

While the ego does many good things for us, like reasoning and logical determinations, it's also the source of all that negative critical self-talk that many of us never learn to quiet.

> *"You're so stupid! You're too fat! What a dummy! You're so clumsy! etc. etc.."*
>
> *"You don't need to exercise. You can skip walking the dog. Your needs are more important than hers. What you really need is to lie down and watch TV. Go ahead and crack another beer…you know you want it. Go ahead and have it, etc, etc."*

I can recall many years ago at yoga class, before I had experienced an epiphany in my practice about disciplining my ego, my ego nattering at me almost non-stop during my practice as I laboured unpleasantly through the asanas.

> *"I don't know why you even come here. You're the worst in the class. You hate it and you know it. You can't even do the simplest postures. What are you doing here anyway? You could be at home watching Monday Night Football. You know you hate this. Let's make this your last class…"*

---

are imprisoned because they are victims of an unjust system. The ability to demonstrate sincere remorse is a major criterion in qualifying for parole.

Now how could someone enjoy yoga practice with that sort of prattle rattling through his head?

And the ego can be very demanding and never satisfied for long. As Stuart Wilde said, as soon as you have satisfied every demand on the list your ego has made for you, your ego will slap another list on your forehead.

> *"You know you could have done a much better job in that discussion with Allison. You could tell by the look on her face that she didn't much like what you were saying. Why can't you ever learn how to talk to people without putting them off? Maybe you should take another course or read another book, you idiot!*
>
> *And while we're at it, how come all your jeans are frayed at the bottom? Don't you care how you look? You'd better go shopping for some new jeans…and buy more expensive ones this time. Your shoes are looking a little shabby too. You want people to think you're a slob? Maybe you <u>are</u> a slob!*
>
> *You said you were going to start getting more exercise. What happened with that? Can't you ever keep your promises?"*

All the examples above are of the ego nagging at us with negative self-talk. The ego can also do damage with unrealistically positive talk, convincing the person that he has positive skills, qualities, and attributes that he doesn't really have, or at least to the degree he thinks he does. I'm not talking about the healthy margin of illusion[56] here. I'm talking about a pathological degree of positive illusion that no one else shares. These people have an inaccurately positive impression of themselves that causes them to have interpersonal difficulties. When you hear people say, "So and so has such a big ego", that's probably what's going on.

My dog Gracie is apparently not bothered at all with ego or self-talk. When she wants to go out, she goes to the door. If she's sick of sitting on the couch with me, she'll get up and lie on the floor. If I'm heading out to take her for a walk, as soon as I grab the leash she starts jumping up and down and running around in circles. She never worries about whether she looks cool or not. After she has a walk, she's satisfied. She lies down and looks content. Ego is just not a big part of her life. But humans have a different sort of consciousness from dogs.

---

[56] See the chapter "Love and Respect Your Spouse" below for an explanation of the healthy margin of illusion.

As humans, we don't have the option of being ego-free. And we don't want that anyway. Our ego is part of us. And a well disciplined ego is a friend and an asset. We don't want to crush our ego or trap it inside a box, like Dr. Venkman does with unruly ghosts in *"Ghostbusters"*[57]. Stuart Wilde and others have pointed out that it's easier and simpler to control your ego with discipline than it is to satisfy it.

So then, how to discipline the ego becomes the question. How you discipline your ego is up to you. For me, a big first step was noticing when my ego was cropping up and causing me issues. Some of us cannot recognize when they're being overtaken by their ego. Being able to do so, take a breath and step back is a necessary skill. If you have a loved one you can trust with something as personal as this, you can ask him or her to point out when your ego is getting the better of you. Chances are, he or she might be able to recognize that situation before you would.

Then of course it will be up to you to drop your defences and take it from there. No one but you will be able to order your ego to stand down. But this approach will not be easy. Your ego's reaction will likely be to throw up a defence. It will insist you deny, perhaps with some outrage, that anything is amiss about its response. It won't want someone else pointing out that the ego is wielding undue influence. It might scream at you not to listen to your loved one.

But one way or another, once you have recognized that you might be falling under more influence than you'd like from your ego, you'll need to order it to stand down. And you'll need to make that order stick. You may be pleasantly surprised in how cooperative your ego is, once you've caught it in the act. After all, your ego is part of you, and you're calling the shots.

Writing this passage reminds me of the image technique Sonia Choquette used for controlling her ego and which she has taught to others[58]. She recommended imagining your ego as a little white dog. When it gets too yappy and uppity, Dr. Choquette advises telling that little white dog to, "SIT!"

Another of my favourite teachers, Stuart Wilde, recommends some

---

[57] In ``Ghostbusters", a 1984 science-fiction comedy film, three unemployed parapsychology professors start a ghost removal service. http://www.imdb.com/title/tt0087332/

[58] See "Trust Your Vibes: Secret Tools for Six-Sensory Living" 2004 by Sonia Choquette.

surprising techniques for disciplining the ego[59]. For example, you could get up at 5 AM on five successive cold mornings and immerse yourself in a cold swift-running river. Or you could get up at 5 AM every morning for two weeks and mindfully move a carefully and sacredly piled group of rocks from one place to another. The next morning you'd rise early again and mindfully move the pile back to where they had been the previous morning, and so forth.

What those techniques have in common, including the 5 AM start, is that at first the ego is going to kick up a big fuss about your doing it. When you demonstrate to the ego that it may as well stand down and be quiet, because you're the boss and you're not listening, the ego will calm down and stop trying to control you. The central point is the discipline. And repeat as necessary.

For me a big part of disciplining my ego has been my yoga practice. Yoga may not be for everyone but it sure does work for me. Thanks to what I've learned from my teachers and from reading the Yoga Journal[60], I'm able to apply some discipline in my practice. I have chronic osteoarthritis in my spine and the joints on the right side of my body, including my right shoulder, elbow, and knee, but especially the knee. These conditions limit what I can do physically on my mat, but keeping the limitations in check is one of my motivations for sticking with my practice. More importantly, those physical conditions cannot limit the psycho-spiritual benefits I derive from my practice, unless I allow them to. Therein lies part of the discipline.

Most of our yoga sessions are 90 minutes. When I'm practicing on my mat I'm no longer distracted by the sort of negative self-talk I exampled above. I may enter the class distracted from the day's activities and sometimes fatigued and not feeling all that great. But when I concentrate on my breathing, my movement and posture, and the teacher's instructions, I have no room in my consciousness for anything else. Early in my practice when I was distracted by ego-chatter, a 90 minute class often seemed to drag on and on forever. Now, within a few minutes, I become locked in the present moment and my mind is still. Having a still mind is wonderful while it lasts. And since I'm not thinking about time, it flies by unnoticed.

---

[59] If you've read Stuart Wilde or listened to his tapes, these techniques wouldn't be that surprising.
[60] The Yoga Journal is a monthly periodical. I recommend it. See http://www.yogajournal.com/

Often when the teacher calls us to Shavasana[61], it seems like we've just started.

When I'm regular and faithful in my yoga practice, I feel better physically, emotionally, and spiritually, and I find it much easier to keep my ego in good disciplined condition. And when my ego is disciplined, it's happy, and I'm happy too.

Conscience and consciousness – Meet your Higher Self

When I say, "…your ego is part of you, and you're calling the shots", just who is "you"? If you are separate from your ego, which is broadly thought to be your thoughts and personality, who then is "you"? It's not your conscience, right? That's the part of your psyche that makes moral judgements. And it sure doesn't sound like your id. If you're observing your ego rising up, who is it that's doing the observing?

If you haven't met him/her before, now is a good time to introduce your Higher Self[62]. If you've ever had an inkling that you're more than your physiology and psychology, you were contemplating your spirit. Your Higher Self is perfect, immortal, and infinite. Your Higher Self exists on a different plane than the one we muck around in most of the time. If you're uncomfortable about my suggesting the existence of your Higher Self, you may be put off by the name. Let's just call him/her Pat.

Pat doesn't care whether you believe in him/her or not. Pat resides in that short pause between your exhalations and inhalations. If you practice yoga or other forms of meditation, you'll catch glimpses of Pat. As I said above, if you've ever succeeded in observing yourself with some separation from your personality, you've done so from Pat's perspective. If you've ever had one of those moments of illumination or clarity when for a second or two, everything seems timeless and perfect, you were momentarily aware of Pat.

Pat is the keeper of your hopes and dreams. When you have a thought, a memory, or a strong emotion that you can feel in your body, are these things no more than charges built up between neural synapses in our brains? Are they no more than hormone surges, or vasodilatation or contraction,

---

[61] Shavasana is Corpse Pose, the final relaxation posture for 10 minutes or so at the end of a yoga session. During Shavasana, we're totally relaxed, alert, and mindful at the same time. After 80 minutes of breathing and exercise, Shavasana is wonderful.

[62] Your Higher Self goes by other names, like "spirit" and "soul".

changes in heart-rate or breathing? Most of us who have wondered about these things[63] believe otherwise.

When we behave badly and hurt others or ourselves, it's not Pat who's doing it. The culprit is the incarnated spirit that we are conscious (or unconscious) about most of the time. It's the imperfect combination of flesh, blood, bones, and personality that we usually think of as ourselves. But Pat is there too, and like Bart Simpson[64], he/she didn't do it.

One level of consciousness is to be aware of and capable of responding to the world around us. If it's cold out, we feel that and put on a coat. If someone is talking to us, we either listen (maybe to a loved one) or try to tune him out (maybe a TV commercial). Some days we're more conscious than we are on other days. In this way, a dog, cat, bird, snake, fish, or ant is conscious, because they all respond to their environments and situations.

A different level of consciousness is to be aware that you're aware. Now it gets interesting in a different way. I doubt whether my dog is aware that she's aware. I'm pretty sure she doesn't contemplate her mortality. Sometime she seems to be deep but mostly she doesn't. I believe she just goes about her business without thinking much about it or contemplating the nature of the canine experience. She's better than I am at being in the present moment.

But I am aware that I am aware. I'm sure of it. Otherwise I couldn't write about the subject. Even if this writing doesn't make sense to you, the only way I could raise the notion of being aware of being aware is if I am aware of being aware.

So where does that second-level consciousness, i.e. that awareness of awareness reside? Is it stored in a neural pathway in the brain? In an enzyme in the liver? In a nucleotide sequence? It is part of our knowledge and part of our personality. So it is likely a pattern in the prefrontal cortex of the brain, where reasoning and problem solving occur.

But who is actually doing this wondering? It could be just one part of the prefrontal cortex firing away and activating other parts, activating neural pathways and so forth. But if I'm separating myself from myself, and observing myself puzzling about it, I can't help but suspect that old Pat is somehow involved too.

Dear reader, you can accept or deny the existence of your Higher Self. That's a personal choice. I have attempted to construct a loose deductive

---

[63] Like, most of us humans trying to understand their world.
[64] Bart Simpson from ``The Simpsons`` Season 5, Episode 12 `Bart Gets Famous` See http://www.youtube.com/watch?v=WTbgsoHDc24

argument in favour of your accepting its existence. I know that the premises and statements are subjective. That's the way it goes in a book like this; it's kind of a subjective book anyway.

But let me try an inductive approach. The people close to me who are all working toward a greater level of consciousness, i.e. a greater understanding of how they interact with the world around them, what that world actually is, how they can create a loving and positive reality for themselves and those they love, all recognize the Higher Self and try to know their higher selves. All the great authors and teachers of whom I have read on this subject of elevating consciousness allude to a Higher Self in expounding their views. It's all but impossible to postulate a spiritual framework without including the Higher Self. The correlation is overwhelming.

Whether you are in touch with it or not, you have a Higher Self. If you want to argue that my inductive argument is a *Fallacy Ad Populum*[65], go ahead. That's just your intellect and ego talking. Your Higher Self knows better.

Accept 100% responsibility[66]

Perhaps the biggest issue in mastering your internal world is accepting 100% responsibility for all that happens to you and every situation in your life. Victor Frankl, the Austrian neurologist, psychiatrist and holocaust survivor, was perhaps the first to write about this principle. Many other thinkers, including Stephen Covey, Wayne Dyer, and Deepak Chopra have expanded on the original idea, in English and more recently than Dr. Frankl.

Let's say you're walking down the sidewalk and killed by a falling safe or that you fall victim to some other statistically unlikely accident. Does accepting 100% responsibility mean that you somehow caused that unfortunate outcome? No, it does not. Bev and I had a friend who died tragically young after a battle with breast cancer. She used to bristle with anger at the new-age pop-psyche types who implied that sort of simplistic cause/effect phenomenon in their preaching.

But accepting 100% responsibility does mean that you are responsible

---

[65] In logic, an argumentum ad populum is a fallacious argument that concludes a proposition to be true because many or most people believe it. The classic illustration of a fallacy ad populum is "10,000 Frenchmen cannot be wrong" when of course, they can.

[66] Victor Frankl is often credited with being the first to articulate this principle. See his book, Man's Search for Meaning: From Death-Camp to Existentialism, originally published in 1946.

(assuming you aren't killed by a falling safe) for how you respond to whatever situation you're in. When Dr. Frankl was suffering in a Nazi death camp, he came to the realization that he could choose his response to the horrors of his situation. He came to the realization that he had a spot or space inside him that his tormentors could not reach. He understood that a gap exists between stimulus and response. Therefore, he was free to **choose** his response. Because of that realization, Frankl found a freedom and dignity that no one could overcome without his consent.

Stephen Covey said that being responsible meant being "response-able", another way of expressing that same idea. The stimulus may be out of your control, but your response is within your control. In a recent episode of Person of Interest, Reece said something like this to a young New Yorker that he was protecting, "Kid, you can't control what happens to you; only how you respond to it.[67]" As you become more aware of your freedom to choose how you will respond, your response muscles and fitness develop, and your personal freedom becomes bigger.[68]

This mind-busting principle can be a life changer. It certainly was for Victor Frankl.

Apply some detachment when appropriate

Consider becoming process oriented rather than being results oriented only. Consider that possibly, the less attached you are to an outcome, the more likely you are to achieve it. This thinking is contrary to a lot of Western culture, which is strongly result oriented.

> *"Keep your eye on the prize"*
>
> *"I don't care how you do it, just get it done. "*

For years I was a management-by-objectives guy too. Back in the 80s I worked for a CEO who preached "Performance is the only reality.[69]" And by "performance" he meant "results". I came to realize that he didn't care much whether we lied or cheated to create the results, only that we

---

[67] Person of Interest "Wolf and Cub" (2012) See http://www.imdb.com/title/tt2178549/

[68] See "Circle of Influence" below. The two concepts are analogous. Your response is within your circle of influence.

[69] This guy had some real values and morals issues. He was not pleasant to be around. I don't know if this is true but I heard through the grapevine years later that he had been murdered. That doesn't surprise me.

delivered the results. He wasn't interested in hearing about our processes, best efforts or our plans to build the business for the long term. What he wanted to hear about was what results we have achieved today. Last month's successes were of no interest either. The culture was, what have you done for the business today? Or as Wayne Gretzky once said, "you're only as good as your last shift."

What do you think the future of this company was? You guessed it. I smelled the stink of rot from the inside out in this company fairly early on. I realized this company was not for me. This realization led to our relocation to Edmonton from Montreal in 1987, prior to the collapse of the company. Of course results are important but paying attention only to results leads to that interesting paradox[70]. Attachment to the outcome does not necessarily lead to that outcome.

If you feel that you absolutely <u>must</u> have something, as if your very life depended on it, you're actually less likely to get it. In a tough negotiation, other things being equal, who holds the power, the person who absolutely must make the deal or the person who can take it or leave it?

As Deepak Chopra says, a good gardener plants his seeds in the ground, covers them up with soil, and waters them every day with his attention. But he doesn't dig them up to see how they're doing. You are walking this road because you want to get to the destination but your real purpose is to be walking the road. If your eyes are on the destination only, rather than on the road as well, you are more likely to hit an obstacle and stumble. Pay attention to <u>what is</u> and see its fullness in every moment. This is life-centred, present moment awareness.

Being detached does not mean being dispassionate or lacking in compassion for another's situation. It just means concentrating on what's happening now and realizing that a space exists between what you sense (see, feel, hear, taste, smell) and how you respond[71]. And as soon as you realize that you are observing yourself in this situation you realize that it's Pat, your Higher Self, that's doing the observing. Pat is detached from the outcome.

I learned this from my teacher when I studied guitar building: Pay attention to the journey and the destination will come. Concentrate on what you're doing at this moment.

And like a lot of big truths, this principle has an important application

---

[70] Luther Lerseth, a strict but wise Lutheran pastor, now retired, once told me, "Michael, some of the greatest truths are expressed in paradox."

[71] In this way detachment is analogous to the space between stimulus and response that I described in the "100% Responsibility" section.

in the practice of yoga. In fact, I first truly apprehended this principle some years ago in a yoga class. This was the major breakthrough in my yoga practice that I mentioned earlier, i.e. the breakthrough that allowed me to separate myself from my ego on the mat, and changed my yoga practice from an unpleasant effort into a joy.

Our normal ego-driven tendency is to move away from discomfort or pain and move toward comfort and pleasure. That statement seems like common good sense. But that dark winter night, our teacher Glenda had decided to teach us a little about yogic detachment. Let's say we're making effort to find a yoga posture. In yoga we never want to push ourselves to the point of pain. Effort is fine; pain is not. We gain strength and flexibility form working at the edge of our pain-free limits of motion. Maybe a little discomfort is OK but too much is not. We want to feel effort in a posture but not discomfort and certainly not pain.

Glenda made the point that we could fully feel the effort and the sensations the effort was creating in the body, but could detach ourselves from the seemingly automatic response of backing off or giving up on the posture if the effort got difficult. Once more, a space existed between stimulus and response and we had a choice. We could step back and observe ourselves making the effort and actually could choose the degree to which we wanted to persevere.

That learning made all the difference and transformed the experience of practicing yoga for me. I could be in a posture where I'd feel like my strength was giving out. My natural inclination would be to pull out and collapse on the mat in disappointment and self-loathing. But with this learning I could step back and observe myself. I might think something like this:

> *"I'm feeling some fatigue in my arms. Look at that...I can see them trembling. That's very interesting. Let's see how this goes..." or:*

> *"I know this spinal twist is limited by the tightness in my lower back. It's probably related to my osteoarthritis. When I twist my knees to the right like this, I can feel a lot of tightness in my left lower side...there it is...it's actually a little uncomfortable. But I know I'm more flexible in the other direction...I guess I'll go back to concentrating on my breath and relax into this twist..."*

That's a whole lot different than having my ego scream at me, like it used to, something like this:

> *"My God! I'm going to collapse onto the floor! This is awful! I hate this!"*

Since making that breakthrough realization of yogic detachment, I have increased my strength, flexibility, stamina, and concentration. The point is that we don't have to be slaves to our sensations. With some detachment, we can choose what's best for us.

Concentrate on your Circle of Influence[72]

Imagine a rectangle with a circle and an oval inside it. The circle is smaller than the oval and is inside it. The oval is smaller than the rectangle and is inside it. The rectangle (1. in the diagram) holds the complete universe of all the cares and concerns possible. You might argue that the rectangle should have no boundaries, but put that argument aside for now. The larger oval inside the rectangle (2. in the diagram) holds all the issues that concern and affect you, e.g. climate change, European economics, domestic abuse, The Oilers, etc. The smaller circle inside the oval (3. in the diagram) holds those issues that you can control or at least affect.

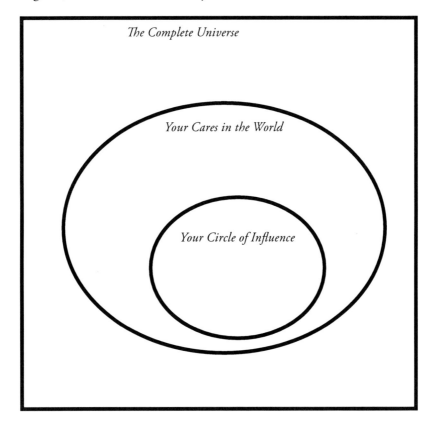

The Complete Universe

Your Cares in the World

Your Circle of Influence

---

[72] This concept is from Stephen Covey's 7 Habits book.

Stephen Covey encourages us to concentrate of our circle of influence. If we spend our psychic energy on issues we cannot affect, we will become frustrated and disappointed, and eventually maybe bitter. Some people put great effort into worrying and fretting over issues that concern them but that they cannot change or even influence to the slightest degree (area 2). Moaning and complaining about it doesn't help either.

Dr. Covey argues that most productive and effective place for us to put our time and effort is in the circle of influence. If we work on the issues that we can change or influence directly, we are at our most effective and impactful. One exciting corollary is what happens to the size of our circle of influence when we concentrate our efforts inside it as opposed to outside it.

Our circle of influence may be smaller than we'd like it to be but if we work at the issues inside the circle, the happy outcome is that our circle expands. The opposite is also true. If we expend our precious personal energy on issues outside our circle of influence, our circle contracts. I believe when you think about this principle, it makes eminent good sense.

We've all experienced folks who moan and complain about all the situations around them[73]. Their externals are always the problem. Here are a couple of examples.

> *"If only so-and-so would wake up and smell the coffee, my life would be so much easier."*

> *"This company just doesn't know how to run a business. If they paid us more, we'd all work harder and better, and they'd be more profitable."*

> *"The weather is so dreary. When are we going to see the sun again? It's been raining for three days now. I can't take much more of this."*

> *"It's so dark this time of year! It's dark when we go to work. It's dark again on the way home. It makes me depressed."*

You can almost hear the whine in the voice can't you? Making negative judgements about the weather or the shortness of the daylight hours during winter has got to be futile. Yet we hear this sort of talk all the time. You might argue that in social situations people connect with others that they don't know well by making small talk about the weather. OK fine. I do that myself when I have a stranger with me in my shuttle van. But that's not the sort of social small-talk that I refer to here. I'm pretty sure we all

---

[73] Of course, we never do this sort of thing ourselves.

can agree that we frequently hear people complaining about the weather to close friends and loved ones. Maybe we even do it ourselves from time to time. And these are sincere heart-felt laments. Up here at latitude 53 we have lots of opportunity to complain about the weather.

For some people, things outside their control just aren't right. I think it's easy to imagine how this self-nullifying[74] behaviour can work to reduce a person's influence. It absolutely never increases it. And the smaller their circle gets, the more frustrated they become, and the more they concentrate on the areas outside their circle of influence. We don't want to be in this cycle. This is not for you.

This notion of the circle of influence is part of mastering your internal world but it applies to your external world also. Concentrating on the circle of influence will make you more effective in the workplace and allow you to complete your work in eight hours, thereby enabling a good work/life balance. Concentrating on the circle of influence will enrich your interpersonal relationships also, because by doing so you will be more grounded, balanced, energetic, and powerful. Everyone wants that, right?

When I first encountered this principle, I felt like the universe had whacked me right between the antlers with a two by four. It's a powerful and potentially life-changing concept. To make it work, we need to discipline the ego and accept 100% responsibility. It's a good thing for us that we know how to do that.

Have a spiritual framework

If you feel uncomfortable with this final topic in mastering your internal world, go ahead and skip it, but I wish you wouldn't. Ask yourself why you feel uncomfortable with contemplating your spiritual nature. Is it because you can't see it, touch it, measure it, like you can your height or weight or blood pressure? When you're flying in an airplane above the clouds, you can't see the ground below, but you're pretty sure it's still there.

I don't know who said this first; I know I didn't. Anyway, some recent thinker said, "I'm not a human having a spiritual experience; I'm a spirit having a human experience". Now that may sound cheesy to the Atheists out there, but just ponder for a minute what that statement means. What if it's really true?

---

[74] A great phrase, from the movie "Wayne's World" (1992).

I think I've always been an innately spiritual person, except for a few years during adolescence when being spiritual didn't seem cool to me. That carried forward into my early adulthood like a bad habit. One day when our kids were little, Bev suggested to me that we ought to take them to church. Her reasoning was that if the boys had some exposure and education in the Christian tradition, they could make their own minds up about religious practice when they were older. Having had this exposure and education, they would be doing so from a position of relative knowledge rather than ignorance.

In those days we lived in West Montreal, in a neighbourhood with a lot of Jewish families. One day when Steve came home from school – he was in Grade 2 – he asked Bev if we were Jewish. I don't think he knew what that meant. One of his classmates had asked him. I have no issue at all with my Jewish brothers and sisters. Many aspects of their faith system and practice[75] are attractive to me. But when Steve asked Bev if we were Jewish, it was clear that he didn't know what being Jewish meant and that he didn't have a cultural faith-based identity. That incident sealed the decision. We started going to church and we took the kids. It was a big deal for me because I had liked it as a pre-adolescent.

From that point and for years following, I was a seriously committed Christian. I attended worship services every week. Every day I prayed and most every day I read the Bible. I enjoyed a few spine-tingling first-hand experiences with the Holy Spirit.

These days I'm more of a pagan[76] yogi. That doesn't mean I'm not spiritual; far from it. I'm familiar with my power animal[77]. His power and temperament match my personality and needs perfectly. I meditate.

[75] For example "Aseret Yemei Teshuva" the ten days of contemplation and repentance leading up to "Yom Kippur" the Day of Atonement, focusing on repentance and forgiveness, make eminent practical good sense to me. These practices parallel Lent and Easter of the Christian traditions, and occur at the same time of year.
[76] Pagan used to mean a person from the country, to be distinguished from the educated elite. Pagan people were attuned to the earth, phases of the moon, the stars and the seasons. They celebrated with festivals the equinoxes, all soul's night, mid-winter and mid-summer. A more modern meaning of pagan, according to the Oxford dictionary is "a person who holds religious beliefs other than those of the main world religions."
[77] Shamans believe that everyone has power animals - animal spirits which reside with each individual adding to their power and protecting them. See http://www. shamanlinks.net/Power_Animals.htm

When I need an answer, some insight to a troubling personal issue, or some spiritual guidance, I go on a Shamanic journey. I know that the answers, insights, healing, or guidance come from the spiritual realm and not my own psychology. If it's a big deal, I consult a Shaman[78]. She will journey with me and for me and tell me what she learns from the spirit world about my issue or question. If it's something I can handle on my own, I meditate and journey in our Spirit Room with the assistance of recorded Shamanic drumming.

When I practice yoga and I'm at my best, I still my mind and ego and encounter the present moment. That is a very positive experience. We folk who practice yoga have ethical precepts we follow to lead good and fulfilling lives. We follow five Yamas[79], or restraints, and five Niyamas, or observances. We also have the Purusharthas, which are the four pillars of a balanced life. See the end of the book for a little more information on the Yamas, Niyamas, and Purusharthas.

Sometimes I miss attending church service. But when I examine where I am on the spiritual path, I am much more in touch with my internal processes than I used to be. I'm more aware of my own vibes and the sensitive to the vibes that others are sending. I have more patience than I used to have both with other people and with situations that require me to wait. I believe I can meet people where they are better than I used to. I judge less and sleep better. I don't get sick often. Generally I feel more at peace and happier than I used to[80]. So for the most part, I can't complain.

Although I no longer participate in Christian worship, I maintain utmost respect for my Christian brothers and sisters. After all, I come from the Christian tradition. And that respect and regard goes out to my Jewish, Muslim, Hindu, Jain, and Buddhist brothers and sisters also. A Hindu friend said to me years ago, "All rivers lead to the sea." The point is, have some spiritual framework.

I humbly recommend to you that you examine your spiritual nature and see what you find. Pat is waiting for you.

---

[78] Shamans are intermediaries between the human world and the spirit worlds. They assist with healing at the soul level.

[79] The Yamas and Niyamas are no big secret. You can look them up. They're in the Yoga Sutra and on line at http://www.theyamasandniyamas.com/ and elsewhere. See Part III for a short overview of the Yamas, Niyamas, and Purusharthas.

[80] I realize this sounds boastful. Please cut me some slack. I am trying to sell you on the benefits of following a spiritual path.

Watch what you think – your thoughts have power

Sonia Choquette said that our psychic ability is always around us. Our awareness of it varies. Kids assume their psychic ability is normal and accept it that way. But somehow as we get older, most of us become separated, even estranged, from our psychic ability. Dr. Choquette says most of us swat away our psychic ability as if it were a fly buzzing around our faces. I think that's a great image.

We emit electromagnetic radiation from our metabolic activity. That's what our vibes are – electromagnetic radiation. They're not some paranormal phenomenon or a construction from science fiction; they're real and they're spectacular[81]. The aura is a field of subtle, luminous radiation surrounding a person. I do not see aura, but most of the time I believe I can feel vibes. Some of us are more sensitive to others' vibes than others. I believe I'm getting better at it than I used to be. Usually I can tell whether someone is feeling good or feeling bad, and I believe that's from more than observing their facial expression, body language, and voice. All those things are important interpersonal cues but I believe being open to feel other people's vibes provides additional information.

Now here's a sobering thought. Being a person on a spiritual path with a higher level of consciousness and sensitivity carries with it a higher level of responsibility. As I see it, this responsibility plays out in two ways. First, you're subject to a higher standard of moral and interpersonal behaviour than the public at large. You may not like to hear that, but that's the way it is. Now that you're vibrating at a higher frequency than you used to, and at a higher frequency than most of the folks around you, you will pick up subtle cues and vibes that other people won't catch. You behave differently in financial and business transactions than most other people do, because you are motivated by different things. You have no obligation to explain your motivations. In fact it's probably better if you don't. Most importantly, you now have the obligation to be gentle and kind in all circumstances to the people around you.

Here's a hypothetical illustration with two players, Larry and Fred. You will pick up vibes when Larry unwittingly causes hurt in Fred. That event may have been inadvertent or purposeful. Maybe Larry was just joking around. You may be able to distinguish that also. Either way, it's not your

---

[81] See *Seinfeld*, Season 4 Episode 19, "The Implant" (1993).

job to rescue Fred. Doing so would likely cause more harm than good[82]. But you will have the duty to be genuinely kind to both Larry and Fred. And now you know what sort of comment or action hurts Fred. You'll avoid making that sort of comment or taking that sort of action yourself in the future.

Can you imagine how it must be for someone like the Dalai Lama when he travels to the West, is interviewed by beef-fed, commercial ratings-hungry media types with big sweaty faces and loud voices? And what would it be like for him when he addresses huge crowds of spiritually hurting people? How do your reckon the Dalai Lama copes with that?

With your increased consciousness and responsibility you will learn how to match your vibrational frequency to the person or persons you are with. That way you can connect. Otherwise you won't. You can reduce your frequency but the other cannot increase his/hers or recognize the need for it.

When you adjust your frequency it's not because you're being judgemental. You're not coming from any position of supposed superiority. Fortunately, a natural inclination toward humility and minimalizing self comes along as part of the package with your increased level of consciousness. You're just being practical and acting from the acceptance of your responsibility to be open and kind. You don't mind making the effort. And it's not much of an effort anyway. Most of the time only a minor adjustment is required, rather than having to close a big gap.

And you're not alone...you will recognize others who vibrate at a frequency similar to your own. For example, I have an easy affinity with Bev. Most of the time we can lock into a matching frequency, either one of us adjusting as the situation dictates. On rare occasions we can't match up for one reason or the other, but that situation passes as egos are told to "SIT!" Most of my yoga teachers and some friends who are also seekers vibrate at a similar frequency to my own. I can't imagine any of these people ever purposely making an unkind action, speaking an unkind word, or performing a dishonest act. Nope.

And I know I can maintain my humility by not kidding myself – these people sometimes have to lower their frequencies to match up with me. I can feel it when that happens. It's a good wake-up.

Second, you need to watch what you think, because your thoughts

---

[82] See Games People Play: The Psychology of Human Relationships (1964) bestselling book by psychiatrist Eric Berne. This book is foundational in the field of Transactional Analysis.

have power. Drs. Deepak Chopra and Wayne Dyer were among the first to write about this, but many others have done so also. I need to introduce the term synchronicity. Carl Jung described synchronicity as the coming together of inner and outer events in a way that cannot be explained by cause and effect and that is meaningful to the observer. Most of us dismiss synchronicity as coincidence. Those of us who feel the hair rising on the backs of our necks know differently.

Dr. Chopra offers the following illustrations of synchronicity[83]:

> *"Perhaps you were out on your bike and collided with another rider in front of a small café you'd never noticed before. Later in the week, you decide to eat lunch there and end up meeting your future wife at the next table". Or:*

> *"Maybe you pick up the Sunday classified ads for no apparent reason and notice a job opening that interests you. A couple of weeks later you find out that your corporation is laying off everyone in your division. You suddenly remember the ad you saw and decide to apply. You go for the interview and the new company offers you an even better position that hadn't been advertised."*

Chopra argues that if you focus your attention, you may recognize that your life is shaped by those moments of meaningful coincidence. I don't know how synchronicity works but I have experienced it in my life and I know it's real. I believe the origin of synchronic events is our thoughts. I'm not claiming that this sophisticated phenomenon is simple cause and effect. It's more likely that our thoughts are components in a complex pattern of flow. But I have no doubt that our thoughts have power.

The law of attraction is the belief that positive and negative thinking bring about positive and negative physical results, respectively. If a person meditates on the phrase "I need to lose weight" likely he will continue to "need to lose weight." If the person wants to change that situation he needs to focus his thoughts on a positive outcome rather than the problem. For example he might focus his thoughts on "I maintain a healthy weight". If he is capable of concentrating on process as well as outcome[84], he might improve his meditation by focusing on:

---

[83] "Harness the Power of Intention, Coincidence, and Awareness", by Deepak Chopra
[84] See the section on the paradox of detaching from outcome (above).

"I maintain a healthy weight by only eating foods which are good for me and by exercising regularly."

Whenever I attend a Yoga-Nidra[85] class, one of the elements is for us to set an intention[86] at the beginning of the class. The teacher instructs us to phrase that intention in positive language and present tense, as if that situation already exists. In my own case, an example of this sort of intention would be:

"I am happily retired, fully engaged in life, in good health, and carefree".

At the end of the class we re-visit the intention we set at the beginning, to feel how it has landed for us.

Dr. Wayne Dyer is one author who has written and lectured extensively on the mind-bending topic of manifestation[87]. Dyer refers to what other's call the Law Attraction. He calls it the Power of Intention. Dyer says:

"The law of attraction is this: You don't attract what you want. You attract what you are. Most people's mistake in trying to apply the law of attraction is they want things; they demand things…"

That's an interesting notion for sure, although at first glance it seems to me to be a little circular. We attract what we are. But part of what we are is what we attract. Wayne's comment seems self-perpetuating to me. But I definitely agree that the Law of Attraction isn't there for us to demand things from an ego-driven perspective. I call that sort of thing "praying for a pony[88]". To me it's childish and superficial to trifle with a Universal force that way. In several books, recordings, and lectures Dr Dwyer has described the Power of Intention. He's a recognized expert on this topic.

But what do I really mean when I say your thoughts have power? I'm referring to the Power of Intention when I say that. We manifest our realities with our thoughts, words, and actions. The more in-the-flow we are, the more powerful our thoughts are. When we're in the flow, we're tuned in and harmonious with Universal forces. When we're in the flow[89],

---

[85] Yoga-Nidra, literally "yogi sleep" is a special yoga practice that combines setting intention, physical asanas and meditation. We intend to reach a conscious awareness of the deep sleep state. It's awesome.

[86] This heartfelt desire is called the "sankalpa"

[87] See especially "The Power of Intention" by Wayne Dyer

[88] That's my own expression, I swear. But you can use it if you want to, royalty free.

[89] When we're in the flow, we're "in the zone".

things seem easier, our interpersonal relationships are smooth, we're sharp, focused, and we get things done. If you're a basketball player, the game slows down, and the basket seems huge. We've all had experiences of being in the flow[90]. And we've all had experiences of being out of the flow. In those dark times, we stub our toes, drop glassware, lose our keys, catch red lights, and say the wrong thing.

As our consciousness and vibrational frequencies rise, we catch the flow more often. And when we're in the flow, our thoughts have more power.

What you think about determines what's in your consciousness. Whether that's true in objective reality[91] doesn't matter when you think about it. Subjective reality is what you experience. The point is, you will find what you think about.

Have you noticed how when you're in the market for a major purchase, when you're thinking about that topic more than you ordinarily would, that you see that item everywhere? Last summer Bev and I were shopping for a car for her. Neither one of us is especially into cars. Each of us likes to drive a nice one that we feel good in, but other than that, the other cars and trucks around us are basically just traffic. Knowing what sort of features Bev wanted, one of the short list candidates turned out to be the Acura TSX. Before beginning the search for a car for Bev, neither of us had even heard of an Acura TSX. Of course we'd heard of Acura, but had no idea about what the Acura models were. But now, Acura TSX (which is not all that common a model) seemed to be everywhere. Every day, I would see at least one of them on the road.

Of course I am not claiming that we manifested an increased number of Acura TSXs on the road in our region. They were always there. I'm only pointing out that since Acura TSX was on my mind I began to notice them when before I had not.

Of course, the same goes for real estate or home renovations or anything else. Bringing our thoughts into our consciousness is by far not limited to purchases or other business transactions. If you think about (look for)

---

[90] Learning how to be in the flow more often and more deeply is one of the central purposes of this book.

[91] I used to have good discussions with Bev about whether objective reality even exists. She argued there was no such thing. I was sure that objective reality existed, although I admitted that every individual's reality is a function of his senses and awareness. Now I have serious doubts about the existence of objective reality, except as a theoretical concept.

beauty and kindness, that's what you'll find. And if you look for ugliness and meanness, that's what you'll find.

Our internal condition affects what we think about. When we're in the flow our thoughts are more likely to be positive and peaceful[92]. By this mechanism, we manifest what we think about into our reality. That's why Bev says, "Concentrate on what you want more of"[93]. If you think big expansive thoughts you will have a big expansive reality. If you concentrate on being prosperous and believe yourself to be prosperous, you will experience prosperity.

Unfortunately the opposite is also true. If you concentrate on scarcity and lack, you will experience scarcity and lack. If your internal self-talk goes something like:

"I'm poor. I don't have enough. I'll always be poor and I'll never have enough. That's just my luck."

Then that's the sort of reality you will experience. That may seem bad enough, but let's say you have discovered the Law of Attraction, want to improve your situation, and concentrate on a thought like, "I need more money". What will happen is that you will manifest "I need more money" and will continue to need more money. That person might tell his buddies over a few pints that the Law of Attraction is just so much B.S. and doesn't work. In fact, quite the opposite is true. That person has manifested needing more money by concentrating on the fact that he needs more money. That person may have been better off to concentrate his thoughts more like this:

"The Universe is abundant and provides for me abundantly."

I should add that manifestation is not instantaneous; it takes place over a period of time. If you're already poor and you concentrate on "I need more money", as I've said above, you'll continue to need more money. If you're poor and start to concentrate your thoughts on the abundant nature of the Universe and your personal abundance, you'll become more abundant. But you will become more abundant on the Universe's schedule,

---

[92] You might argue the corollary here, i.e. that if our thoughts are positive and peaceful, we're more likely to be in the flow. If you were to say that, I would respond YES!! You've got it!

[93] See Preface at the beginning of the book.

not on your own. Be patient, keep your thoughts positive, and you will manifest what you think about.

So watch what you think about – your thoughts have power. When you hear someone say, "Don't even put that thought out there…", that's what that person means. He or she is exhorting you not to manifest a negative outcome. Concentrate on what you want more of, not what you're trying to avoid. As illustrated above, that's very important. The more in the flow you are, the more powerful you are. And the more powerful you are, the more you will manifest your concentrated thoughts into your reality. And this principle will become more obvious and clear to you.

Your Interpersonal World

Now that you have learned how to master[94] your internal world, we can move on to how to enjoy enriching interpersonal relationships. Everyone wants enriching interpersonal relationships. Some people work really hard at it. And the harder they work at it, the interpersonal life they want remains just slightly out of their reach. So I am not going to recommend that you work really hard at it.

Instead, I am going to recommend that you learn who you are, assess what you want in an interpersonal life, and act in the outside world in harmony with whom you are in the inside world. We are going to "minimize incongruity." To minimize incongruity, you will need to know and understand yourself thoroughly and maturely. So first, let's get to know who we are.

Know yourself

With so many tools now at our disposal for mastering our internal world, we should be able to get a good handle on who we are. Some people make fun of psychological testing or personality inventories, that sort of thing. I don't make fun of them; I think they're fascinating and valuable in understanding myself and appreciating others.

I'll give you some examples. The Myers-Briggs Type Indicator (MBTI) is designed to measure psychological preferences in how people perceive the world and make decisions. The purpose of the MBTI personality inventory is to

---

[94] Note that I say, "…learned how to master…" rather than "…mastered…". Doing so is a life-long journey.

make the theory of psychological types described by Carl Jung understandable and useful in regular people's (i.e. non-psychologists) lives[95].

The MBTI inventory has four preference pairs representing different levels.

> The first level measures your inner vs. outer orientation, i.e. do you prefer to focus on the outer world or on your own inner world? This is called Extraversion (E) or Introversion (I).
>
> The second preference pair measures how you process information, i.e. do you prefer to focus on the basic information you take in or do you prefer to interpret and add meaning? This is called Sensing (S) or Intuition (N).
>
> The third preference pair selects between how you make decisions, i.e. when making decisions, do you prefer to first look at logic and consistency or first look at the people and special circumstances? This is called Thinking (T) or Feeling (F).
>
> The final preference pair selects on structure, i.e. in dealing with the outside world, do you prefer to get things decided or do you prefer to stay open to new information and options? This is called Judging (J) or Perceiving (P).

When you decide on your preference in each category, you have your own personality type, which can be expressed as a code with four letters. Since a person can be either of each of the four preference pairs, that produces 16 types[96]. All types are equal in their value; there is no "best type". The goal of knowing about personality type is to understand and appreciate differences among people.

The 16 personality types of the Myers-Briggs Type Indicator® instrument are listed here as they are often shown in what is called a "type table."

ISTJ	ISFJ	INFJ	INTJ
ISTP	ISFP	INFP	INFP
ESTP	ESFP	ENFP	ENTP
ESTJ	ESFJ	ENFJ	ENTJ

---

[95] See http://www.myersbriggs.org/my-mbti-personality-type/mbti-basics/
[96] $2^4 = 16$

My MBTI is ENTJ[97]. To review the preference pairs above, that type indicates Extroverted, iNtuitive, Thinking, Judging[98]. Some qualities of that type are "*frank, decisive, assume leadership readily…quickly see illogical and inefficient procedures and policies, develop and implement comprehensive systems to solve organizational problems…*"[99]

While part of the value in taking personality typing tests like the MBTI is to come to understand yourself better, part of the value is also in understanding others better. If you understand others better then you'll get along with them more smoothly, have less friction and fewer interpersonal conflicts. When you think about the fact that the MBTI has 16 types, it may strike you that other people may be different than you. In fact the truth is that people interpret their worlds differently and process information that comes to them differently.

I believe that one of the major reasons why people have difficulty with each other at all is because they don't respect the seemingly obvious fact that the other person is a different person. This is called "Respecting the Otherness.[100]" While truly we're all connected in the fact that we're mostly empty space and vibration, recognizing and apprehending[101] the otherness can be a life-changing insight.

Other people may not process the same information the same way that you do. That doesn't make them wrong, and you have no obligation[102] to help them see things "correctly", i.e. the way you do. And yet we see this sort of thing happening all the time, and it's unfortunate. Everyone is exactly how he/she ought to be, given their inherited and experiential backgrounds.

---

[97] The exception to the rule of there being "no best type" is ENTJ, which is the best type.

[98] Having J vs. P for the final preference pair in the MBTI does not mean you are judgmental.

[99] These words come from the myersbriggs.org website.

[100] Many authors, philosophers, and theologians have written on the concept of "respecting the otherness". You can find the topic in the Koran and in the Bible.

[101] I use the word "apprehending" in some applications where others might use "comprehending". Both words mean to understand something. But apprehending carries the other meaning of to catch something or "get it". Apprehending captures the "Aha!" moment a little better than comprehending does. Also, to me at least, apprehending carries a meaning of understanding that transcends the intellectual to include the spirit and body as well.

[102] In fact, you have no right to do this at all. To do so does not respect the otherness.

So where does this lack of respect for otherness come from? For the folk with this issue of not respecting otherness, I believe that it comes from not mastering their internal world. Maybe I ought to say "never even attempting to understand their internal world" because lots of people live largely unconscious lives. To be able to concentrate on the external world, where all those other people are, we need to have a peaceful and quiet inner world. To be able to see that other person as separate but still connected is a matter of mature spiritual development. I believe that many people are tortured by a noisy and fractious inner world, with their ego screaming and complaining to them a lot of the time. For people like that it's difficult to see the other as anything but an extension of themselves. And that might explain a tendency for them to want to convince others to see things as they do.

But as Brian Tracy said, this is not for you. For those of us who are working on mastering their internal worlds, we're quiet and grounded enough to realize that other people may interpret the world differently than we do. So to sum up this thought, personality inventories like the MBTI help us to appreciate and respect the varied nature of humankind.

Another fascinating personality tool is the Enneagram, which is an ancient symbol of unity and diversity, change and transformation. The Enneagram is one of the most powerful tools for understanding ourselves. The Enneagram system was designed primarily to help elucidate the relationship between essence and personality, or ego[103]. The Enneagram is a nine-pointed symbol, representing nine natural orientations or types. It draws meaningful distinctions about the nine different ways that people approach their lives and relationships.

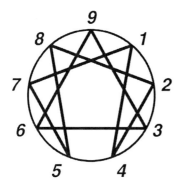

The Enneagram has a host of practical applications. We can use the Enneagram to understand a multitude of business applications, relationships, parenting, cultural differences, and personal growth...to gain more insight into academic psychology, philosophy, education, biography, the arts (and the styles of composers and creative artists), mythology and the study of archetypes, religion and mysticism, prayer and

---

[103] See the website: http://www.enneagraminstitute.com/

ascetic practices, spirituality and spiritual direction, psychological testing, and more[104].

Many full books have been written on the Enneagram, its interpretations and its applications. My purpose here is only to make you aware of it and encourage you to look into it for your own journey, as part of getting to know yourself.

I've taken several Enneagram tests and I always come out as a Type 8. I know deep down that typing is accurate for me and knowing that helps me understand my inclinations to act certain ways under certain circumstances. As a refinement I know that I'm a Type 8 with a 9 Wing, which is even more accurate. The literature tells me that I desire to appear solid. I see myself as earthy, simple, honest, practical, authoritative, solid, wise and considerate. That fits for me.

From studying the Enneagram, I know even more about myself. I know that when I am under stress and pressure and not at my best, I may behave like the down-side of Type 5, and become emotionally detached, analytical, and distant. When I'm in the flow and at my best, I can become like the healthy side of Type 2, i.e. more caring, empathetic, sincere, and warm-hearted.

As a Type 8, my word is my bond. I believe that being true to myself means that I try to say what I mean and mean what I say. I stand up for my beliefs and perceive backing down as a sign of weakness. Behind what some who don't know me well might consider a "tough exterior", actually I tend to be gentle, playful, childlike and sometimes innocent. Always one to laugh and joke around I try to see the humour in situations, even painful and difficult ones, sometimes inappropriately. I am also unusually devoted to and protective of those in my 'inner circle.' That last part is definitely Type 8.

---

[104] This is mostly a quote from the above website.

Here are some additional characteristics of Type 8. I believe that people close to me would verify this is pretty much true for me.

Need	You need to be your own authority, and seek independence to be master and commander of your own life. You have the need to feel confident, self-reliant and in charge of your emotions.
Avoid	You avoid being weak, vulnerable, controlled or manipulated. You fear being caught off guard, harmed and/or humiliated. You resist and defy anything that is imposed upon you.
Virtue	Your greatest strength is your sense of justice and desire to protect the weak and vulnerable. Big hearted by nature, you protect others even at your own expense. You deliver what have you promised.
Vice	Your vice is excess and going to extremes. Whatever you like, you want more of. Quick to respond, you can over react and come on too strong. You can be too much, too intense, and unwilling to self-limit.
Attention	Your attention goes to issues of power - who has it and if it is being used fairly. You are not interested in subtle nuance but rather in the big picture. You search for truth, justice, power and influence.
Spiritual Path	Your spiritual journey is to reclaim your sense of innocence. Spiritual growth will come when you can acknowledge a higher truth and a higher power.
Mantra	True strength comes from surrendering the need to have power and control. Showing sensitivity to others and acknowledging your own tender emotions are signs of strength, not signs of weakness.

That seems to be a lot of information about Type 8. If you study the Enneagram literature you'll see that the information I gathered and presented here about Type 8 barely scratches the surface. I chose Type 8 because that's my Enneagram type and the type I understand best. But every Enneagram type is fascinating and has a wealth of analogous information to describe it. My goal here is to illustrate the sort of self-awareness and understanding that can arise from studying the Enneagram, i.e. to learn about your own type and the types of those close to you.

The point of this section is to know who you are to help you to have a meaningful and successful interpersonal world. When you know yourself and have a grounded enough inner world to respect the otherness, interpersonal interactions come more easily. And if you know yourself, you have a much better likelihood of minimizing incongruity[105].

---

[105] The Encarta English Dictionary defines incongruity as "…something that

Minimize incongruity

We have gone to some extent to learn about mastering our internal world, controlling ego and so forth. And we have gone to some extent in getting to know and understand ourselves. That must be leading up to something important. After all, this section is about our interpersonal world and so far our focus has been internal and introspective.

Well no surprise: that is indeed the case. I am going to introduce here the notion of minimizing incongruity[106]. One of the keys to minimizing incongruity is to have mastered your inner world and to know yourself.

I ought to be clear about what I mean by minimizing incongruity and why that is important in maintaining healthy interpersonal relationships. When you act or speak in harmony with what you think, believe, and feel, you are acting congruously. Of course then, the only way you can act congruously, is if you are self-aware enough to know what you think, believe, and feel. That's why we have put so much emphasis on mastering the internal world and knowing ourselves.

Conversely, people who act incongruously pay a big price. I'd like to tell a short story from personal experience that I hope will illustrate what I mean. Five or so years ago when I was still working full time, our company's management team, including me, was obliged to attend a weekend management retreat. This management retreat had a metaphorical military theme, you know...teamwork, sacrifice, capturing hills, that sort of thing. Our CEO, whom no one ever accused of being in tune with or connected to his people, had a military background and continued to serve in the reserves at the time. I guess he figured a management retreat with a military theme was just what the company needed.

Just try to imagine a collection of 20-30 intelligent, independent, and opinionated scientists and engineers in a setting like that, force-fed unpalatable military metaphors for 12 hours a day. Military metaphors were not particularly meaningful to people usually immersed in the scientific method. I felt forced to maintain a huge incongruity gap. I wanted to stand up and scream "Enough already! This is madness!" But of course in

---

does not seem to fit in with or be appropriate to its context." That's the meaning we use in this book, i.e. behaviour that is inconsistent with the inner state and preferences.

[106] You might see fewer footnotes in this section. That's because I believe, to the best of my knowledge and recollection, that this notion of minimizing incongruity is my own thinking. If I first heard it somewhere else, then I don't remember it.

a corporate setting, you cannot behave that way. The tension and unease within the group grew steadily.

The retreat was an absolute disaster. It ended in anger, frustration, and resentment, with hard feelings and bitter cynicism as the aftermath. In my own case, it took me about 6 months of concerted effort to get my balance back. I had a smouldering pain in my gut from being forced to maintain such a huge incongruity gap for three intense long days.

Projecting a personality or values that are different from what they actually are consumes a lot of psychic and emotional energy. The need to act incongruously is unfortunately common in our culture, especially in the workplace. Western culture and the western workplace tend to value confidence, extroversion, and assertiveness. Dis[playing these qualities may not come naturally to some people.

Bev has told me many times that our society favours extroverts. She may be right on that one. No doubt introverts can also be confident and assured. Extroverts may not recognize this fact because introverts don't exhibit it their confidence the same way that extroverts do. Gentle people who by their true nature are introverted, introspective and reflective may feel they need to project more extroverted qualities to succeed in the western workplace. Maintaining that projection can be exhausting for some introverted people.

But this section is about our interpersonal world, which is a broader context than the workplace[107]. You might wonder what minimizing incongruity has to do with having a successful and enjoyable interpersonal world.

The element that connects minimizing incongruity to our interpersonal world is the BS detector[108]. As it turns out, we're all equipped with a BS detector, which like intuition and psychic ability is sharp when we're children but sometimes atrophies from lack of use as we mature. But all of us have a BS detector. Its function is to detect disingenuous and duplicitous behaviour in other people with whom we interact interpersonally. When you're interacting with someone and act incongruously, you will set off their BS detector. You know what it feels like to have your BS detector go off because certainly you've experienced it from the other side of the transaction, i.e. having your own BS detector activated by someone else.

When our BS detector goes off we feel uneasy and wary. The hair might

---

[107] We'll explore succeeding in the workplace in a later chapter.
[108] The BS Detector was discovered by Bernard Samson, an English "wet work" MI5 agent, gastronome, and philosopher.

stand up on the back of your neck. Your stomach may flutter. Depending on your own personality your BS detector may make you want to keep your distance from the source. Incongruous behaviour does not endear you to others. The only way you can get away with incongruous behaviour without alienating others is if you hang with people who have disconnected their BS detectors. That may appear to work OK for celebrities[109] whose entourage is composed of people with deactivated BS detectors, but it probably won't work for you[110].

Some people act incongruously inadvertently and unconsciously. It's difficult for these people to act consistent with their deep values because they have not done the work of mastering their inner world or learning who they are or what their values actually are. For people in this condition, I'm not sure that the concept of minimizing incongruity even applies. How can a person act inconsistent with their values if they don't have a conscious knowledge of what those values are?

So clearly, one good reason for minimizing incongruity is to avoid setting off the BS detectors of the people with whom we interact. If you are not genuine in the way you interact, if you're putting in an effort to act differently than who you really are, whether you realize it or not, other people are going to be put off.

But the bigger reason for minimizing incongruity is from the other side of the interpersonal transaction. As I said above, people who act incongruously pay a big price. Projecting a false self, whom you mistakenly imagine will be more interesting, entertaining, or engaging to the other, is tiring and not worth the effort. The larger the gap between the essence of who you are, and what you really feel, value, and think, and how you behave, i.e. what you actually say and do, the larger the cost to you in psychic and emotional energy.

Now that we have gone to such effort to master our internal world and get to know who we are, why would we ever act incongruously? Once you come to the realization that people actually do not have to like you for you to survive, everything will come easier for you. You do not minimize incongruity solely because you want people to like you. Actually, you do not need everyone to like you. Your higher self is entirely independent of others'

---

[109] Tracy Jordan with his entourage of Griz and Dot.com on NBC's "30 Rock" is a good example. See: http://www.imdb.com/title/tt0496424/

[110] If it is working for you, or seems to you to be working for you, you might want to take a look at the genuineness of your behaviour and the people with whom you're hanging, and why.

judgements, approval or disapproval. You mainly minimize incongruity to avoid the leak of your precious psychic energy[111]. You minimize incongruity to minimize the cost burden of behaving incongruously. And as a pleasant offshoot bonus, you might actually become eminently more likeable, because you won't be setting off BS detectors all the time.

It's time for a reality check. We live in an imperfect world inhabited by imperfect humans. Some situations will arise when you will need to act in certain ways if you want to get by. Imagine having a family commitment with your in-laws on a beautiful summer week when you had planned to go camping with a buddy. Or imagine having uninvited house-guests who sit on the couch, expect to be wined and dined, while not pitching in to help with cleanup, or contribute anything other than their needs. You're basically their host and butler at the same time. Situations like these demand that you conduct yourself with grace and good manners, even if what you're doing so is not necessarily what you might choose to do in a theoretically perfect world. Changing your attitude to the situation eases the strain of incongruity. If you change your mind about it, you become more congruous.

Situations like these don't call you to express exactly what you think and feel or to do exactly what you would like, as if you were five years old. We have a civilization, which like it or not demands that we be civilized. The keys to making the most out of situations like these lie outside the realm of minimizing incongruity. They lie in a different set of skills, including apprehending and accepting the situations exactly like they are, without resistance, and in controlling our own internal orientation toward the situations[112]. That way, you will be minimizing incongruity, *given the circumstances*.

Be trustworthy

I believe that most of us want others to trust us. So what's the key to having other people trust us? Well, it's being trustworthy. If you want other people to trust you, be trustworthy. That's the part you can control with a little discipline.

---

[111] If you study and reflect on the Yoga Sutra, you'll see that minimizing incongruity is consistent with following the Yama of *Brachmacharya,* at least in my opinion.

[112] See sections on behavior, attitudes, and values, and no resistance later in this chapter.

So how does a trustworthy person behave? Let's start with talking straight. Mean what you say, say what you mean, and do what you say you're going to do. If you talk straight, that's the first step in becoming trustworthy. If you consistently do what you say you're going to do, other people will notice that you mean what you say.

Another important part of talking straight is not to gossip. This may seem obvious but some people cannot resist the lure of gossip. Don't do it[113]. I read somewhere that good minds think and talk about events, great minds think and talk about ideas, and small minds think and talk about other people. I know I feel uneasy when I'm in a small group of people, perhaps another couple, and everyone (but me) starts talking about someone else who isn't there. That discomfort occurs even if the comments seem on the surface to be positive. Even if the comments are positive, that still implies judgement, doesn't it? My BS detector goes off. I also feel uneasy when I'm with a small group or even one other person, and that person starts asking me questions about someone I know who isn't present. Like, how old is she? Where does she work? Is he married? It's as if they want me to provide a little bio on this person. Usually I don't know the answers to the questions they're asking anyway.

Sometimes in a setting like that, when I have a chance to speak I'll say something like,

> *"Don't we have something bigger or more interesting to talk about than Larry (or Fred, or whomever)? I feel a little uncomfortable talking about someone who isn't here. Why don't we talk about our own ideas or plans?"*

Of course that sort of interjection doesn't always go over well. But I don't care that much. I've tried it. Everyone will stare at me for a brief period and soon enough the conversation drifts back to other people. I think talking about other people is small minded and I avoid doing it as much as I can. When I'm in the presence of people who are gossiping I can feel my stomach tightening up, which indicates that one of my values is being violated.

Another way to build your trustworthiness is to keep your promises and pay your debts. If you promise to do something, make sure you do it. Similarly, if you owe somebody something, whether it's a favour or a debt, pay it. Get that debt off your shoulders. If it's your turn to pay for

---

[113] Once more, as Brian Tracy would say, "this is not for you."

lunch, make sure you pay for it. If you have promised to drive a friend to the airport, take him to the airport. Never make a promise you can't keep. That way, you will be able to keep your promises. And when you promise to do something, everyone knows that you will do it.

Finally, if you want to be trustworthy, don't worry about being liked. Stick to your values. This section isn't about pleasing others or manipulating others into liking you. It's about being trustworthy. Being trustworthy entails being true to yourself. If you disagree with someone's opinion, and they ask you what you think, say so. If they don't ask you what you think, you can speak up or hold your peace, as you wish. But keep in mind that if you stifle yourself too much from speaking your truth, you will block the free flow of chi through your throat chakra[114]. You don't want to reduce the flow to your upper chakras. You need energy up there.

When you stand your ground and stick to your values, you keep your integrity. Others can like it or not like it. That will be up to them and you will not worry about it. When you are solid in your values, you will build a reputation of integrity. And others will trust you because of that.

Behaviour, attitudes, and values

I like to think about behaviour, attitudes, and values to be like a set of Russian dolls. Behaviour is like the largest doll – the one you see. It is on the surface. You can observe and measure behaviour. For that reason, you could argue that behaviour is objective. Behaviour is more or less within our control, depending on the circumstances. And because behaviour is within our control, with some effort and determination, we can change it.

Habits are patterns of behaviour. We'll respond in habitual ways to stimuli that we link to the habit. For example, if a person smokes tobacco, they will light up when they get in their car for the commute home after work. They will light up again after dinner, and so forth. We have all heard how difficult it is to quit smoking. But most of us believe that habits can be broken with motivation, effort and willpower.

As we get older, perhaps more and more of our behaviour becomes patterned and habitual. But in the final analysis, as long as we're conscious, behaviour is under our control.

---

[114] To learn about the throat chakra, see: http://www.chakra-colors.com/Throat-Chakra/

Attitudes lie beneath behaviour. They are the Russian doll inside the largest, Behaviour one. Where behaviour can be observed and measured directly, attitudes cannot. Attitudes can only be discerned or apprehended indirectly, from observing behaviour. When we believe we can identify patterns in behaviour, we can attribute those behaviours back to the attitudes which may underlie the behaviours. Our attitudes predispose us or motivate us to behave in certain ways when faced with certain situations. Basically our attitudes are a set of positive or negative judgements about other people, objects, events, activities, ideas, and other elements in our environments[115]. Attitudes are learned. Most attitudes are the result of either direct experience or observational learning from the environment.

We form attitudes at an early age from hearing what our parents say and watching what they do under different circumstances. As adolescents we form attitudes from our peers, which are ultimately important to us at that age. As adolescents, we form our attitudes to conform to group norms, because fitting in is of prime importance to us. If our peer group likes this, we like it too. If our peers think this is cool, we think it's cool too. If our peers think this is gross, we think it's gross too. You get the idea.

And we continue to form attitudes as adults. We are just a little more discerning and discriminating and self-driven about what attitudes we form than we were as teenagers. We may take a little longer to form our attitudes as adults than we were as teens, and we have become a little more sophisticated about what attitudes we form. As I said above, our attitudes predispose us or motivate us to behave in certain ways when faced with certain situations. In that regard, they're kind of a behavioural shortcut for us. They are kind of lightly burned-in behavioural program.

So as we continue to form and re-form attitudes as we go through life, we have to ask ourselves to what degree we can consciously change our attitudes. Well, I can tell you here that the answer is yes, of course we can consciously change our attitudes. If we understand that attitudes influence behaviours and we want to change a particular behaviour for the better, the way to go about that is to look at the attitude underlying the behaviour. We can work at the behavioural level and consciously modify our behaviour each time a situation arises. That is one way to do it. But that approach requires a lot of repeated effort and not fool-proof. Our behaviour can slip into old habits if we are not right on the spot in control at the moment we need to change it.

Or we can examine what underlying attitude is predisposing us to

---

[115] Zimbardo et al., 1999

behave in a way that we want to change. Let me provide some illustrative personal testimony here. Before I tell this story, I want to start by saying that I maintain love, compassion and respect for the memories of my parents. They lived in a different time from ours. They did not have instant electronic communication, available information, and exposure to a diversity of people like we have now. Their view of the world came from what they read in books and newspapers, heard on the radio, and saw on TV. I believe their social attitudes were for the most part normal for their time.

With those disclaimers aside, I was raised in a racist home. I'm not proud to say that but I believe it's the truth. Neither of my parents is alive so I am not going to hurt anyone's feelings by saying so. My parents expressed racist thoughts and opinions that were largely unconscious and certainly uninformed. I was raised in Winnipeg during the 50s. I don't believe Winnipeg was unusually racist; I believe adults were fairly casual about racism all across our culture during those days. I have no way of knowing this for sure, but I expect a lot of men and women my age who grew up in North America during the 50s were raised in an environment of casual racism. Winnipeg was a good example of a cultural melting pot. We had lots of immigrants and people of different religious and ethnic backgrounds. So maybe the adults around me had plenty of opportunity to express their racism. I expect that other cities like Toronto and Chicago were probably similar, but who knows and that's not the point. I have had to work hard to overcome the negative and racist attitudes my parents so casually passed on to me.

The point is, I heard things at home all the time that parents today would never say around their kids, with their peers, or to each other. My parents were equal opportunity racists. They casually spread it around equally to Jews, gays, Eastern-European immigrants (like Ukrainians and Poles), and aboriginal peoples, basically anyone with a background different from ours.

My most recent recollection of that is actually fairly recent. I can recall one incident when my mom was visiting us when our sons were teens. That would have been in the early 90s. We were driving in the car, my mom beside me and Steve in the back. I can't recall the actual conversation or even the topic. But what I do recall was my mom saying some extremely racist things about aboriginal people. Now, this woman was a warm hearted and loving mother and grandmother. At the same time, she harboured some racist attitudes about aboriginal peoples. When she was making these racist remarks, I felt distinctly uncomfortable because I didn't want to be rude or disrespectful to my mother. But at the same time, I didn't want my teenage son hearing this racist nonsense. It was a tough situation. I tried to get her to stop gently. When that didn't work (I guess Mom felt she was correct in what she was saying) I had to ramp it up and state very clearly that she was violating an important value. I said something like, "Look! Stop talking that way. I don't want my son exposed to such racism." She stopped but I don't think she liked it much.

My point is that attitudes are fluid compared to values. We can change our attitudes if we want to make the effort. Perhaps our values evolve during our life also. The Russian dolls analogy is a good one but it only goes so far. That image implies a discreet boundary between where an attitude begins and a value leaves off. The point I want to make is that the deepest changes are the most difficult to make. The deeper based the attitude is, the harder it will be to change the behaviour that derives from that attitude.

And before I forget – minimizing incongruity is not an excuse for bad behaviour. Of course you don't want to behave incongruously. We already know that doing so activates other's BS detectors and creates a psychic cost for us. But your wanting to act in harmony with your attitudes does not give you license to act like a jackass. If your attitudes need changing, change them. The section on minimizing incongruity assumes you have healthy attitudes based on information, experience and solid values.

At the deepest level we have our values. They are the smallest of the set of three Russian dolls, inside the middle-sized Attitudes one. A lot of psychologists and other scholars believe that our deepest values are formed very early in life, maybe by age 5 – 7. Up to the age of seven, we are like sponges, absorbing everything around us and accepting much of it as true, especially when it comes from our parents[116]. Human organizations in both private and public sectors will be happy to list their core values for your inspection. They want us to know what they stand for. Problem is, some of these value statements activate our BS detectors. Back when I worked full time in management, I remember my immediate supervisor, the VP of our research division, confiding in me about a senior management retreat where the top management group worked at establishing one of these value statements for our corporation.

Now this guy had a tendency toward straight talk, i.e. saying what he meant and meaning what he said. That to me was a positive attribute

---

[116] See: http://changingminds.org/explanations/values/values_development.htm

but it meant this guy could not stay with our corporation very long. He could not minimize incongruity as much as would have been healthy for him. His work environment was too toxic and too woven with insincerity and duplicity. For the time we had him in the senior management group, he was like a breath of fresh air to work with. He was trustworthy. He reported to me how he and his senior management colleagues had come up with this value statement and they were pleased with themselves. It was the kind of value statement any corporation would be proud of. The problem was that the value statement was false. If it really were a statement of our values, then we sure were not acting that way. So either the value statement was inaccurate or we were acting out of step with our values. You would think that if the organization said we value respect and we value transparency then the people who work in the organization would behave in accordance with those values. But that draft value statement seemed to have no attachment to reality. Have you ever read the value statements on the wall of a hospital and yet you had a distinctly different experience during your stay? Some spiritually awakened people say we teach what we most have to learn. Maybe inadvertently that's what corporate value statements really are – what the corporation has yet to learn.

My supervisor pointed out this glaring inconsistency at the management retreat. He said it got kind of sticky for a while after that. But his BS detector had been activated and he had to speak up. That's the kind of thing a values-based person will do. The possibility that had he not been there, no one else would have realized the inconsistency makes me think.

What does it mean to be value-driven? I remember many years ago attending a time management seminar[117] to learn some skills. I expected to be taught some behavioural based techniques, like sharpen your pencils in the morning, make a to-do list, and so forth. Instead, the seminar leader asked each of us to write down privately what were the five most important things to us. He was asking us to examine our values. He was taking the first important step in teaching us to organize our lives around our priorities and devoting our time accordingly. Bingo! That was one of those lights-on moments for me.

One major key to leading a purposeful and impactful life is to act in harmony with your values. Your values are the things that matter most to you, the things you want to experience in this life, and the things you most want to stand for. Of course I cannot tell you what your values ought to be. That is an intensely personal matter. Acting in harmony with your values

---

[117] We'll explore managing our time a little later in the book.

includes but goes beyond minimizing incongruity. To act in harmony with your values, of course you need to know what those values are. Do you know what your values are? What if I asked you to write down the five most important things to you in your life – would you be able to do that? If you have never taken quiet time to examine your values, I suggest you do that sometime soon[118].

But what about values clash, you ask. When values clash, people go their separate ways. People leave jobs over clashes in values. If a place of employment claims to value family and work/life balance but actually does not, their employees who do value family and work/life balance will eventually find it impossible to work there without huge personal cost. Marriages and other intimate personal relationships end because of clashes of values. That's tough but that is the way it is, and to my way of thinking the way it ought to be.

Bev and I have had plenty of disagreements over the years. Sometimes, these disagreements have been because of different interpretations of facts and events. Different experiential backgrounds will lead to that sort of thing. If you have been following this section, you will know that this implies we may bring different attitudinal orientations to the situation under debate. That is no big surprise; no two people can have identical experiential backgrounds. So we may disagree strongly on some issues. It would be difficult to imagine how it could be otherwise for two bright, reflective, opinionated people with strong personalities. But when you cut to the heart of it, I believe Bev and I share common values. We were both raised during the 50s in Winnipeg in working class homes. We have been able to overcome these disagreements and enjoy each other's company in an intimate relationship for more than 40 years because we both value the same things. Our values are aligned.

So if you happen to be a young person reading this and contemplating marriage or cohabitation with someone you love deeply, I recommend you have a serious heart to heart with your significant other and examine your values. Take a weekend away from distractions specifically for this purpose. Find out what your own values are. Write them down. And find out what the values of your loved ones are too. To a great degree your values define you.

You do not need a big sophisticated process to do this. Just follow the outline of this section. Let us assume you have taken a weekend away

---

[118] See: http://www.decision-making-solutions.com/personal_core_values.html. See also: http://beanoriginal.net/my-five-core-personal-values-and-how-i-use-them/

J. Michael Curtis

without interruptions to honour this process. For Day 1 of your couple's values retreat, start with a blank sheet of paper each and a pencil with an eraser. Work separately at different tables. Take 15 minutes without conversation and write down the five things you value most, and put them into priority order. When the 15 minutes are up, get together and compare notes. One person speaks at a time without interruption from the other. Then take a coffee break.

For the next round, start with a fresh sheet of paper and work quietly and separately as before. Write down three behaviours you'd like to change and link them to attitudes that could be driving the behaviours. Get together and compare notes as before, one person speaking at a time without interruption. Then take another break and a walk outside, followed by a leisurely lunch.

For the third round, start with a fresh sheet of paper and work quietly and separately as before. Write down some strategies you will employ to effect the changes in the attitudes you identified in the previous round. Be as specific as you can about actions you will take. Then get together and compare notes as before, one person speaking at a time without interruption. Go back to your notes separately and prepare an action plan for yourself based on the discussion you've just had and the insights you reached. Then take another break.

For the final round, start with a fresh sheet of paper and work quietly and separately as before. Write down the five things you most love and appreciate about your partner and why you value them, i.e. how those things affect you. Get together and compare notes as before, one person speaking at a time without interruption. End with a hug. Then open a bottle of good Cabernet Sauvignon, drink a glass each and celebrate an awesomely successful Day 1. Go for another walk outside before a nice dinner for two.

Day 2 is a free day. Have fun and treat each other with love and respect.

No resistance – this is a big one.

If you're in a situation that you don't particularly like, offer no resistance. Apprehend reality; don't judge it. As grown up people in a developmental path, we need to deal with reality as it is, rather than wasting our valuable physical, emotional, and psychic energy lamenting that reality is not what we'd prefer it to be. As cool dudes say these days, "It is what it is."

86

If reality isn't what you would like it to be, offer no resistance. As The Borg[119] were so fond of saying, "resistance is futile." Resistance to reality is a huge waste of energy. When you resist what you do not want, you are not allowing what you want to come to you. When you resist, you are sending out a contradictory vibration along with your desired intent[120]. A double minded state creates a duality that prevents you from being fully present. As I said in the previous chapter, concentrate on what you want more of. Don't concentrate on the situation you don't want, or it will persist.

In the meantime, theory aside we will still need to cope with that situation that we don't like. Shutting your eyes and squeezing them tight and wishing the situation away, like some modern-day Peter Pan, will not change the present reality. Let me illustrate with a personal story.

About 12 years after moving back West from Montreal, Bev and I visited the Maritimes. I was in Fredericton New Brunswick for a conference. Bev came along because we planned to take a vacation after the conference ended. When we'd lived in Montreal we had become close friends with a woman through our church named Shirley. She and her husband Ted, being about 10 years older than we were, had recently retired to a rustic rural acreage home in the woods of rural New Brunswick. Shirley had encouraged us to visit them if were ever out their way. So this was an opportunity to have a nice afternoon visit while we were on our way to somewhere else.

The only potential complication was that Ted, a dry alcoholic and retired airline pilot, was the most unhappy, bitter, and unfriendly man we had ever encountered. We'd met him when we lived in Montreal and remembered him. He wasn't the sort of guy you forgot. He made Oscar the grouch seem like Kermit the frog[121]. He was estranged with everyone except Shirley, including all his adult kids. He had written each of them off one by one after they had disappointed him or slighted him in some small way. Ted and Shirley were comfortable financially on their retirement savings and Ted's generous Air Canada pension. But he refused to help

---

[119] The Borg are a pseudo-race of cybernetic beings from the Delta Quadrant. Their ultimate goal is perfection through the forcible assimilation of diverse sentient species, technologies, and knowledge. As a result, they are among the most powerful and feared races in the galaxy.

[120] See: http://www.mindreality.com/offer-no-resistance-to-what-you-do-not-want

[121] Oscar the Grouch is a Muppet character on the television program Sesame Street. He has a green body and lives in a trash can. As his name would imply, Oscar is grouchy. Kermit the frog, on the other hand, is a happy-go-lucky guy who is always optimistic and cheerful.

his kids because they had all disappointed him. He'd just closed his heart to them. Anyway, 12 years had passed, we wanted to see Shirley, and Ted could have mellowed by this time. We figured how bad could it be?

And it turned out to be not bad at all – for Bev at least. After the first few minutes, Shirley said to Bev with some cheery enthusiasm, "Why don't we leave the boys to get re-acquainted and you and I can have a nice chat outside?" With that, they went up the stairs and outside and left me alone in the dark basement rec-room with Ted. Just like that, there we were – Ted and me - just the two of us. It seemed like a scene from a Stephen King movie.

This was a situation that I wouldn't exactly have chosen to be in. Yet here we were. This was not the time for me to minimize incongruity by speaking my mind and heart…maybe give old Ted some of his own treatment back. It was a situation that called on me to act graciously, compassionately, and with good humour. To enable me to do that I, applied the "no resistance" principle. Breathe – centre – focus.

I tried some polite small talk. Ted nearly bit my nose off. Then I had the idea to ask Ted for his assistance with something…draw him out, get him talking about something he knew about. This was our first time in rural New Brunswick. Why not pull out our road map and get Ted's opinion on the best route to our next destination? Although Ted continued to grumble and complain about the country roads and the impossibility of getting anywhere quickly, that approach did help some.

The only problem was that with Ted's angry and jerky movements, he tore my map pretty badly. He gave it a good foot and a half rip. But pretty soon after he tore my map, Bev and Shirley returned, and with them, some feminine civility. Soon we had a nice cup of tea and we were on our way again. The only damage done was to the road map.

When I was left alone with old Ted, I knew that the situation would pass. Most times, when you feel unsettled, it's because you're not in the present moment. You may be reliving the past or worrying about the future. During those times, it helps to bring yourself into the present moment, which when you examine it, usually is not really so bad. In this particular situation, the present moment was actually fairly crappy. Knowing that this situation would pass helped me to ground and centre myself. I could live with the present moment because I realized that it was just a passing moment.

So how do you not resist a situation that you don't like much and maybe even resent a little? It comes back to the central issue of mastering the internal world. You need a disciplined ego. Good thing we know how to discipline our egos, right? Of course, it's your ego that's screaming at you and causing you suffering when you're in a situation you don't like. And "suffering" is an important choice of word here. A few years ago in a yoga class Glenda taught us that when we face a task or situation, we can respond in three ways: 1) with enjoyment, 2) with enthusiasm, 3) with acceptance. Responding in any other way than one of those three will create "suffering for yourself and for those around you". That suffering is largely under your control. You create it with your response to the situation. Choose not to suffer. Discipline your ego. And offer no resistance.

I've been getting my hairs cut by Theresa for about 10 years now. Theresa is a good haircutter but she's also a grandmother with a tough exterior, a sense of humour, and a keen eye for the human condition. By her station in the hair studio hangs a little framed cartoon of an arch-looking mature woman who says, "Put on your big girl panties and deal with it." That's the other element in coping with situations you don't like. The complete package is: choose not to suffer, discipline your ego, offer no resistance, and adopt a mature attitude.

Don't give advice

Here we are in a book full of opinions and recommendations, basically a book which provides advice, and we come to a section titled "Don't give advice." I am aware of the irony. Please read on nonetheless. You may be surprised that in my day to day life, I do my best to minimize providing advice, and that's what I'm going to advocate in the paragraphs that follow.

In the Introduction I quoted Bev's expression, "Everyone has a suggestion for someone else." She was the first to say that, at least to me. We're going to expand on that idea here. Bev said that a few years before I began to appreciate Stuart Wilde's broader principle[122] to avoid giving advice at all. I believe Bev's comment was a wry observation of human behaviour. No doubt it's true. We see it all the time. How do you like it when someone says to you:

"Look – your problem is..."

"You know what you should do? What you should do is..."

---

[122] Stuart Wilde - *Infinite Self: 33 Steps to Reclaiming Your Inner Power*

I think most of us would just as soon skip advice like that. And the reasons are fairly obvious. It's trite and disrespectful for anyone to think that they understand someone else's situation better than they do themselves. And it's hubris[123] to believe you're somehow in a position to tell that person what they should do. None of us can possibly be able to comprehend and appreciate the complex web of experiences and preferences another brings to a situation that is confounding them. If we're only half-conscious, we likely want to be a little less arrogant and a little more humble than that.

Jesus of Nazareth, who taught a lot of good truth, said *"first take the plank out of your own eye, and then you will see clearly to remove the speck from your brother's eye."*[124]

The two examples above are of the rude unsolicited variety. I believe it's fairly clear that to offer unsolicited advice is impolite and disrespectful. If we have a habit of doing this, we want to take some steps to break that habit. It's abrasive and insensitive to offer unsolicited advice.

But what about when someone asks us for advice? What if someone says, "What should I do?" Stuart Wilde would say to refuse to give advice then too. And I would agree. Avoid giving advice even when you're asked, even if you believe that you know what the person should do and assuming that you want what's best for them.

I can think of two good reasons for avoiding giving advice, even when you're asked to do so. The first reason is fairly obvious. If you give advice and the result turns out unfavourably, that looks like you gave bad advice and it's your fault it didn't turn out well. Do you want someone else's misfortune to be the result of bad advice you provided? I don't think so.

The second reason is a little more subtle. When you give advice, in a sense the person to whom you have provided it has become dependent on you. He/she will expect you to provide advice the next time a difficult decision comes along. And if you refuse to provide advice in a different situation in the future, the other person may resent you for it. Stuart Wilde's image for this situation is memorable. He says it is as if you have swept up the other person, who has become miniature, in your big strong hand and lifted them off their feet. Their little legs are dangling and kicking in the air. Then when you go to put them back down on their feet, they ask indignantly, "Hey, what's this?" They don't like being put back onto their feet.

So the next time someone asks you, "What should I do?" try answering

---

[123] I really like the word "hubris". I use it when I can but it's never enough.
[124] Matthew 7:5, New International Version.

something in a calm and kind voice like, "I don't know what you should do. What would you <u>like</u> to do?"

That question is powerful. You'll probably hear back something like, "Well, what I'd like to do is abc, but I'm concerned that if I do that, xyz might happen". As long as the other person is analysing the situation himself, delineating alternatives, and imagining positive and negative consequences, he's taking care of business and you are truly helping him out. Help him with his analysis by asking good questions, e.g. "What do you think might happen then?" "How would you feel about that?"

Do that and you're helping. But don't offer advice. When you do that you rob the other person of his power and remove his responsibility for managing his own affairs.

Before we leave the question of not giving advice I'd like to say a little more about the difference between giving advice and helping. Helping is kind and generous. Helping is a good thing. When you have an opportunity to help someone out, do that. If helping includes passing on information that you have and the person who needs help does not have, that situation is a little different than offering advice, in the way I have been describing it. By all means, pass on that helpful information.

Let me illustrate with a little story. All the stories in this book are my own stories except this one, which comes from a friend. But I think it is the perfect story to illustrate what I mean. The story goes like this. My friend's family included an older couple who were retired, living in their own small house. The man had served in the Second World War and had become disabled. They had no income and little savings. They did not know that he was eligible for veteran's assistance and disability assistance from Social Security. Without this supplemental income, the couple was in danger of losing their house. Who knew what would have happened after that? Another family member, unasked, took it upon herself to advise them that they could get this financial assistance and helped them to apply for it. They were successful and both lived in their little home until they died.

The person who passed along that important information about the availability of financial assistance helped that elderly couple keep their home. That is helping.

Expand your outward orientation

I believe that one of the major reasons people have difficulties with interpersonal relationships is that they do not have the discipline or make the effort to direct their attention outward when they are interacting with someone else. I know that's the case with me. When I have had difficulties, it's been because my orientation has been too much inward and not enough outward. Consider this superb quote from a recent publication.

> *"We can't see people as they really are because we are too busy reacting to our own internal experiences of what they evoke in us, so we rarely relate to reality. We mostly relate to internal remembrances of our own history, stimulated and evoked by whatever is externally before us."*[125]

As Bev has said, our job when relating to others is to get ourselves out of the way. When we are relating to someone else, we need to quiet our inner world and focus our attention outward, i.e. on that other person. This principle applies to your relationship with your spouse as much as it does to your relationships to others, including new people you meet. I believe marriages fail or fall into difficulty because of the inability of married people to quiet their own inner processes and see their spouse as a separate person with a full life, and worthy of respect. But we will cover that topic in a later chapter[126]. For now let's return to the everyday circumstances of encountering and relating to another person who is not your spouse. When you meet someone, quiet your inner processes, call them by name, look that person in the eye, and when you shake hands, see if you can apprehend that person's vibrational state through the hand touch. The important thing is to quiet your inner chatter and focus outward.

Most of us want to be an interesting person, the kind of person others are drawn to and find interesting. The key here is, if you want to be interesting, be interested. I am reminded of an old story from my Dale Carnegie training, which I will paraphrase here.

Back in the days of ladies and gentlemen, a well-bred lady put on a fine dinner party. This was the sort of formal dinner party where you would meet strangers and have a seat at the table assigned to you with a place card. As it turned out, a single gentleman faced a single lady across the table whom he had not met before. He looked at her as if she were the only person in the room, smiled, and started asking her questions about herself…her opinions on current events, her favourite books, that sort of thing. The evening passed very pleasantly. The gentleman and

---

[125] "Synchronicity the Inner Path of Leadership" by Joseph Jaworski (1996) BK publishers
[126] See the "You are connected but don't lose yourself" section in "Love and Respect Your Spouse" chapter, later in this book

lady had a long and animated conversation, which was characterised by the gentleman's asking the lady questions that got her to open up and talk about herself. The gentleman never talked about himself. The next day, the lady sent a note to the hostess thanking her for the invitation, and especially for seating her across from the fine gentleman who was a "brilliant conversationalist". I believe that the point is obvious: direct your focus outward.

Give that other person your complete undivided attention. Want to have success with someone you find attractive? When you are with a person you want to know better, treat her (or him) as though they are the only other person there. Make eye contact, smile, and ask that person questions about herself. Forget about telling her what a cool dude you are, with all your cool experiences and cool possessions. If you can get her to open up and talk about herself, you'll be a brilliant conversationalist too. The way to do that is ask her questions that call for her to offer her opinions and preferences. The dinner party story may be almost a hundred years old but that doesn't matter. Human nature has not changed that much. Dale Carnegie training teaches that people love to hear their own names and they (by and large anyway) love an opportunity to talk about themselves. A person's name[127] and the sound of his own voice are music to his ear. I'm not being cynical; that's just the way it is.

I just mentioned the use of names. Before I close this section, I want to say a couple of things about remembering other people's names and using them. All of us have run into people who say things like,

> *"I just can't remember names. I never forget a face, but I'm no good at remembering names."*

I have no doubt believing that is true because we hear it all the time. But the fact is anyone can remember names if they make the effort to do so.

When you are introduced to someone, all it takes for you to remember his name is to calm down, quiet your interior clamour, including all that ego-self-talk, and focus on the other person. I do not want to sound high and mighty here because I have forgotten names lots of times. I am usually pretty good at remembering names but sometimes when I am introduced to someone new in a social setting, I will forget their name in

---

[127] Some of my more introverted friends have told me this is not the case for them. They find it inappropriately intimate to have someone they barely know call them by name. Dale Carnegie taught otherwise. I guess he was an extrovert seeing the world through extrovert's glasses.

a few minutes. But I know why that happens. Whenever I have difficulty remembering someone's name, it happens because I was not grounded or properly outward focused at the time of the introduction. When that happens, I say something like, "I'm sorry, but I have forgotten your name and I want to remember it. What was it again?" And when they tell me, I look them straight in the eye, use their name and say something like, "Thank you Larry. I will remember."

Don't say, "I just can't remember names…" because basically, I don't believe it's true. I believe that when people cannot remember names it's because of their noisy internal world and their own interpersonal anxiety. Those conditions are potentially controllable by anyone who wants to learn how to do it. People who have given up on remembering names do that basically because it is not worth the effort for them. Remembering names is within your reach. Anyone can do it.

Remembering and using other people's names is important in interpersonal relations because it is affirming to the other person. Remembering names is good manners. It tells the other person that you value having just met him. It also affirms you as someone who was paying attention at the time of the introduction. When you forget the other person's name (and tell yourself the truth, they can tell when you have forgotten their name) you send a message that meeting the other person just was not that important to you. Also, sad to say, when you make no effort to remember names, in my opinion that kind of labels you as a bit of a lightweight or a flake.

In 1997, I met Manitoba Premier Gary Filmon one evening at a stand up social event at the Canadian Embassy in Warsaw, Poland. We were there for separate reasons and just happened to meet by chance at this event over Polish vodka and finger foods. Someone introduced us. Of course I had no problem remembering Mr. Filmon because he was the premier of Manitoba and semi-famous at the time. We made some small talk; I told him I was originally from Manitoba, that sort of thing. Then we went our separate ways and mingled with the other guests. An hour or so later, we ran into each other again, each of us having spoken to several other people since our introduction earlier. Gary looked me right in the eye and said something like, "How are you doing Mike – having a good time?" I felt affirmed. That's how it's done folks.

Raising Children

If you have children, raising them so that they have a chance to be happy in their life is the most important thing you will do in your life. It's a sacred responsibility. Can you think of anything more important?

I believe that we have two distinct phases in our lives. The first is when we do not have children. That period is composed of our childhood, adolescence and young adulthood. For me, that was my first 30 years. The second phase is when we become parents (and later grandparents), and that lasts the rest of our lives. Our sons are grown men now, but they are still my kids, I want what's best for them, and I help them out when I can. They do not need me to shape their values any more. I could not now if I tried and it would be disrespectful for me to do so. But from time to time when the need arises, I believe I still have to model behaviour, attitude and values.

I had better be clear right away that I do not consider myself to be any sort of expert on raising kids. Subject experts have published volumes and volumes of scholarly work on childhood development. Whole sections in bookstores are devoted to the subject of effective parenting. Monthly publications, both scholarly and non-scholarly fly out to private homes and physician's and psychologist's offices.

As Steve Earle would say, I'm just a regular guy. All I know about parenting is what I have picked up from my own observations and experiences[128] and the little I have read.

In one way, I am specially qualified to write on the topic of fathering. If you read the Introduction, you will know that my own father died shortly after my 14th birthday. Up to that point, he had not been a particularly

---

[128] Some people define experience as the lessons learned from making mistakes.

positive role model anyway[129]. After that point, I had no role model for fathering at all. After his untimely and tragic death, no one from my immediate dysfunctional family stepped in to fill the void. I was pretty much left alone to fend for myself emotionally. So basically I was raised without a father. What that turned out to mean was that when I became a father myself, I had no instinctive grounding to know how to respond to different situations.

I can recall many times when Steven[130] was a little toddler, Bev would have to cue me to respond with a normal fatherly action that would have been natural for most guys. If Steve fell and scraped his knee, I would stand there and look at him. Although I would feel bad for him, Bev would have to say something like, "Pick him up and hug him." Pathetic, right? Well it's true. I did not have quite as severe a compassion shortcoming with Robert because by the time he came along I had learned some basics with Steven. Whatever compassion I have learned by now, comfortably into my 60s, I can thank my kids and Bev for. When I was suddenly a dad at age 29, compassion and empathy were not strongly developed in me yet. I had to learn them.

Now Steve and his wife Jill have two sons of their own. When I observe Steve fathering his sons I'm amazed at his natural tenderness, compassion, and empathy for them. He does not seem to have to work at it. When Steve is fathering his sons he is totally present, outwardly focused, and committed. When one of the boys is crying or having a difficult time, Steve's concern is not how the situation affects him, how inconvenient it is for him and so forth. His concern is focused on his child, what the child is experiencing, how he is feeling and why. When I see that sort of naturally good fathering behaviour (the kind that did not come naturally to me), I think, "Whew! – that's a relief". Steve must have picked it up somewhere. It must be from his mother.

Believe it or not, this history has a positive spin. When I said above that I was specially qualified to write on fathering, that is because I did not learn any bad fathering habits from my father. I had not learned much of anything from him at all, which meant I was pretty much a blank slate on the topic. I believe I learned some fathering skills fairly quickly, because

---

[129] My father was an unemployed alcoholic with anger and depression issues. My childhood memories of him are his lying on the couch drunk and dozing on and off.

[130] I mention Steve rather than Robert because by the time Rob came along, I had learned a few things and had some rudimentary fathering skills.

the situations demanded it but also because I did not have to unlearn any bad habits.

Fortunately, children are resilient. Otherwise as parents we would mess them up even more than we already do. It takes years for your children to grow into adults themselves and realize that when you were raising them, you were just another schlump doing the best he could but still reading his own autobiography into every situation.

With one more disclaimer and my autobiographical biases out of the way, I will tell you some things you can do and some things to avoid in raising your kids. Before we get going with my recommendations, I want to make sure you know that these recommendations are not all based on things Bev and I always did right. A lot of them are based on mistakes we made, which we now comprehend looking back. If my recommendations seem obvious, do not be surprised at that. As I said, I am not a renowned expert in the field.

Maybe raising kids is a little like shooting pool. Being a good pool player is not about all the jaw-dropping fancy or trick shots you see in the movies. Being a good pool player is more about not blowing the easy shots that you ought to make every time. If you watch good pool players in a match on TV, they seem to make easy shot after easy shot...like 15 in a row after the break. And they never miss an easy shot. If you are a recreational pool player and you are in the flow and having a good night at the table, your good results might be 20% because you are making difficult shots that you usually do not make. But I suggest to you that your unusually good game will be 80% because you are making all the easier shots that you sometimes miss.

Being an effective parent is like that. It is about showing up, being 100% present, keeping your mind on what you are doing and your eye on the ball, doing the simple things well and consistently, and following through...as I said, just like shooting pool.

Some things you can do

1. <u>Relax</u>. Just like in pool, you need to relax. You cannot shoot a good game of pool if you are all tense about it. If you are tense, you will choke on an easy shot that you should make every time. Similarly, you want to relax when you are raising your kids. No one is diminishing the awesome importance of raising your kids. But you still need to relax into it so that you can be present and outwardly focused. You also need to be relaxed to enjoy what you are doing. While you are raising your kids, it seems interminable and the responsibility seems crushing. When you look back on it, that period of time seems brief.

2. <u>Be loving.</u> This one seems obvious. Sometimes when I see our grandsons and whip them up into the air so we're eye to eye, I feel like my heart is going to burst out of my chest. I can't imagine such love that I feel for these little guys that is both tender and fierce at the same time. And back when it was our own little sons, I felt the same way. Loving your children seems like the most natural thing in the world. But the truth is they're noisy, needy, messy, and expensive. They can be tiring and frustrating too. If you don't have your own kids yet, you won't understand what I mean. You may think you do but you don't. But if you do have your own kids, you will know what I mean.

   The thing is, your little ones are just learning what it means to be embodied in this incarnation. You need to show them that you love them. They learn to have a capacity to love from their parents. You cannot love your children too much and you cannot show it too much. They're just little. Be gentle and tender in the way you speak to your kids. Pick them up and hug them. When they squirm, put them down. You need to respect them too. When they want down, they want down.

3. <u>Be supportive but provide guidance</u>. Your kids need to know that you are in their corner unconditionally and no matter what. But when they need guidance, give them guidance. That is your job as a parent. If your kid needs to learn to share his

toys, tell him he needs to share his toys. If your kid needs to learn not to whine and pout in attempting to get his way, tell him that whining and pouting is not the way to go about it. Your kid needs to learn to say please and thank you. That's your job too. You see what I mean? You can be supportive and also provide guidance. The two are not mutually exclusive.

4. <u>Be consistent</u>. If you want to turn your kid into an insecure nervous wreck, the best way to do that is to be inconsistent. Being consistent with your kids is very important. Don't be strict about something on Tuesdays and Thursdays and soft on the same issue on Wednesdays or Fridays. Don't take one position on a question when you have had a good night's sleep and a good breakfast and take another when you are tired out and cranky. If you do that sort of thing, your kid will be bewildered. They count on you to be a rock in their life. They need to rely on you to teach them what's up and what's down, what's in and what's out, what's allowed and what's forbidden. And you need to teach them those things consistently.

    And for goodness sake, get together with your spouse on these issues and present a consistent view to your kids. A kid going to Dad to get the answer she wants after not getting the answer she wanted from Mom is so hackneyed and clichéd that it's in comic strips and on TV sitcoms[131]. Only it's not funny. If you don't hold a consistent view with your spouse and allow your child to play one of you against the other to get the outcome she prefers, you will teach her to be duplicitous and manipulative. Even if you don't agree with your spouse, back him/her up in the heat of the action and present a consistent position to your children. You can sort out your differences with your spouse later.

    Another aspect of being consistent is to allow the law of natural consequences to apply, unless of course your child will be endangered by your doing so. You don't want your child to learn not to play at the top of the stairs by letting him fall down them. But all kinds of opportunities arise for an inquisitive toddler to learn that his choices will bring certain predictable

---

[131] Many TV sitcoms are all about duplicity and manipulation, so this isn't a big surprise.

consequences. This is important learning, because it's one of the earliest applications of the personal responsibility principle we examined in an earlier chapter. It's also an opportunity to demonstrate to your child the value of saying what you mean and meaning what you say.

For example, let's say you have a general rule with your small child that as long as he packs away all his toys by 7:00 PM, he gets to watch his favourite TV show before bed. If he packs away his toys on time, he's sitting in front of his favourite show with his glass of milk. But if he doesn't pick up his toys on time, he doesn't watch his TV show. And this is not a topic for negotiation. I'm not trying to advocate that picking up your toys is some sort of big deal; that's just an example.

With a slightly older school-age kid, you might strike a deal. For example, if she maintains a perfect attendance record at school with no late arrivals, you'll take her and a pal to the mall for shopping, food-court and water-park at the end of the school year. If she produces those results, you keep your end of the bargain, without fail. But if she doesn't, no mall trip.

When our son Robert was a little tyke and we were living in suburban Montreal, he had an unfortunate experience with the law of natural consequences. Rob was about 6 and had just learned to ride a 2 wheel bike. He had a cool little black bike which he loved. And he loved to rip around the neighbourhood on his bike. When he came home he used to leave it on the corner of our front yard, right where it joined the foot of the driveway in one direction and the edge of the lawn in the other direction. I reminded him a few times that his bike might be more secure in our back yard, which was fenced. Sure enough one morning Rob's bike was gone. That was life in the big city I guess. Rob had to do without a bike for a while.

Some things to avoid

1. <u>Don't tease</u>. Your child might get teased when she starts school. Don't make the mistake of thinking you're going to prepare them for that somehow by teasing them at home. In more than 60 years I have not met anyone yet who actually likes to be teased[132]. Some potential effects of teasing your child are passivity, withdrawal, hostility, and anger[133]. No one wants that result for their child.

    Don't tease your kids. Nothing good can come of it. If you are even tempted to tease your child, go to your room and take a time out. You might be acting like a child yourself. Seriously, if you are tempted to tease, examine your motivations. I believe that hostility and resentment are at the basis of teasing. You don't want to act out on feelings like that toward your vulnerable little child. If you're a 200 lb. man or 130 lb. woman remember that your 4 year-old is 35 lb. and relies on you for everything, including milk, bread, bedtime stories, and a safe and loving environment. Don't make teasing part of what she can expect from you.

2. <u>Don't be sarcastic</u>. We see lots of sarcasm on TV shows, especially American sitcoms. Does using sarcasm make those characters seem witty and sophisticated? I can tell you I don't much like it.

    Strike sarcasm from your repertoire entirely. Don't make sarcastic comments to your spouse, your work colleagues, your friends, or your children. I remember my Mom telling me once when I was going through a difficult phase as a teenager, "You know Mike, sarcasm does not endear you to people." That was 50 years ago and I still remember her saying that to me and how I felt when she said it. I can't recall what I had said to her – I guess it must have been something sarcastic – but she caught me up short. I asked myself, "Why would you want to say something sarcastic to your mother? You love her. Smarten

---

[132] I'm not talking about naughty "adult" teasing here. I wouldn't know about that. This isn't that type of book.
[133] See: http://www.ehow.com/info_8735692_psychological-effects-teasing.html

up!" I may have slipped up occasionally since that incident, but at that point 50 years ago, I swore off sarcasm in principle.

Sarcasm mocks its victim and demonstrates a lack of respect. When you examine what sarcasm is, you'll never want to make a sarcastic comment to your child. When you say something sarcastic, you actually say the opposite of what you really mean to mock the other person. The other person has to go through the mental exercise of realizing that you didn't mean what you said; you actually meant the opposite. Then wham! The joke's on him. Ha ha. Have cheap laugh at the expense of someone else's feelings. That's your kid, remember.

So for example let's say you tell your son that he has to clean up his room. Then you go in 30 minutes later and see that the job he did doesn't meet your expectations. If you say something in a dry voice like, "Hey nice job with the cleanup, Josh!" that would be sarcastic.

If you make sarcastic comments like the one above to your child you're messing with his mind. Your sarcasm will contribute to his feeling insecure. It may erode his confidence. Of course he'll feel insecure because he'll learn that people – even the ones closest to him that he relies on the most – don't always mean what they say. He'll begin to question the motives and genuineness of every comment he hears – and not just from you. It's a difficult enough world out there as it is. Don't make it more difficult for your dear child than it needs to be by using sarcasm. As a parent, you're a role model and a teacher with everything you do and say. As the Dixie Chicks said in one of their songs, "Our children are watching us.[134]" You don't want to teach your child to feel insecure and undermine his self-confidence.

3. <u>Don't shame</u>. Shame is a technique parents use to cause children to change or stop a behaviour by creating negative thoughts and feelings about themselves[135]. It involves some sort of a comment about what the child is, e.g. "you're a bad girl!" "Don't be so selfish!" Shaming makes the child wrong for feeling, wanting or needing something. Shaming your child is

[134] From "I Hope" from the Album "Taking the Long Way" (2006)
[135] http://www.naturalchild.org/robin_grille/good_children.html

an effective means of controlling your child's behaviour, which may be one reason why it is as common as it is. Shaming occurs in the "nicest" of family and school environments. A recent study of Canadian schoolchildren, for instance, found that only 4% had not been the targets of their parents' shaming; including "rejecting, demeaning, terrorizing, criticizing (destructively), or insulting statements"[136]

No-one is born ashamed. We learn to be ashamed by being shamed by someone else. For little kids, that is most commonly their parents. As I said above parents resort to shaming maybe as a last resort, but in the final analysis because it works. The problem is that shaming your child can harm them in the longer term, by damaging self-esteem and diminishing spontaneity. When a child feels ashamed they tend to withdraw into an inner world. On the surface their behaviour may appear better but inside the child may be suffering. A child who begins to feel he is "bad" or "naughty" or "clumsy" or "stupid" will begin to inhibit his behaviour and the expression of his emotions. This is not a healthy outcome.

This may seem really difficult. Actually it is. But remember, kids are resilient. You don't need to be perfect as long as you're loving, supportive, and as consistent as possible. If you make a mistake, learn from it and don't repeat it. If the situation fits, tell your child you made a mistake and apologize to her. Saying sorry is difficult for a lot of people. Modelling that behaviour for your child is a good thing. And don't beat yourself up with negative self-talk. You can't be a positive role model and teacher to your children and a loving support to your spouse if you aren't feeling good about yourself.

So what alternatives do we have if we don't want to shame our children? Teach your child to identify with positive self-statements. You can use experiences as a positive learning lesson. Instead of shaming your child, point out how the child could reassess the situation for positive results. Focus on the impacts that positive and negative behaviours will have. If you say something like, "Fred, I want you to stop abc. When you do that, xyz might result, and we don't want that to happen."

---

[136] Solomon & Serres, 1999

When you say something like that, you aren't shaming your child but you're still providing guidance.

Teach your children to become decision makers. You can help them identify when they've made a good decision and to help children think of alternative options if they've made a poor choice. This sort of approach will help your children "own" their decisions and gain confidence in their own abilities.

Encourage your child to ask questions when in doubt. When your child does ask a question you have a great opportunity to teach. How you answer the question will teach your child much more than the factual content of your answer. You will teach him that when he's unsure, if he asks an honest question, he'll receive a straight answer, without sarcasm or shame. Whew! What a relief! Now you're building your child's confidence and sense of self. Children with a positive sense of themselves, and a sense of humour, have a better ability to deal with life's challenges.

4. <u>Avoid food fights</u>. Relax about food. Your kid won't starve. I have to own up here that like every other pair of parents, Bev and I fell into the trap of fighting with our little kids about food. I don't know why this is such a common issue between parents and their little ones. But in North America we seem to think our kids' stomachs need to be full all the time. Perhaps young parents are tired and sleep deprived, and therefore is unconsciously concerned that their kids will be more likely to wake them up at night if their little bellies are not absolutely stuffed. But that's no more than wild speculation.

Consider what message we give our impressionable young children when we badger them to eat more all the time. To me it seems a little offbeat. The kids probably get the message that their parents think eating as much as you can hold – even eating more than you feel like eating – is somehow a desirable thing. Of course I don't know this to be true from empirical research, but common sense tells me that this practice likely contributes to obesity, either childhood obesity or adult obesity or both. I believe this practice certainly contributes to unhealthy attitudes about food.

Don't bargain over food. Striking a deal with your child whereby she gets a reward for eating something seems borderline crazy to me. If you say to your child, "If you finish your peas, you get to watch a TV show before bed" you're linking food with secondary gratification. When she gets older, when she sits down to watch TV, she'll want to eat something while she watches. If you say to her, "If you finish your peas, you can have a cupcake for dessert" you're linking eating something healthy with eating something more, which is less healthy but maybe more fun. You might argue that there's nothing wrong with that. And maybe you'd be right. After all, I said I wasn't any kind of expert on raising kids. I am just offering up my opinions here. But after saying that, I would rather you just had a rule that you eat dessert once you have finished your meal, and stick by the rule. The parents have to abide by the rule too for the child to accept the rule as reasonable. So make sure you don't put too much on your plate.

And what's with the snacks all the time? Does your kid need to eat three meals a day plus have snacks between the meals and then a snack before bed? If she naps until 3 PM and then you give her a snack when she gets up, maybe don't be too surprised if she doesn't have much of an appetite for supper at 6 PM.

Keep your humility

Anyone reading a book like this one probably doesn't need to be told this, but being a parent does not make you into some sort of big wheel power figure. Your child is an awesome blessing and raising your child is a sacred responsibility. You want to raise your child with a firm but always gentle touch. You never want to overpower or dominate. Your job is to help your child grow into a healthy adult who can then leave you and become independent of you. That may seem like a paradox but it's true. If you do a good job of parenting, your child will not depend on you as an adult. Your responsibility in this is so awesome that alone ought to keep you humble. Sorry to say so, but anyone who has a 30-something living in the basement has not succeeded in raising a fully functional independent adult.

Actually for most parents, the corollary is what's applicable. Your kids will absolutely help you stay humble. When you're raising your children you learn a lot of lessons from them and you learn a lot about yourself and your shortcomings as part of the process.

Bev's dad Ernie Harris said some noteworthy and wise things that I will remember all my life. One of them was, "You really know you're married when you have children". He said this before we had children. It didn't mean that much to me at the time. But a few years later when we became parents, I remembered what he had said. It's true. When you are raising children, you and your spouse are working in the deepest, most meaningful, and most impactful partnership you will ever be part of. You rely on each other for so many things, so often and so deeply that your marriage will never again be the light-hearted and carefree relationship it was before you had kids. That doesn't mean you won't have light-hearted and carefree times, because you will. But your relationship will have a depth, commitment, and meaning that you could not imagine before you embarked on parenthood together.

Our elder son, Steven, had a difficult start. He was born prematurely with underdeveloped lungs and digestive system, and cerebral irritability. He was so tiny as a newborn that he slept in a wicker basket inside a doll's crib. He didn't sleep much and had trouble nursing. He cried a lot and was difficult to comfort. Steve's first months were very hard on him, and of course hard on us too. Bev and I had had no preparation for this period. Another wise and kind comment Ernie made to Bev was, "Sometimes it just takes a while to get them started." That simple comment implied that first, the situation wasn't our fault, and second, we could have hope that eventually the situation would improve and Steve would turn out OK. And that's exactly what happened.

When Robert was born we braced ourselves for another hard go at it. But Bert was a different boy than Steven from the start. First, Rob was born late rather than early. He was in no hurry. As an infant, Robert was good natured, relaxed, and easy to comfort. He slept well too. After getting up several times a night every night when Steve was a baby, we expected the same with Rob. Both Bev and I would wake up in the middle of the night to a silent house. One or the other of us would run across the hall to check on Robert. He would be sleeping peacefully. Anyone who has raised kids knows that they arrive with personalities and preferences. They're anything but blank slates. Go figure.

Now that Steve and Rob are both grown men, they're not exactly two peas in a pod. But they're good guys, good brothers to each other and I know that they share common core values. As Ernie said, "You really know you're married when you have children" and "Sometimes it just takes a while to get them started". How true.

My point here is how we need to keep our humility as young parents and how our little kids help us with that. Many times raising our little boys I was reminded of my own personal shortcomings, how assaholic I really was, and how dreadfully unprepared I was to be a father. But I learned some important lessons from the boys too. With their open innocence, love, acceptance, and tendency toward positive self-confidence in spite of my incompetence, I learned that being assaholic and recognizing it was actually near the centre of the human experience.

Honour your dharma

Dharma is a big and broad concept in Indian philosophy, referring to natural law and all the behaviours, values, and practices necessary to maintain the natural order of things. Here I use the word dharma in the narrower and more common sense of a person's duties as dictated by the circumstances in his life. Using the card playing metaphor, we're all dealt a hand in life. We need to play those cards. Eddie Vedder of Pearl Jam cleverly illustrates the idea of dharma with his lyric "*Born on third, thinks he got a triple*"[137], referring to George Dubya Bush's station in life. Some of us are born on third, but most of us aren't. Most of us are born to assaholic imperfect parents, who though they may honestly try their best, are damaged goods themselves and can't help but pass along some dysfunction.

As parents we have the responsibility of identifying the dysfunctions that we don't want to pass along to our kids, and then making a conscious effort to act in ways to make sure you don't. That's what I mean by "honouring your dharma" in the context of parenthood. Every generation of parents wants things to be better for their kids than they experienced themselves. In that way, our species evolves and moves forward. When our sons became young men, I recall Bev saying to them several times, "When you're in your 40s, your first 6 months of therapy are on us." Steve and Rob may have thought Bev was joking a little, but I know she wasn't. Both of us have tried hard to honour our dharma as parents. And both of us have spent a great deal of time, effort, and expense with psychologists, "doing our work", i.e. working through and healing issues of dysfunction from our

---

[137] From "Bushleager", the Pearl Jam album "Riot Act" (2002)

childhood and adolescence that would otherwise limit our development and growth as humans and our effectiveness as parents.

And as a result of that kind of important work, parents can honour their dharma by understanding their sacred duty, by choosing not to pass on identified issues of dysfunction. In my own case, I can vividly recall, although it was many years ago, participating in a weekend retreat[138] where we identified personal issues and worked through them for healing in a supportive environment. I had indentified that my father's alcoholism and emotional absence had left a big hole and big hurt in my life that was limiting me as a person and as a parent. I vowed to the group, "The dysfunction stops here!" meaning that I vowed that I would not pass that dysfunction on to our sons. I would not be an alcoholic and I would remain emotionally present and available.

And I think I have done that. I am not an alcoholic and I am emotionally connected, in a healthy way, to both our sons. When I look at them as objectively as I can, I'm sure they are both emotionally stronger and healthier than I was at their age.

Being a parent for the long term – Parenting your adult children

When our children are grown adults we may have a tendency to want to treat them as pals or peers. I know it's been that way with me. I've come to understand that may be a mistake. It may be the path of least resistance and it may be the easy way, but that does not make it right. It's tempting to become pals with your adult offspring. In our case, I could add two healthy young men with many admirable qualities to my list of friends. But as Brian Tracy would say, "This is not for you."

Treating your adult children as pals may be nice for you but it may not be fair to them. We look through our glasses and we see young people that we like and would like to have as friends. But when they look at us through their glasses, we may not look like that to them. We need to remember that. While we're no longer guiding them and helping them understand the difference between right and wrong, and we're certainly no longer shaping their values, but whether we like it or not, we're still their role models.

If you're fortunate enough to have an open and trusting relationship

---

[138] These events were called "Shalom Retreats" and they were wonderful, life changing experiences.

with your adult children, they might still seek your advice from time to time. And when they do that, the problems they are looking to solve are a lot more complex, adult, and sophisticated than the problems they had as kids or adolescents. When they ask for your advice or viewpoint, they're not asking you as a peer; they're asking you as a parent, because they respect the way you have encountered and responded to problems and issues yourself.

Remember that this kind of situation is a not peer-to-peer. For you to respond the way your adult offspring needs you to respond, both of you need to respect that. You need to respond as an elder to your adult child. And here's another application of the "Don't Give Advice" principle I examined earlier. This is not the time to say, "What you should do is…". This is more one of those times where you might be better off saying, "What would you like to do?" or "How do you feel about that?" Help your adult child by guiding him through an analysis and resolution process.

At a time like that, you can describe the experiences you might have had that are similar or relevant. It might be OK for you to say, "Well, if it were me in that situation, I would probably do abc…but then, this isn't me; it's you. What does your experience tell you and what does your gut tell you?"

The point is, when you sign up as parents, you sign up for life. Even though your kid may have a good job and have kids of his own, he is still your kid. And from time to time he still needs you to be a parent. He already has pals.

Steve and Jill: Happy couple at their wedding, Punta Cana DR

Robert: Robert at a family gathering in Winnipeg MB

Steve and Jill family: Steve, Jill, Cole, and Caden

Love and Respect your Spouse

Much as I came clean on not being a child-rearing expert, I'm no expert on marriage either. But I am a veteran with more than 40 years experience in marriage. I may not know much in general about the institution of marriage, but I do know about one particular marriage, i.e. ours. I know what works and I know what doesn't work. And I do believe that I have identified a few critical success factors. In the sections that follow on this topic, when I refer to spouse with feminine pronouns like she and her, I don't do that to be sexist, so please don't interpret it that way. It's natural for me to think that way and that's all it is. The principles are not at all gender specific. In that way, this section is decidedly non-sexist. I believe these principles transcend gender.

Expect and celebrate growth and change

Most of us have heard the old saying that every cell in the body is changed over a period of seven years. It's true. You are not the same person you were a few years ago. And that's more than just the experiences you've gained. You, in the most basic physical sense, are not the same person you used to be. Every cell in your body has been replaced. And if you're like most of us, you won't look the same as you did seven years ago either. If you're committed to a long-term intimate relationship[139], you'd better expect it to change also. Your marriage is an organism, just like you are. I suggest you expect your marriage to go through changes, just as you do. If you expect

---

[139] When I use the word "marriage" in this section, I mean it in the broader sense of intimate committed relationship, whether or not the relationship has been formalized by church or state.

it to stay the same, you're not being realistic. A living organism cannot be healthy without undergoing change.

Bev has said many times that we've had several marriages. That is true. The nature of our relationship now is quite different from what it was in 1971. Of course I loved Bev as a 20 year-old but I wouldn't want to be married to a 20 year-old now. Mignon McLoughlin said, "A successful marriage requires falling in love many times, always with the same person[140]".

What happened to the girl I married, the old saying goes. Well hopefully, growth and development is what happened. Recently at an extended family event, I met a younger man who is a distant relation through marriage. So actually, we're not related at all through bloodlines. He looked as though he was in his late 30s. He said something that made me think. I can't quote exactly, but it was something like, "Every woman wants to change her husband and every man wants his wife not to change". And he said it with a certain world-weary conviction. My vibes told me that he actually meant it. When he asked me if I agreed, all I could do is stare. What a sad and diminishing thought.

Anyone who has been married 40 years will have had a few people ask "what's your secret?" as if some simple answer existed. That question calls for a short, non-preachy answer, so I usually say something like, "Give your spouse some room to grow and change. Don't expect her to stay the same."

In reality of course that's true, but it's also more than that. By all means, don't be threatened by change. Welcome change. Life is about change. Your marriage relationship has to have elastic bonds. During the course of your marriage one of you may be evolving at a rate that exceeds how the other is evolving. If you're younger, like in your 30s or 40s, your spouse may be growing more rapidly than you are and in a direction you don't want to go yourself. No matter how threatening that might seem, you need to be OK with that. You may feel like you are losing your spouse as she grows in a different direction. Indeed her centre may move a little away from you during that time. However, latching on and trying to hold her back will only cause her to strain harder to pull away. Either her centre will return or it won't. Or maybe her centre hasn't moved at all with her growth; perhaps you've misinterpreted that. But attempting to restrain that movement will not help the situation. Do not resist it. Your turn

---

[140] http://www.brainyquote.com/quotes/authors/m/mignon_mclaughlin.html

could be next year or in five years. And you may find yourself growing in a harmonious direction. Just let it be and do not resist.

The last thing you want to do is to try and confine your spouse in some sort of limiting psychological and emotional prison. For you to love your spouse, you need to respect her also. She will need room to grow and expand and she'll need room to exercise her expanding thoughts, discoveries, and beliefs. Celebrate that. Life is for learning, growth, and development. You won't get bigger by trying to remain small.

When I say the key to a healthy long-term committed intimate relationship includes "give your spouse some room" but is more than that, I don't mean to imply that it's terribly complicated. Actually I believe the key boils down to a few relatively simple concepts. The difficult part is actually in living those concepts consistently. This factor is especially important yet especially difficult for you to apply to your relationship to your spouse. If you wonder how and why that is the case, I promise more on that later.

The principles that are important to maintaining a mutually respectful and healthy intimate relationship are the same principles that I've already described in the "Master Your Internal World" and "Your Interpersonal World" chapters. I don't think that ought to come as a big surprise. Yet lots of people don't live that way. Control your ego, strive for consciousness, accept responsibility, know yourself, minimize incongruity, offer no resistance, and so forth. It's the same good stuff. Now that you know that good stuff, bring it to your most important and intimate relationship.

When we celebrated our 40th anniversary, we received many rich well-wishes from friends and loved ones. But I want to mention one in particular. Our daughter-in-law Jill gave us an anniversary card. In it she wrote, "You make it look easy." That brief message touched me deeply. Jill is a smart young woman with a deep well of solid character. And she's the mother of our grandchildren. We couldn't love her any more if she were our own daughter. So when she writes something like that, it means a lot. Jill doesn't write down messages in her cards unless she means them. It had never occurred to me that we made it look easy. I guess I hadn't realized that Jill had been watching either. I'll never forget that card.

Let your spouse out of the box

I could have put this section in the interpersonal world chapter. I decided to include it here because I believe this principle applies especially to married relationships or intimate partnerships and because it follows logically from the previous section. Sometimes when we form an impression of another person, we store that impression away as if it were permanent. Once we know a person, we ascribe qualities and attributes to him, like:

"In this situation, I know he will react this way. He always does"

"She doesn't much enjoy this sort of social event"

"No way would he enjoy watching this movie with me"

"She never likes this sort of music"

"He drinks too much beer and watches too much TV".

I don't recall whether Bev or I coined the expression "Let me out of the box". But it was one of us. Married couples sometimes keep their spouse "in a box" by forming a composite impression of their preferences, tendencies, strengths and shortcomings, habits, and other personal attributes that is highly resistant to change, as if it were an old photograph in a box. The impression may be much more resistant to change than the actual attributes of the other person are.

One spouse may be working hard, making an honest best effort to change in one way or another. And that individual may actually make big strides in that improvement effort. This individual may be breaking old habits and opening up to new ideas and ways of thinking and doing. Yet his/her spouse may be the last person to recognize and appreciate that change. Rather than supporting and encouraging that change for the better, the spouse may be insensitive or oblivious to it. When this happens it can be disappointing and frustrating for the person who's trying to grow and develop.

If the couple is conscious and aware enough of this concept to have language for it, one can say something like this to the other:

"Hey! Let me out of the box! I've left that old habit behind."

In our own marriage, both of us have used that expression a time or two. So here's my suggestion. Remain sensitive to your spouse, her personal aspirations and struggles, and her efforts to grow and develop. Be supportive and encouraging of those efforts. Remember that you can't capture your spouse's path to fulfillment with a still photo. Don't keep her in a box.

And the other side of the coin applies also. If your spouse asks you to let her out of the box, do so. Don't get defensive and ask her to justify why she thinks you've been insensitive to her change. And when the time comes that you feel that you're being held in a box, be assertive and speak up about it.

Avoid "Always and Never" thinking and speaking.

How do you feel when your spouse says to you?

> *"You always complain about going to visit my family. You never want to spend any time with them".*

> *"You're never satisfied with what I do. You always have to criticise me!"*

Chances are, when you hear words like that, you feel defensive, resentful, or angry. That sort of "always or never" statement is off-putting. Want to start a fight with your loved one? One of the best sure-fire ways of achieving that outcome is to lodge a complaint in the form of an always or never statement.

The fact is, "always" and "never" rarely apply truthfully to human behaviour. We may have tendencies to do act in certain ways preferentially or more often than some alternative ways. But always or never? Not really. As a species, we just aren't wired that way. So when we hurl an always or never statement to our spouse, her most likely first response will be to feel defensive. That's reasonable, considering that the always or never statement is probably inaccurate. And if you persist, that defensiveness will escalate to anger or hostility.

If your spouse tosses an always or never statement your way, remember the space between stimulus and response that makes you response-able. Take a breath before you dig in your heels and start ramping up the situation. You can defuse the situation by reeling in the rhetoric. You can say something like,

> *"Perhaps you're right that I don't like to visit them as often as you'd like me to. But to say I never want to simply is not true. In fact, I recall suggesting that we do that last fall. Would you like to talk about it?"*

And watch your own thoughts. Anytime you think in terms of "always" and "never", you want to go on alert. Something is likely out of whack if you're thinking along those lines. Pull yourself together and ask yourself what's going on if you feel inclined to spit out an unkind always or never statement. Resolve yourself not to make always and never statements to your spouse. As the pug said, "Them's fightin' words!"

The exception to avoiding always and never statements is when you're saying something positive or nice. It's perfectly OK to say something like,

> *"You always buy such thoughtful gifts" or*
>
> *"You never disappoint me".*

In fact, that sort of statement is preferable to the remote and intellectual phrasing like,

> *"You usually buy such thoughtful gifts" or*
>
> *"You disappoint me infrequently"*

If you talk like that, you will sound like Dr. Temperance Brennan on Bones[141]. You probably don't want to adopt her interpersonal mannerisms with your spouse.

Listen – don't discount

Stephen Covey's fifth of his Seven Habits[142] is seek first to understand, then seek to be understood. One of the best things you can do to understand your spouse is to listen to her. Listen and empathise but whatever you do, don't analyse, don't offer advice and don't discount. When I say listen and empathise I mean consciously discern what your beloved is expressing about how she feels. Quiet yourself, still your self-talk and concentrate on her, what she's saying and what non-verbal messages she's sending.

Let's start with an illustration that's fairly straightforward. Imagine you and your spouse are visiting at the end of the day and she's telling you about an incident that occurred that day. She may say something like "When abc happened, I felt xyz[143]." That's the simplest example I can provide. Real-life examples could be a little more complex, like "Then she said abc and

---

[141] See: http://www.tv.com/shows/bones/

[142] The Seven Habits of Highly Effective People, by Stephen R. Covey. (1989)

[143] I use 'abc' and 'xyz' because I'm trying to describe a <u>type</u> of statement that has that form, where abc and xyz are variables. It could be something like "When Alison said my work was below standard, I felt crushed and humiliated." I use the abstract rather than the particular form because I don't want the reader to get sidetracked by the content of the example.

I'm like 'what was that?' I was just xyz". In either example, your spouse is sharing an experience that held some meaning and emotional content for her. She's sharing it with you because sharing her feelings is part of being intimate. She's looking for understanding. She may be looking for affirmation. But she's probably not looking for your analysis and advice on how she could have handled it better. You can pretty much take that to the bank.

Instead of analysing and offering unsolicited advice, this might be an opportunity to apply some of your active listening skills. You could calibrate by saying something affirming like, "I can see how you'd feel xyz. If I were in that situation, I know that's how I'd feel too." The absolute last thing your spouse needs to hear from you is that she doesn't need to feel the way she does. Trying to tell someone else not to feel what they feel is one of the most insensitive, disrespectful, and discounting things you can do. If you have that habit, break it, starting today.

A few years ago Bev and I attended a couples retreat. The retreat leaders had just finished a session focusing on this important concept, i.e. to listen to your spouse, especially for descriptions of feelings. We took a break and stepped out into that beautiful late winter mountain air. Bev was talking about the session in which we'd just participated. And she included a description of how and what she was feeling. I can't remember the specifics but I do remember blithely brushing aside her feelings and telling that she didn't need to feel that way and why. "Aaah, you don't need to feel that way…". Fortunately we were in a positive and loving environment. Bev gently and kindly pointed out to me that I had just done specifically what the seminar leaders had been trying to teach us not to do. And she was right. What a donkey I was. Boy did I feel like a putz. I promised not to do that again.

Tell yourself the truth.

Psychologists have coined the term "Margin of Illusion[144]" to describe the process healthy people follow whereby we imagine ourselves to be little better looking, smarter, more charming, and better dancers than others see us as being. This practice is healthy because "…highly accurate [self] perceptions are associated with depression and other maladaptive patterns[145]." In other words, if we were to see ourselves as others see us, we'd probably get depressed. That's not even funny. Bev sometimes seems to enjoy reminding me that I have a healthy margin of illusion. Be that as it may, I'm glad my big fat margin of illusion keeps me from feeling depressed.

But one of Bev's teachers would say to her from time to time, "Tell yourself the truth." I would interpret that to mean that we are to be honest with ourselves about our feelings. I think for the most part we can maintain a healthy margin of illusion and still tell ourselves the truth. Most of the time, the topics we're being truthful to ourselves about won't be those well-protected margin of illusion topics, like how good-looking, smart, and charming we are. They're more likely to be about how we really feel about something.

Perhaps sometimes our self-concepts doesn't allow for feelings we'd just as soon not admit to ourselves that we have. Maybe your self concept doesn't include having petty little ugly feelings like jealousy, resentment, humiliation and so forth. And maybe your margin of illusion includes denying feelings like that. The principle of telling yourself the truth has to take priority here. If you harbour feelings like that, face them, call them by name and accept them. If you deny having them, that's just your ego popping its head up trying to protect itself. Some content experts have said that we all have a dark side. We need to get to know our dark side rather than suppressing it and pretending that it doesn't exist.

If you have feelings like that, tell yourself the truth. You can't minimize incongruity if you're not honest with yourself about your feelings. And you can't have an open, trusting, and intimate relationship with your spouse if you aren't straight with her about what's going on for you. If you don't want to have feelings like you have, you don't need to. But the way to find

---

[144] "The Optimal Margin of Illusion" by Roy F Baumeister Journal of Social and Clinical Psychology (1989) Volume: 8, Issue: 2, Publisher: Guilford Publications, Pages: 176-189
[145] Ibid.

peace in that situation is to do your work, i.e. face your feelings and work through them. If you deny having those feelings, they will smoulder and rot inside you. You don't want that.

Don't criticize or complain

In the early 90s I took Dale Carnegie training and after completing it I was invited to serve as a graduate assistant, which I gladly did. One of the first principles we learned was "Don't criticize, condemn or complain." We weren't learning specifically how to be good marriage partners, but that principle certainly also applies to how you treat your spouse. Katherine Hepburn said, "If you want to sacrifice the admiration of many men for the criticism of one, go ahead, get married." Wow what a concise indictment.

Do not criticise your spouse. She needs your support, affirmation, and encouragement. She most certainly does not need your criticism. Criticism implies judgement. Any dictionary will tell you that criticism includes evaluating merits or their lack and passing judgement. I would suggest that most people don't much enjoy being criticised by their spouse. The whole notion of passing judgement on a loved-one seems borderline absurd, yet we see it all the time. All the time I say. Criticism is hurtful.

If you want to be pleasant to live with, do not criticise or complain. If your spouse slips and criticises you or complains about something you did or didn't do, do not respond in kind. Break the cycle of criticism by not participating in it. If you have a habit of criticising or complaining, break it.

Anne Bancroft and Mel Brooks were married for many years before her death in 2005. Someone asked her how she felt when Mel came home. She answered something to the effect that she felt happy when Mel came home because that meant the party was about to begin. What a loving little story! You want your spouse to be happy to see you when you come home?

Forgive – Anger bites the angry

In the 1986 move The Mission, Robert De Niro plays Rodrigo Mendoza, a Jesuit Missionary with a sinful past, in 18th century South America. As his penance for having killed his brother in a duel over a woman, Mendoza drags behind him a large and heavy bundle of weapons and armour. Dragging this heavy bundle as Mendoza and his Jesuit brothers scale the steep Iguassu Falls is both a figurative and literal penance. In a memorable scene, the senior monk cuts loose Mendoza's bundle, to make his effort more bearable and less perilous. Wracked with guilt for his terrible sin, Mendoza cannot let go of his penance. He climbs back down to retrieve it.

Carrying anger is like Mendoza's carrying his bundle. When you hang onto anger you carry a heavy bundle with you. When you let go of your anger, you also let go of that heavy bundle. If you have difficulty with forgiving, I encourage you to examine that. For your own benefit, you want to learn to forgive.

Forgiveness is a wonderful gift, not only for the person being forgiven but also for the person doing the forgiving. Forgiveness benefits the forgiver at least as much as the forgiven. The reason for this is that sometimes the person who has wronged you is completely unaware that you are holding anger or resentment against him. Confucius said, among a few other things, "Anger bites the angry."

The other day when I was in the waiting room of an X-Ray clinic, I picked up a women's fashion magazine[146]. I look at those magazines sometimes, partly because they're full of photos of beautiful women but also because I pick up clues about the complex female psyche from them. This issue had an article that touched on forgiveness and holding anger. The author said that the bitterness that comes from holding onto anger "is like taking poison and expecting the other person to die.[147]" That's what Confucius meant. When you hold anger, you're the one who experiences the pain in your stomach. And when you're the one holding anger, you're the one who can do the most about it.

Let's imagine for a minute that your spouse has actually wronged you and that you're filled with righteous indignation, anger and resentment over it. You're not imagining it; it actually happened. She did something or said something that has hurt you and she was in the wrong for doing so. It is, in reality, a truly unfortunate and crappy situation. And boy are you feeling chapped.

Let's say your spouse realizes she was wrong and apologizes to you. Do you forgive her? That pure anger and righteous indignation is pretty delicious. It's burning in your gut like a hot flame. Now that she has apologized, you're kind of in a power position. She's a little vulnerable

---

[146] Unlike the guys who read Playboy, I read women's fashion mags for the photos not the articles.
[147] Flare, March 2012.

having made that apology. Do you use this opportunity to vent that righteous indignation and really give it to her?

Well, let's hope not. In a situation like this that's pretty clear in terms of who's in the wrong, by all means accept that apology and forgive her. What else can she do but apologize? And when I say forgive her, I mean do so and mean it sincerely down to your toes. It may or may not be your style to say, "I forgive you". If it is, say that. If that doesn't come naturally, then say something else to your beloved that ensures that she understands that you have forgiven her. Forgiving her is kind to her but its kind to you too. That pure white-hot righteous indignation will burn an ulcer in your stomach unless you let it go. Anger bites the angry.

But what if the situation is not so clear cut? What if that apology is not forthcoming? Do you really need an apology to forgive the other? Not really. You need to forgive the transgression whether you receive an apology or not. So first forgive in your heart, then seek out a way of making clear to the other that you have forgiven the wrong. You don't need to say "wrong" because that word could be a hot-button. But you might consider saying something like,

> *"Look, about that abc situation, I feel like we just don't see eye-to-eye on that topic. I can accept that. I want you to know that I don't hold any hard feelings about it...".*

Be pragmatic about it. You are forgiving because it's good for your own health to do that. You don't want to carry Mendoza's bundle away from the situation. If you hold onto anger the other person may not even realize that you're doing that. So it seems to me that holding onto anger is not in your own interest. Don't do it. This is not for you.

Or what if both of you have been wrong? That may be the case more often than not. Remember, believing that you're 100% right and your spouse is 100% wrong may not be realistic or mature. The notion of "wrong" may be a little subjective. Don't let resentment smoulder. Doing something to rectify the situation is within your control. Be big about it and do the right thing. Forgive the other in your heart and apologize to her for your part in creating the mess. Hopefully she'll forgive you too. Part of being less assaholic is damage control and mess management.

You are connected but don't lose yourself

This *"you are connected but don't lose yourself"* principle may be the most difficult one in this chapter. So I have saved it for last. Celebrating growth and change, listening without discounting, being truthful to yourself, avoiding criticising or complaining, and forgiving are all fairly easy to understand. They may be challenging to practice, but they're not difficult to understand as principles. But for some reason, being connected but yet not lost as an individual in your marriage seems to be a difficult idea for many people.

You might be wondering what it is that I'm going on about. For some wacky reason, many married people seem to save their most selfish, impolite, judgemental, negative, critical, and sometimes downright rude behaviour for their spouse. Although their spouse is supposedly the most dear and important person to them on earth, their partner in life, these people sometimes treat their spouse with disrespect and meanness. They say things to their spouse that they would never say to anyone else. Naturally you're not one of them, right? You wouldn't be reading this book if that applied to you, right?

That sort of behaviour obviously imposes toxicity on the most important and intimate relationship, yet some people do it anyway. And they do it apparently without any idea that just maybe they ought not to. I believe that the source of this problematic behaviour lies in apprehending the notion of being connected in marriage yet still retaining your individual nature. Many marriage ceremonies charge the couple with words to the effect. Once they embark on their new life as a married couple, they go forward united as one, in an intimate relationship honoured by church, state, and the tribal members gathered for the ceremony – yet – also as two individuals.

I've been to several weddings ceremonies that quote from Khalil Gibram[148] on just this topic:

> *"You were born to be together, and together you shall be forevermore.*
> *You shall be together when the wings of death scatter your days*
> *Ay, you shall be together even in your silent memory.*
> *But let there be spaces in your togetherness,*
> *And let the winds of the heaven dance between you.*
> *Love one another, but make not a bondage of love.*

---

[148] The Prophet: Khalil Gibram (1923)

Let it rather be a moving sea between the shores of your souls.
Fill each other's cup, but drink not from one cup.
Give one another of your bread, but eat not of the same loaf.
Sing and dance together and be joyous, but let each of you be alone,
Even as the strings of a lute are alone, though they quiver with the same music.
Give your hearts, but not into each other's keeping,
For only the hand of life can contain your hearts.
And stand together, yet not too near together,
For the pillars of the temple stand apart,
And the oak tree and the cypress grow not in shadow."

Those are wise words that capture very nicely the idea I'm trying to express here. Sometimes I wonder if no one is actually listening at those wedding ceremonies. The first time I heard those words at a wedding, I was lot younger, and I found them to be a little troubling. Now that I'm older and more experienced, I appreciate what Khalil Gibram was exhorting the young couple to understand.

Your spouse is not merely an extension of yourself. She is a whole and separate person, no matter how intimately connected you are. She is a breathing warm-blooded human with emotions, hopes and fears, preferences, a separate set of life experiences, and assaholic in her own ways. That person is absolutely worthy of your respect and the benefit of the doubt. When you respect your spouse, you will treat her with deference and kindness. You have a right to your own thoughts, preferences, beliefs, opinions, and space – but so does your spouse. We all need to respect the otherness of our loved ones, and especially of your spouse.

So what's behind this? Why do some people find it to be harder to be kind and respectful to their spouse than they do to other people that they barely know, like work colleagues, customers, shop-keepers and outright strangers? People who are pleasant and smile all day at work then come home, kick the dog and are mean to their spouse are not behaving like someone who has put much effort into mastering his or her internal world. I can hypothesize that this has to do with not minimizing incongruence. If you haven't mastered your internal world, you cannot minimize incongruence. Some people must make a great effort during the day, when they're away from home, being nice to others and appearing to be cheerful and polite. The persona they project during their public day might be at times hugely different from how they really feel. As we know from examining what goes into minimizing incongruity, the projection of a positive image has a cost to the person who projects. The person who does that all day may not have much left in the tank when he gets home to his family in the evening. Then he balances the books149 by taking it out on them.

The way to minimize incongruity is not to start being nasty and grouchy to strangers during the day so you can save your niceness for your spouse and kids when you return home in the evening. The way to minimize incongruity is to master your internal world, so your outer demeanour of kindness, compassion, friendliness, and good cheer is in harmony with your inner world. Control your ego with discipline, remain conscious and in touch with your higher self and the present moment, accept responsibility, control your thoughts…all that good stuff. Just stay grounded in your values and with what you know, and loving and respecting your spouse will be like falling off a log.

If you're in a committed, intimate relationship, remember to master your inner world and stay in charge. If you haven't begun to master your inner world yet, start now, and you'll become a more loving spouse. If you have never even thought about mastering your internal world prior to reading this book and you're not married yet, considering doing some honest important work on mastering your internal world before you get married. Then once you're married, you'll be mature enough to be a good spouse.

Maintain your sense of humour and perspective. Remember who you are and who your spouse is. The keys to experiencing pleasure in loving are trust and acceptance. Become aware of the subtle expectations you bring to your relationship. If you want to be trusted and accepted, be trusting and accepting yourself. And make sure you're trustworthy.

I wrote "Bev's Song" in 2001 to commemorate our 30th anniversary150. I don't want to brag, but this is a pretty good little country song. Many people have told me so. Bev's Song is about the breakthrough realization of your life's partner as brand new, even across the breakfast table when she's just got out of bed. The experience of suddenly seeing your loved one that way, so dear, so connected, so familiar, so rumpled – but separate, is startling, utterly exhilarating, and potentially life-changing. The central words are in the chorus:

> *"Today I looked at you for the thousandth time, and I saw you as Brand New."*

---

[149] By "balancing the books" I mean closing the incongruence gap.
[150] "Bev's Song (Brand New)" by Max Doubt (2001)

When you see your beloved as brand new, just like when you first met, with all that breathless excitement, you will find it so much easier to be loving. And to see your lover as brand new, you need to be intimately connected – but still separate.

Bev and Mike: Bev and I at her 60th birthday party.

Bev and Cole: The boys love Grandma Bev

Mike and grandsons: Cole, Cade, and I at Christmastime last year

Mike and Cade: Cade likes it when I whisper sweet nothings in his ear

Finances and Being at Peace
With your Money

I'm no financial expert. And I'm bored by financial planning and budgeting.
I don't do either. I have worked with an intelligent and spiritually developed
financial planner for the last 25 years. She does excellent analysis and
provides me with good advice. Like the guy in Steve Earle's song, "Regular
Guy[151]", I'll never get rich, never did try, never get rich but I'll always get
by. I think I have an OK attitude toward money and that's what I'm going
to share with you in this section.

Both Bev and I grew up in modest[152] homes in families that were
anything but wealthy. So neither of us had any sort of attitude of entitlement
when it came to financial wealth. But neither of us went hungry or cold
either. When we married, both of us had bikes and we slept on an air
mattress from Canadian Tire. As Kenneth the NBC page said on the TV
show 30 Rock, "We had plenty of rock soup and squirrel tails – and we
knew lean times too."

Now skip ahead more than 30 years. For a few years after our kids
were grown up and on their own, when we were both working full time
in responsible professional jobs, our combined income was well into the
six figures. We were shocked when our financial advisor told us we were
in the 80th percentile for income. That was shocking news to us. We sure
didn't feel like we were in that group. We see wealthy people all around us.
Being in the 80th percentile means our income was as much as 80% of the

---

[151] From Steve Earle's song "Regular Guy" from the album The Hard Way (1997)
[152] That's being on the generous side. We're from working class neighborhoods that
some would call inner-city slums.

population. But that's all it means. The people in the higher percentiles[153] make much more. In our culture probably 20% of the people have 80% of the money. But that's not the point; we had enough.

So we've seen both sides. We were never wealthy but we weren't worried about money either. In fact, that's exactly the point that I'm going to expand on here. We've been married for 40 years and we have never had a family budget. When our kids were little, Bev wasn't working, and money was tight, we didn't budget. When our kids were teens and becoming more expensive, both us were working. We had more income but we had more expenses too. We didn't budget then either.

Now I'm semi-retired with a low-paying, menial, hourly part-time job and a small business that doesn't make much either. Bev's working half-time. We still don't budget.

Since we married in 1971 until now, if someone asked us how much we paid for groceries or utilities, neither of us would be able to tell you. I realize that's unusual. I'm not going to advocate that you avoid budgeting. That's a worthwhile and necessary practice for some people – just not for us.

What I am going to advocate is some restraint and some common sense. And I am going to advocate that you recognize when your ego might be trying to get the best of you and stay on top of that. And perhaps most importantly, I am going to advocate what may for some people be a radical shift in their attitudes and philosophy towards and relationship with money.

The Overriding Principle – Spend less than you make.

This is going to sound a little like "The Wealthy Barber"[154] by Canadian David Chilton. That's because common sense never goes out of style, and sometimes common sense isn't all that common. Many people (and governments) fall into debt and resort to bankruptcy because they can't seem to grasp that self-evident principle.

Sine we're talking common sense here, let's clarify. It's perfectly OK to use debt sensibly. Very few regular folk can buy a house without taking on a mortgage or a car without a car-loan. By all means, take out a mortgage to buy that house for your family – just make sure you can handle the

---

[153] Professional athletes, celebrity entertainers, bankers, etc.
[154] "The Wealthy Barber: The Common Sense Guide to Successful Financial Planning". David Chilton. Stoddart Publishing Co. Limited, 1989.

payments. When I say "spend less than you make" I really mean cash-flow.

If for example, you're income is $4000/month clear, you'd better not have financial obligations that exceed that, or you're headed for inevitable trouble.

Temper your big purchases with some common sense and proportion. If you're the sole bread-winner for a young family and your salary is $60,000, a $750K new house and a $75K BMW is likely too much for you. Those two big fixed payments will have you living in a house with no (or cheap) furniture and feeding your family with Kraft Dinner and Hamburger Helper. Buy a less expensive house and car until you can afford it. Otherwise, you'll be an anxious mess, worrying about every dime and quarter. That's no way to live.

When the US banks collapsed in 2008, the basic reason was greed and callous disregard for their clientele and the economic impact of their practices. The banks were loaning sums of money to people that common sense would indicate they could never pay back. An example would be someone with unrealistic expectations (and maybe being a little stupid) borrowing $500K on a $50K salary. Now that defies common sense, right? But the banks enjoyed collecting payments from those borrowers that were almost entirely interest. Basically, the money just rolled in. When the borrowers inevitably defaulted, the banks could seize the properties[155] for resale. That worked fine as long as the banks didn't run out of suckers who wanted to buy more than they could afford or until the whole immoral and greedy scheme collapsed, which it did.

The influence of popular media in creating unrealistic expectations in the minds of young people doesn't help. Everyone knows that TV commercials encourage us to spend, spend, spend to achieve instant gratification. But some TV shows do the same thing. I could cite many examples but the one that springs to mind immediately is "Friends"[156]. This show ran for 10 years and featured the lives of six young New Yorkers. It was a nice, good-natured, easy show to watch. The problem with the show was the way it portrayed the easy affluence of its characters. People in their 20s living in Manhattan and working in normal jobs could not afford the apartments, clothes, and lifestyles of Monica, Ross, and the others. Their easy and elegant affability was not portrayed realistically. I was in my

---

[155] That's precisely what a mortgage loan is, i.e. the house the loan pays for is the collateral for the loan.

[156] Friends NBC (1994 – 2004). See: http://www.imdb.com/title/tt0108778/

mid-forties when the show ran, so I knew better. But viewers who were teenagers might form an unrealistic idea of what their lives would be like in 10 years. That sort of unsophisticated unrealistic set of expectations can lead young people into financial problems.

Years ago, when we were contemplating buying our first house, an accurate rule of thumb was that you would pay back roughly three times what you borrowed with a 25 year mortgage. So if you borrowed $50K, you would pay about $150K over 25 years. This is how the banks get increasingly wealthier on the backs of hard working young people.

These days, interest rates are a lot lower than they were back in the 70s, but people are borrowing much larger amounts than we did. As a consequence, their mortgages are spread over longer periods, so interest costs are almost as high in proportion as they used to be. It may not be three times principal like it was for us but it can be almost twice the principal. These days 30 year mortgages are common. If you borrow $500K at 3.5% over 30 years, you can expect to pay about $305K in interest. That's a great scheme for keeping the banks profitable and the shrinking middle class slaving away.

To me, the notion of a young couple borrowing that kind of money is borderline nonsensical.

The rest of this section follows from this basic principle, i.e. given that you don't spend more than you make, the rest applies.

Tell yourself the truth about your priorities

Some guys say one thing then do another. Almost any working man will say that his family comes first. In fact a lot of the time, the job comes first. Acting in manner that is incongruous with your stated priorities is one of the sure-fire ways to make yourself crazy with stress and anxiety.

One of the best reasons for not getting yourself badly into debt and under the crushing weight of burdensome financial obligations is to have the freedom to act in accordance with your priorities. To the extent that your financial obligations control you, you become a wage slave. These days, it's normal for a young man to have financial obligations that would have him defaulting within one month of having his salary cut off. Now that's pressure! And employers know about this too. And some of them are unscrupulous enough to exploit their wage slaves.

So, the boss wants you to work late and your son has a soccer game that you want to take him to and watch. What do you do? You always say that your family comes first but my God, you need that job or you won't be able to meet your payments. You can't even afford a performance evaluation where the boss questions your dedication to the job. What to do? No matter what you do, you lose. Who got you into this mess?

So how much money do you need? You need an amount that exceeds your financial obligations (thereby providing some discretionary income for fun and living) in accordance with your priorities. If your financial obligations and lifestyle are out of step with your priorities, you'll need to change your financial obligations or change your priorities.

But you need to be honest with yourself about what those priorities are. Don't tell yourself or your family that they come first, when in reality, your priority is the accumulation of financial wealth and all the trappings that make that obvious to everyone around you. If your priority is work and wealth, then by all means go for it, but don't be surprised if you don't have much of a family or social life.

The important thing is to tell yourself the truth about your priorities, then act in accordance with your priorities.

So given that we understand the importance of the overriding principle that, at least in the long run, you cannot spend more than you earn, we can move on to the central principle that can change your life for the better.

Distribute your money lovingly

When Jesus of Nazareth said, *"Then you will know the truth, and the truth will set you free"*[157], He was referring to a much broader truth than I'm going to describe here. He referred to the fact that we are limited by our small thinking and world views, and that real freedom comes from the inside, not from a change in eternal circumstances[158]. Although I've studied the Bible and for years used to worship faithfully, I now describe myself as a "Recovering Lutheran"[159]. So I don't want to fall into the trap of comparing this financial principle of mine to that immense one in terms of importance or scope. But I will say that's it's conceptually similar in its life-changing potential, and at least somewhere on a continuum of potentially life-changing principles.

I referred to this principle in my Preface, so that you already know that

[157] Gospel of John 8:32
[158] Like the overthrow of the occupying Roman Empire.
[159] That's another story, not that interesting, and certainly beyond the scope of this little book.

I believe it to be one of the most important principles in this book. We're not talking about regular oil changes here.

I first heard "distribute your money lovingly" from Bev. The first time she said this to me was around 20 years ago. It might have been at tax return preparation time. I used to get really uptight about preparing my tax return. This was in the days of sharpened pencils and electronic calculators. Revenue Canada provided two forms: one to work out your return in pencil and the other to write out in pen when you were sure you were done. It wasn't the overall idea of paying taxes that bothered me. I understood why it was necessary and I looked forward to receiving an income tax refund. It was the hassle of preparing the forms under threat of penalty for error that got me a little tense. In any case, in that time of struggle Bev suggested that I distribute my money lovingly.

When I first heard that phrase, I thought it was one of the most preposterous things I had heard in a while. I didn't get it. But now I do get it and live by it, and it's made me a more contented and peaceful person.

I have observed that some folks are obsessed in every financial transaction with keeping as much money for themselves as they can and giving the other person as little as they can. Of course I haven't measured this but going by what I have observed and what people have told me, I believe this value and behaviour is more common than the value and behaviour I'm going to describe and recommend here.

I believe this money-gripping value is pervasive in our culture. I have found it to be more common than not. In social gatherings, I've often heard people proudly boasting about how they were able to out-manoeuvre or manipulate another person in a transaction into selling for as low as possible or buying for as high as possible.

Why do people do this? This philosophy of scarcity is damaging for the person who acts this way and can create suffering for him/herself and the people around him. If they have been able to negotiate a buying price that was unexpectedly low or a selling price that was unexpectedly high, what does this imply about the fairness of the transaction for the other person? Is that something to feel good about and boast about? I don't think so.

The Law of Attraction applies to your relationship with money too. If you believe that everyone is out to cheat you in every small purchase and major transaction, that's what you will expect and that's what you will manifest into your life. And then unfortunately, you will act that way yourself because acting that way is consistent with your expectations from others. It's a dog-eat-dog world out there. You'd better do it to someone else before someone else does it to you.

Recently I was chatting with a young man at a social gathering. He proudly told me how he had been undercharged at a big-box retail outlet because of a scanning error by the clerk. He paid $15 instead of $250 for an RV battery. He had had two $250 batteries in his cart, one $15 item and a few other items. Somehow the clerk scanned in one of the batteries at $15, using the "two @..." function. So I asked him, "You pointed out the error and offered to pay the correct amount, right?" He looked at me like I was either joking or crazy and replied no. I pressed him a little further about his motivations and he explained that he figured that the establishment naturally overcharged all the time for everything and made too much profit anyway, etc, etc. It never occurred to him that he was taking money that was not his. He evidently saw every purchase as a win/lose competition and that he had won that particular skirmish. This guy has two little kids. I wonder what their attitudes toward money will be when they grow up.

The fact is that hanging onto money this way makes you a prisoner to it. It also implies a lot of unhappy things about the world view of the person who lives this way. It implies that he believes that money is scarce resource, when in fact it is not a resource at all, but only a potential. It also implies that the person believes that the world is an unfair and unscrupulous place, when in fact we all create the world around us with our thoughts, feelings, expectations, and behaviour. If you believe that the world is mean-spirited and unscrupulous, then by George, that's what it will be. You can absolutely create that reality for yourself. And once you're in that reality, it's difficult to recognize that another reality might be possible.

Many authors have said that everything we think and do there comes from either fear or love[160]. This clinging-to-money behaviour comes from fear and a world-view of scarcity. It does not come from a place of love and a world-view of abundance.

So here's the central idea. You're in a situation and you're going to have to pay. You could be paying for a car repair, a restaurant bill, some new clothes, an airline ticket, or many other things. The fact is, you're going to pay. So given that you're going to pay one way or the other, you have a choice. You can pay with a smile or your face and a light and generous heart, or you can pay with a scowl, a frown, and a sour stomach. Which one feels better? Which one would you choose for yourself?

---

[160] The Dream Manifesto is one of many sources for this belief. See: http://www.dreammanifesto.com/.

How many times in a week do you pay? Whatever the answer is for you, you have that many chances to distribute your money lovingly. When I said at the top that this is one of those truths that can set you free, I meant it. Think deeply about it. Examine this question at the feeling level, deeper than the thought level, and see where it settles for you. To start, you might just see a little glimmer of light at the bottom of the door in a dark room. But that little glimmer can grow to bathe you in a beautiful white light that you can enjoy from here on.

This central principle is still bound by the overriding first principle. We all still need to control our expenses so we don't go broke. But even as you manage your finances responsibly, we still need to pay for things. I refer to **how** you go about doing that.

Let's say you're on a vacation with your spouse, whom you love dearly. You knew at the planning stage that the vacation was going to be expensive, but you decided that even so, you both wanted to go. You knew this vacation would be good for both of you. So here you are at a nice restaurant near the end of what has been a perfect day. You're both happy and relaxed. You look at the menu and you see that all the dishes are $10-$15 more that you are used to paying, compared to back home.

How do you handle this situation? Do you feel cheated, unhappy, sour, deflated? Do you grumble into your shirt about the rip-off prices? I sure hope not. Maybe the restaurant bill is going to be $25-$35 more than you think it ought to be. So what? That's chicken feed compared to the value of how you are feeling. You came into the situation wanting a beautiful meal at the end of a perfect day with your spouse, whom you love dearly. And you can absolutely choose to have exactly that. Be big, be generous, pay the bill gladly, and enjoy yourself. Your response is your choice. Choose to distribute your money lovingly.

What if you actually are cheated by some unscrupulous person? First, assertively try to get your money back. After all, being cheated of your hard-earned money is far different from animating with your money. If you can recover it, that's good. Do your best to move on. If you can't recover it, you need to make the best of the situation. That probably means making your best effort at forgiving and letting go of your anger about the incident. You've already been cheated and that's a loss. You don't want to lose your mental health, emotional stability and spiritual grounding also.

Money is energy

Money is not a commodity and it's not in short supply. Governments can print more whenever they want to. That's essentially what the U.S. government did when they bailed out the banks and automakers after the collapse of 2008. A barrel of oil is a commodity. Soybeans are a commodity, as are wheat, barley, and canola. The values of those commodities are determined by what people will pay for them, i.e. by demand and supply. I've heard people complain that the governments ought to control commodity prices somehow, but in a global economy, sellers will sell to buyers for what buyers will pay. The only way governments can control commodity prices would be to buy them all up and then sell them for a controlled price. First, that wouldn't work because governments don't have that kind of money. Most of them are already in debt. Second, doing that sort of thing would be Socialism, and no one wants that, right?[161] Third, should a government or cartel try to control prices by holding back supply[162], other suppliers will step into the void and start selling.

Anyway, enough Economics 101. It's clear that money is not a commodity. In and of itself, money has no intrinsic value. Commodities do have value. Oil is a source of energy, which all of us consume. Wheat makes bread, barley makes beer and feeds livestock, and so forth. But if you ask yourself what money actually is you're going to have a hard time explaining it.

Back when we had dollar bills and my eyes were better, the bank note (i.e. that dollar bill) said that the Bank of Canada promised to pay the bearer of the bank note one dollar. Now what does that mean? If that dollar bill is not in itself a dollar, then what is? The fine print on the front of today's $5 bill or $10 bill says in both official languages "This note is legal tender." I think what that might mean is that a $5 bill is worth $5. I'm not sure that gets us a lot closer understanding what money is. Although it seems to imply that we can exchange the bill for something else that's valued at $5.

Perhaps originally, wealth was based on gold, and a one dollar bank

---

[161] Heh, heh, heh.

[162] That's what OPEC does, to limited success. The global demand for oil is such that suppliers want to sell before someone else does. Oil isn't a good indicator because global demand is increasing and since supplies are finite and practical limited by production costs, will continue to drive up prices until all reserves are spent.

note meant theoretically you could cash in the bank note for $1 worth of gold. I doubt you could go into TD Bank today, present a $5 bill, and get them to give you $5 worth of gold. And if you could, what would you do with that $5 sliver of gold?

The puzzle gets even more confounding when you realize that only a small fraction of today's financial transactions are done with cash. Just line up at Sobey's or Canadian Tire and you'll see how few people transact business with cash. Money is now bits and bytes in computers. I haven't had an actual paycheque (is a cheque money?) in years. I do all my banking on-line. Money comes into my accounts and leaves my accounts according to computer keystrokes that I and others make. This is one of the reasons why we were all concerned with Y2K[163]. Remember that? What if all our wealth and debts disappeared because all the computers got confused?

So then, what is money exactly? It is potential; it's purchasing power; most importantly, money is energy. When the energy flows, it's easy and pleasant.

Cash money in and of itself seems to have no intrinsic value. The paper and ink are virtually worthless. But if I have a few $20 bills in my wallet, I can go to a retail shop and exchange the paper for something with practical functional value like an iPod, a digital camera, or a yoga mat. Those bills represent my potential to do that. Chances are very low that the shop sales person is going to reject my cash in exchange for any of those items. He will make the exchange even though the bills have no intrinsic value and those items do. Everyone ascribes purchasing power to those bills. As long as everyone does, the system works.

After the transaction, I can take my new item home and put it into use. And what can the shopkeeper do with the bills I exchanged for my new item? This is where the paper money takes on value. The shopkeeper can include those bills in his monthly revenues, to pay taxes and other fixed expenses, pay staff, invest in new inventory, and contribute to profit for the owners. And you can bet he does that by depositing the cash in the bank and converting the cash into electronic bits and bytes.

I feel good about my new iPod. Shouldn't I also feel good also about the benefits the shopkeeper realizes with what I paid him? The point here is that when I turn over the payment to the shopkeeper, once I understand what's going on, I don't do it with regrets and mixed feelings. I do it consciously, mindfully and in good cheer. I am realizing the buying potential of that money with the transaction. With that exchange, both of

---

[163] Y2K was when December 31, 1999 turned to January 1, 2000.

us are enriched. I have passed along **energy**. I have **animated** that retail shop with my purchase.

Money is not something to grip. It's an energy to distribute lovingly. Money does you or no one else any good if you're hanging onto it. I'm not advocating against having a responsible savings account. And I'm not advocating "spending like a sailor"[164] either. I am advocating that you spend your money mindfully and lovingly.

Now that we understand what money is and why we should distribute it lovingly, a few other principles follow naturally.

Be Generous

Be generous with your money. Always pay your share - and maybe a little more - and always pay your debts.

If you're contributing to a cost-sharing scheme with friends or family, pay your share and maybe a little more. If you've agreed to split a restaurant bill with another couple, do the same thing. If their share is more than yours, pay half. If their share is less than yours, suggest you pay the bill and they leave the tip.

Don't be the guy that hangs back or goes to the washroom when the bill comes[165]. When it's your turn, pick up the tab and pay it gladly – not like some sort of big-shot, more like a person who has enough self-confidence and self-esteem that paying the bill comes naturally.

And when you're tipping, tip generously. Remember you are animating that server, or hair-cutter, or whatever. If you're in doubt if the tip should be $5 or $6, or maybe $18 or $20, **always** choose the higher amount. There - now I've made it easy for you. You'll never have to stew again about how much to tip. When you tip generously, you feel good and so does the person you are animating.

And the same principle applies if you find yourself on the other side of the transaction. If someone is generous to you, the right thing to do is accept that generosity with humility and gratitude. Now that I'm retired from full-time professional work, I work part-time as a courtesy shuttle driver for a car rental company. Occasionally, my passengers tip me. The

---

[164] The image comes from the old notion that a sailor would blow all his money on wine, women, and song while in port. When they shipped off the next day, he had no further need for money. While at sea, the ship supplied their food and rum rations.

[165] Larry David did a good bit on that in his show "Curb Your Enthusiasm".

first couple of times this happened, I was taken aback. Here I was over 60 years old, and I had never before been in a situation where someone was offering me a tip. I turned the first couple of tips down, telling my passenger something like, "you don't need to do that" or "thanks but we don't accept tips" – that sort of nonsense.

That didn't feel right in my gut. Actually my gut told me that something had been wrong with that transaction. Then like a two-by-four across the forehead, I got it. Those people who were offering to tip me were being kind and generous, wanting to offer a gesture of appreciation for the service I had provided. And by turning down the tip, I was slamming the door on the flow of positive energy.

Yikes! Like, who did I think I was turning down those tips? Now when someone offers me a tip – and it's always a surprise because it happens infrequently – I accept graciously and with gratitude. I feel good about it and I know the tipper feels good also. If a passenger tips me $5, I figure that's a sub sandwich at Quizno's. I take the $5 and pass it along to someone else.

Buy good quality - Don't buy cheap merchandise

I first apprehended this important principle in a Brian Tracy tape seminar on Self Esteem. A surprising truth is that buying good quality merchandise is often a better economic choice than buying cheap merchandise. The good quality merchandise will perform better and last longer than the cheap merchandise. This principle applies to all sorts of consumer goods, like musical instruments, furniture, clothing, and motor vehicles.

Buying cheap is often pretty much like throwing your money away because you'll end up throwing away the cheap merchandise before long. And what are you saying about how you value yourself when you buy cheap? Buy good quality, pay a fair price for it, and feel good about it.

I want to share the story of my dear old Guild D40SB acoustic guitar here. Back in around 1977, we were finally hauling ourselves out of poverty[166]. Both of us were working. I was making about $12-14K and Bev about the same. We sure weren't wealthy, but we had just bought our first house[167] and we were meeting our financial obligations.

I wanted to buy a good acoustic guitar. I had had a pretty good one

---

[166] The first four years of our marriage, 1971-1975, one or the other of us was in University while the other worked.

[167] Our first house was a 2 bedroom bungalow for which we paid $40K.

for a few years previously but I had wrecked it by slamming an unfamiliar trunk door down on it. Since that unhappy incident, I had been doing without. In 1977, $500 for a guitar was a huge amount for a young couple with our income and expenses. It would probably be like $5000 today.

Bev, who was even then was wise and far-thinking beyond her years, encouraged me to make the purchase. She reasoned that it was a good quality instrument[168] and I would enjoy it for a lifetime. So I did, although with some reluctance. This was years before I understood what money was and that it was to be distributed lovingly. But nonetheless, we made the right decision.

That guitar has been all over with me. I have written songs on it, performed in front of drunks with it, played it on the deck in the sunshine, and taken it on camping and vacation trips all across our country. It's sitting beside me as I write this. Although its face is a little beaten up with the years, my 1977 Guild D40SB has only improved in sound and responsiveness as it has aged.

Whenever I consider the principles of generosity (Bev's) and buying quality, I think of the story of that guitar. We really couldn't afford it (of course we could – because we did) but we took the plunge and never regretted it. I love that old guitar as much as a person can love an inanimate object. In fact, I think I will pick it up right now and take a break from writing.

Be scrupulously honest with money

I practice yoga and have been doing so for many years now. Yoga is much more than a physical exercise; it's the mastery and integration of the activities of the mind, and a way of life. Our lives are guided by the Yamas, or restraints, and the Niyamas, or observances. One of the Yamas is *Asteya*[169], or non-stealing.

As a yogi[170], my life is guided by the Yamas and Niyamas. Because of *Asteya*, I choose not to steal or cheat anyone and I choose to pay my taxes. For me and others like me, it's out of the question to do otherwise. This discipline, like distributing your money lovingly, can change your life for

---

[168] Bev doesn't know about guitars. She knew that it was good quality because I had told her so. She trusted my assessment.
[169] The Yoga Sutras are written in Sanskrit, an ancient tongue.
[170] "Yogi" is not an exalted term. I don't claim any status by calling myself a yogi. It's just a fact. A yogi is a male who practices yoga.

the better, as it has changed mine. It's liberating to an extent that's difficult to realize if you don't live this way yourself.

I believe that you cannot put a price tag on your integrity. How do you live in accordance with *Asteya*? I want to tell four short stories that illustrate how it's done. The stories are in chronological order, beginning with the oldest.

1. The Wallet

    This story features my late mother–in-law Ellie, who lived and loved in modest circumstances but knew the difference between right and wrong. One day as she was getting into her car in the Zellers parking lot, she found an open wallet on the asphalt right beside her car. She could see that the wallet contained a big wad of cash. Ellie picked up the wallet, knowing that if she left it there, someone else might pick it up and keep it. She took the wallet home and called the police. The police came and picked it up, contacted the owner, and returned the wallet to him with all the cash intact.

    It turns out that the owner was a young man about my age at that time (around 30). He had just cashed his monthly paycheque and had more than $600, a huge sum in 1979, in his wallet when he lost it. He was floored with gratitude and the impact of Ellie's honesty. Bev and my infant son Steve were visiting with Ellie when the man dropped by her house to convey his gratitude. He offered her $20 as a reward and Bev was there to witness it.

    Not to make too much out of it, but an act of integrity like that could well have been life-changing for that young man. I hope so and choose to believe so.

2. The $100 bill

    A few years later than the wallet incident, I was a young technical rep with a job that included a lot of business travel. One day I was gassing up my company car at a Shell station just North of Calgary for my return trip home to Edmonton. In those days, they didn't have "Pay at the Pump" like now. I walked into the station to pay for the gas. Right under my nose on top of a display of motor oil was a $100 bill. The cashier couldn't see it so I could have stuffed it in my pocket easily.

That was before I started yoga and I had never heard of *Asteya*. I had this strange feeling that I was being watched even though I wasn't. This was in 1982 or 83. $100 bought a week's groceries in those days. I must admit I was a little torn. But I knew that $100 bill wasn't mine. So I picked it up and gave it to the cashier. For all I know, she kept it. But I did not, because it wasn't mine.

3. The Canada Trust teller
    A year or two after the $100 bill incident at the Shell station, I had another $100 bill experience, only this time it was with $100 that actually was mine. It was a beautiful summer day. Bev, the boys and I were vacationing in our home town of Winnipeg, visiting friends and family and having fun.

    We banked with Canada Trust, which subsequently merged with Toronto Dominion and became TD Canada Trust. But in those days, it was just Canada Trust. I had this $100 bill in my wallet that had been difficult to use. I wanted to exchange it for smaller denominations. So I walked into this downtown Winnipeg branch full of enthusiasm, confidence, and good spirits. I smiled at the teller and asked her, "Would you please change this hundred for four fifties?" She returned my cheery smile, peeled of four fifties and replied, "Certainly sir, here you are" and handed them over.

    Within a second, both of us had funny looks on our faces. Something didn't feel right. I beat her to the punch. "Wait a minute. That's not right." We both laughed, I apologized, and handed her back two $50 bills.

4. The Green Machine[171]
    This recent story features Bev. A few months ago, Bev walked up to a Green Machine ready to do a little routine automated banking. The screen did not display its usual appearance when you first walk up to begin a transaction. In fact, the screen said "Would you like to perform another transaction?"

    The previous customer had absent-mindedly left his bank card in the machine and walked away. Much like the guy who

---

[171] The Green Machine is what TD Canada Trust calls its automated tellers located at the TD branches.

had dropped his wallet had been lucky that it was Ellie that found it, this guy was lucky that it was Bev who walked up to the Green Machine after he had abandoned an active session with his card still in the machine.

So what do you suppose Bev did? Do you reckon that she quickly withdraw $500 from that person's account and stuff the money in her purse? No doubt some people might do that. Bev took the card into the branch and turned it over to one of the staff, explaining how she had recovered the card. The person who had left his card in the machine was not short one dime.

5. The Canadian Tire Guy

    This incident happened recently. In the final stages of writing this book, I was on my way for a meeting with one of my editors to discuss the changes he recommended when I stopped in at Canadian Tire to pick up a few items. I mention this because I was not in a mindful state at the time. I was thinking more about the editor's meeting that I was about what I was doing at the self-checkout.

    So there I was walking out of the store with my purchase when I heard someone behind me call out, "Sir! You forgot your change!" This regular-looking guy in his mid-forties, another customer, had followed me out as quickly as he could go, likely losing his place in line. He smiled and handed me $5 plus two 5 cent Canadian Tire bills. Then I remembered how I had put in 12 cents so I would get a $5 bill back rather than a bunch of coins. But, not being in a mindful state, I had walked out without my change. I thanked him.

    As I said in one of my country songs, the time's always right to do the right thing[172]. Whether it is five, fifty, or five hundred dollars at stake, the right thing to do is not to take or keep what is not yours. The man who handed me the $5 understood that. Good on him.

Those stories all had a happy ending. And in each case, good energy was passed forward. Don't put a price tag on your integrity. You'll be happier and you'll sleep better when you are scrupulously honest with money.

---

[172] Lyrics from "Not Trying to Change Him" by Max Doubt (2002)

The Corollary – Don't give your money to someone you don't want to animate.

Distributing your money lovingly carries with it a certain mature responsibility. Now that we're spending our money mindfully and kindly, we understand that we're also passing along energy when we do that. Consequently, just as you're happy to pass along that good energy when you feel you're making a good and fair transaction, now that we understand what we're doing, we have the option – actually the responsibility – not to give your money to someone whom you don't want to animate.

We may have decided that we will never cheat someone else and that all our transactions are good and honourable. But not everyone shares that belief or value. Don't do business with another person or organization that you don't like or trust.

If you walk into a restaurant and the vibe doesn't feel right, leave. Don't distribute your money there. If you enter a shop where the shop owner is mean to his young staff, don't buy there. If you don't like the fact that modern big-box retailers can sell cheap because they carry goods that were produced by child labour in Asian sweat-shops, don't spend your money there. Or if you don't support how some retailers market their products by unfairly exploiting less powerful players in the supply chain, don't buy from them. See what I mean?

It's not that your money is sacred. It's not; it's just money. But your energy is sacred. Don't pass along your positive loving energy to a place that isn't worthy of it. I only offer examples above. I'm not trying to preach about what's right and wrong in business.

The point is, it's up to you where you participate in the marketplace, according to your own values and preferences. You aren't absolutely obliged to buy from the cheapest seller. And neither are you obliged to buy from the most expensive and prestigious seller, or the one closest to your home, or the one owned by your boss's bother. But you have a choice where and to whom you distribute your money lovingly. Pass along your energy to places and people that you feel good about animating. And avoid the ones you don't.

Working for a Living

When I say "working for a living" I mean more than working for pay. If we work an 8 hour day, we spend 1/3 of our adult lives working, at least on work days. And with the extended work hours many people are putting in these days, maybe it's safe to say that we can spend up to 1/3 of our overall adult lives working. If you work that way for 40 years, say from age 25-65, that's a seriously big chunk of your life devoted to the workplace. So, we want your work life to be as healthy and rewarding a part of your life as is possible. Your time at work is not a prison sentence; it's part of your life. So when you're "working for a *living*" I want you to be *living* while you are working.

I started off previous sections with disclaimers, making it clear that I wasn't claiming to hold any particular expertise in the topic area. I haven't written any books or done any exhaustive research on this topic either. But I did work hard and long, and had some successes along the way. I'd like to share with you some principles that will contribute to making you succeed and enjoy the workplace. I'm going to provide a little introduction to my time in the workplace, so you'll know where I'm coming from.

After graduating with my second degree in 1975, I went to work for Canada Packers in the Chem Lab as a foods chemist, performing in-process and finished product compositional analyses. Starting there, I worked 34 years for three organizations without any break between successive jobs. My older brother has called me "super-responsible". I thought that was interesting. I have never gone out of my way to be super responsible. But looking back, I can recognize at least one common trend. In all three organizations, I got promoted a lot. Maybe other people also thought I was responsible. Without any effort on my part to impress anyone in authority with my skills or personal attributes, my supervisors always placed me in positions of increasing responsibility. And this for a guy from an inner-city slum with distinct problems with authority and a lack of sophisticated breeding. As Joseph Heller[173] would say, "Go figure".

I enjoyed a 34 year professional career in the sciences without the usual Ph.D. requisite. I hold two bachelor degrees and a half of a business degree. Most guys with a B.Sc. will work in industry selling equipment or in some administrative function, or perhaps for a consulting company. Or maybe they'll become realtors or stockbrokers and make a pile of dough. But I loved science and wanted to work in my field. When I graduated with my B.Sc. in 1975, Bev and I had been married four years and had experienced four years of poverty. The first two years of our marriage I worked while Bev finished her degree. The next two years Bev worked while I earned my second degree. At that point, I had six years of University education. I was sick of being a student and sick of poverty. I didn't want to go to graduate school. I wanted to start working. And being a young dude of 26, I had the hubris[174] to believe that I was bright enough, tough enough, and street-wise enough that I could work in the sciences without a post-grad degree. Basically, I didn't know any better.

And I pretty much did that. But I think they slammed the door shut after they let me in. So kids, don't try this at home. If you want to work in the sciences, put your mind, time, and effort to it and earn that doctorate.

After I left the science and technology supply-side profit sector where I had held a management position, I worked my final 23 years in a research and technology organization, side by side with scientists and engineers who were doing actual research in applied science, trying to improve the lot of humankind. At the apex of my working life I led a research and development business unit with more than 70 scientists, engineers, technologists and support staff with a budget exceeding $8 million. I succeeded in a sometimes cutthroat and always highly political environment until eventually I reached an impasse with our CEO over a matter of honour and principle. That sort of event that can come during difficult times[175] when you're in a position with a lot of responsibility. In my

---

[173] Joseph Heller (1923-1999) was an American satirical author who wrote some of my favorite novels, including Catch-22, Good as Gold, Something Happened, and God Knows

[174] Again with the hubris. That's still my favorite word.

[175] Like in 2009 after the global financial collapse of 2008.

own case, I wouldn't back down from what I considered to be a matter of principle. And being an Enneagram Type 8, of course I absolutely needed to protect my people. That meant I retired about a year and half before I had intended to. But, since I had a contract, I left with a big settlement that left me better off financially than I would have been had I worked those last 18 months.

So, from that perspective, here is some of what I learned about surviving and succeeding in the workplace, distilled down into principles.

Bring your A-Game to the workplace

Many years ago my direct supervisor told me, "You come to the rink to play." I took that as a compliment then and I still do. He was using a hockey metaphor that any Canadian male would understand. That's the kind of comment a hockey commentator might make about a player who "gives it a 110% every night." What my supervisor meant was that he appreciated my effort. Remember how pumped you were when you first landed your job? Of course it's not realistic to keep up that giddy enthusiasm indefinitely but you still owe your employer an honest effort every day.

A lot of people will tell you this – and add my name to the list – you need to be technically competent at your job but what really makes for success in the work place is your behaviour and attitudes. In this section I'm just going to introduce this notion. I'll get more into it later in this chapter.

The point is I've seen lots of people with excellent technical skills fail in the workplace. That happens for two reasons: First, because they aren't sufficiently careful with their behaviour and don't pay sufficient attention to their relationships with their work colleagues. Second, because they begin to take their job for granted, as though somehow they were entitled to it, and don't consistently make their best effort every day.

Bring your A-Game to the workplace. And put in an honest day's hard work in exchange for your pay. You aren't entitled to your job. By your work, you need to add value to your employer. Make sure he gets his money's worth. If your employer pays you $x/day, make sure you add $(x + y)/day in value. That's the ethical way. To do less is not ethical.

No one gives you power and authority – step up

In the heading to this section directly above, I don't mean that you ought to become a power or authority grabber. But I do recommend that you show initiative. From my years as a manager I can tell you it was plain to me that some staffers had an inclination to step up assertively and take action to get done what needed to be done. Other staffers were more inclined to wait passively for direction when they weren't clear what to do, how to do it, or whether they had the authority to do it. The workplace has room for both types of people. But only people in the first category have the natural inclination toward leadership. I much preferred staffers to take a little risk, even when they made a mistake[176], to act proactively and effectively in the interests of the organization.

Since in my later jobs, my direct reports were all professionals with responsibilities of their own, I didn't have to worry much about whether they could or would take initiative. That was an assumed part of their job. I had promoted them because of their leadership qualities, including initiative. But still, we can always observe that the tendency to assume authority is on a continuum.

When I was in my twenties and first promoted in my first professional job I had to learn about assuming authority. I hadn't asked for a promotion or anything like that. I had just been beavering away at the bench doing my chemical analyses. I assume the boss must have thought I showed leadership potential. In any case, he offered me a promotion. My promotion meant taking over a different group whose leader had just been promoted into the production part of the plant. I'd been on the job for a year or less. I didn't know the guys I would be supervising and I didn't know the work that they did. I would need to be trained for a while in their work, by the guys I would soon be supervising and then take over leadership of the group. And perhaps predictably, the guys were not all that enthusiastic about "… having a rookie crammed down our throats[177]", as one of them succinctly put it to me. That situation was fraught with many ways to go wrong.

I found this career development to be a difficult challenge. All of a sudden I had responsibility and I wondered if I had the authority I needed to deliver on my responsibility. I found that I didn't know what authority

---

[176] In an organization "making a mistake" sometimes just means doing the job differently than the boss would have done it. A good leader will look at the results as well as at the process.
[177] Lorne Macamus, 1976

was. I sort of had a vague idea from what I'd seen in the movies and on TV. I reckoned that authority meant that if you told someone under your authority what to do[178], they had to do it or risk being fired. That was at best a rudimentary appreciation of what authority or leadership meant, but then I was 25 or 26 years old, and pretty green. I sure didn't figure I had the clout to fire anyone. And of course I didn't want it to come to that anyway.

I could write a whole book about the mistakes I made, but I don't want to and I can't remember much about that time anyway. It was more than 35 years ago. But I can remember how it felt in my stomach. Wow – leadership and assuming authority is tough. And in that job, I didn't really have any mentor to trust for teaching.

Skip ahead about 30 years in the workplace and now I'm the grey haired guy with all the experience and seasoning. Over the years since 1975, my role had evolved so that I was now on the other side of the desk, so to speak. Now I was one promoting younger people whom I thought displayed leadership skill or potential into group leadership roles. The difference was that I was available to help them when they had difficulties adjusting to their new responsibilities and came to me for help. I found this to be a rewarding experience because I understood how they felt, having been there myself.

I can remember one case well. I had recently promoted this young man who was obviously bright, ambitious, with good values and clear leadership potential. I know he was a born leader because he knew what he knew and he knew what he didn't know, and had the confidence and self-esteem179 to ask for assistance for the latter. This guy wasn't sure how to grab authority with his new group. He understood very well his new responsibilities. And I had made it clear to him that he had the authority he needed to deliver on his responsibilities. I had also made sure he knew that he was free to use his good judgement, act as he thought right, and that I would back him up as necessary. The question came down to how he would act with his new group. He had just been promoted from a group that previously had been his peers. He felt uncomfortable in his new role as leader, especially with one member of his group who seemed to hold some resentment, and he asked my advice on how he should act.

---

[178] On TV shows like Star Trek or others with paramilitary themes like cop shows, the leader would bark, "That's an order!" and expect his subordinate to comply. The real life workplace isn't much like that.

[179] He also made good eye contact and spoke with a level, respectful, and confident voice.

I told him something like, "Act like a Program Manager". He admitted that he didn't yet feel like a Program Manager and experienced some unease about that. He asked me to expand and tell him how a Program Manager acts. I told him something like, "Act like you're in charge. You have the responsibility and the authority to back it up. Just act like it. If you want to feel confident, act confident." I'm not claiming that was especially sage advice. But it did work. This guy went on to become a successful leader who delivered on all his responsibilities, all the time. Taking command, assuming authority, and acting like a leader comes from the inside. The big secret here is that no one can really confer authority onto you. Your boss can promote you but it's up to you to assume your authority, become comfortable in it, and act as though you have it. Authority does not reside in having three stripes on your sleeve. Authority resides in your character. Step up. No one else can do it for you.

Use your Interpersonal skills

As I said above, the two big reasons why people don't succeed in the workplace are that they don't take care of their interpersonal relationships and they don't apply themselves to their work. In this section I'm going to provide some principles that apply to the former reason. In the following section, I'll provide some principles that apply to the latter reason.

Want to work and play well with others? Apply your knowledge from the previous chapters. The vast majority of the interpersonal skills y0ou need for success in the workplace are the ones we've already discussed. Master your inner world by controlling your ego, accepting responsibility, staying conscious and present in the moment, and applying some emotional detachment when appropriate. Stay grounded in your spiritual values. Be a genuine person by knowing yourself and minimizing the incongruity between your inner and outer selves. Be trustworthy. Conduct yourself in a manner consistent with your deepest values. In my 34 years of professional work, I never read a company employee manual with HR policies, business ethical principles and so forth. I'm not bragging about that; my point is that I never felt a need for my employer to tell me what my values ought to be or how I ought to behave it certain situations180. I always felt confidently grounded enough in my own values. If you apply the inner

---

[180] As I said earlier, I have problems with authority...not _my_ authority – the kind that others might think they have over me. It may be part of being a Type 8.

world and outer world principles we've already examined, those are skills will cover off about 80% of the situations you'll meet in the workplace.

But the workplace is a special enough environment that we need to fill in the remaining 20% with some principles that are especially important for that environment.

First, the workplace calls for assertive behaviour. You can like it or not, but this is a fact and you may as well get used to it. Entire books and seminars can teach you all about assertiveness. We can't get into all that here. If you're not naturally inclined to engage in assertive behaviour, I suggest that you learn about it. You'll find that practicing assertive behaviour will drastically improve your life in the workplace and elsewhere. In the workplace, I believe your boss, your colleagues, and your subordinates will all prefer that you conduct yourself assertively. Let's make sure we don't confuse assertive behaviour with aggressive behaviour. They are not the same thing. In the workplace, we want assertive behaviour and for the most part, we don't want aggressive behaviour.

The Oxford English Dictionary says that "To assert" means to state an opinion, claim a right, or establish authority. If you assert yourself, you behave in a way that expresses your confidence and power and earns you respect from others. Assertive people own their feelings and communicate clearly about what they want and expect. They're straight shooters. Assertive people say what they mean and mean what they say. They raise questions, ask for favours, open and close conversations. Assertive people state their opinions, while still being respectful of others. Aggressive people attack or ignore others' opinions in favor of their own. Passive people don't state their opinions at all181. And passive-aggressive people express their thoughts, feeling, and preferences indirectly or obliquely182, with sarcasm and throw-away comments.

Remember that when you're assertive, you still need to be polite and respectful. But given that you remain polite and respectful, you have a right to hold your opinions and preferences and you have the right to speak up about them. When you're assertive, you own your own feelings and you aren't responsible for others' feelings. If assertively expressing your opinion results in someone else becoming defensive, angry, or aggressive, that's his problem, not yours. And when I say you own your own feelings, I mean you have the right to speak up if someone is trying to manipulate you with passive aggressive behaviour.

---

[181] See: http://www.mtstcil.org/skills/assert-3.html

[182] And in my opinion, pathologically.

Let's say you have a colleague who sometimes rolls his eyes up when someone else says something he doesn't like, as if to imply, "Duh! Is that stupid or what!?!" People behave that way in the workplace because it works for them. Many people don't want to confront passive-aggressive behaviour. It's easier to let it slide. The passive-aggressive behaviour like eye rolling works for them until they run into an assertive person183 who calls them on it. Next time you make a sincere and assertive suggestion and old Fred rolls his eyes, say something like,

> *"Fred, when I made that suggestion just now, I noticed that you rolled your eyes. I'm puzzled by that. What do you mean when you roll your eyes like that?"*

Fred may get defensive and fire back something aggressive at you. If that happens, don't back down. Stay grounded, maintain steady eye contact, keep your voice level and conversational in tone, and ask again,

> *"What does it mean when you roll your eyes like that?"*

If you think you could never behave that way, let me tell you – you can. I know this is true because I tried it myself after attending a seminar on assertive behaviour in the workplace. You may have a lump in your throat or a knot in your stomach when you try it the first time, but the other person doesn't have to know that. When you act assertively like that, you are teaching others how you want to be treated. Fred will think better about rolling his eyes the next time you suggest something. Don't worry for a minute about what old Fred might say about you behind your back. Think about the reputations both of you are building. You're building a reputation of someone who's a straight shooter, someone who communicates clearly and openly and won't be intimidated by passive aggressive manipulation. Fred is building a reputation as a manipulator and someone who gossips about his co-workers.

If you want to learn about how to be assertive, your local bookstore will have an entire shelf devoted to the topic. But take this to the bank: assertive behaviour is your ally in the workplace.

Second, avoid using sarcasm at work. Sarcasm is for the passive aggressive folks; it's not for you. The principles of assertiveness call for you to be clear and straightforward in your communication style. That rules

---

[183] Or some fortunate person who had the good judgment and acumen to buy and read this book.

out sarcasm right there. If someone is really getting on your nerves with his habitual use of sarcasm, you can approach the issue in a similar fashion to how you approach the eye rolling. Just make it clear that you'd prefer if he cut it back some. But be careful with this. You don't want to come across as pompous or superior. Remember your role in the workplace is to get your work done. It's most definitely not to "improve" your co-workers. If someone's habitual use of sarcasm is interfering with your ability to do your work, then speak up assertively. If it's just some poor soul who doesn't seem to have a clue, then be like Sir Paul McCartney and let it be184. The main thing here is to make sure your <u>own</u> use of sarcasm is zero. Your own behaviour is the behaviour you control. Your personal standard for the use of sarcasm is zero.

Third, mind your manners, every day and for the long-term. Employ common courtesy but maintain a polite distance from your co-workers. Maintain a standard of politeness from which you never waver. Remember that your colleagues are your colleagues; they're not your closest intimates. If you want long-term cordial working relationships, keep it that way. Don't encourage your colleagues to confide in you their deepest secrets fears and concerns or personal problems. Nothing good can come from it. That's for their loved ones, not for the workplace. And likewise, keep your most private thoughts private. Keep your own counsel. After all, you have work to do.

Always be polite. Say please, thank you, good morning, good night, smile, and get back to work. If you are troubled with personal concerns, keep that to yourself or seek help through your employee assistance program or a private psychologist.

Fourth, avoid gossiping in workplace185. Keep your conversations at work on task. When you gossip you send all sorts of unfavourable messages about yourself along with that juicy gossip. Be interested in getting your work done and getting it done well, not in what other people are doing. Most workplace gossip is negative. In that case, the reasons for avoiding are rather obvious. But avoid what superficially seems to be positive gossip too. Nothing good can come of it, so don't do it.

If you feel the urge to gossip, go to a quiet place and ask yourself why. You need to understand your motivation for wanting to gossip. Elevate

---

184 "Let It Be" Lennon–McCartney (1970) written by Paul McCartney. See: http://www.youtube.com/watch?v=ajCYQL8ouqw&feature=related
185 Avoid gossip altogether, anywhere and anytime. But we're talking about the workplace here.

your thoughts. Concentrate on what you want more of. When you gossip, you're sending out negative energy. We already know that thoughts have power. For a host of good reasons, you don't want to be the source of negative energy.

Finally, pack care and compassion into your briefcase when you leave for work in the morning. Especially if you're in management, you need to care about your people. Have compassion for your employees' shortcomings, and try your best to create a work environment that values and recognizes the contributions that employees make. If you think demonstrating care and compassion is inconsistent with maintaining a polite distance, we'll just have to disagree on that one.

When managers don't care about their staff, it shows and the employees can feel it. When the company says something like "Our people are our most important asset" and then doesn't actually act that way, the result is that saying it causes harm rather than good. We want to be genuine in the workplace just like we do in our personal lives. People bring their BS detectors to work with them. Uttering insincere platitudes breeds mistrust. Avoid that.

On the other hand, whether you're in management or not, consistently bringing a sincere caring and compassion with you to work, coupled with common courtesy and a polite distance, will contribute over the long term to a positive working environment. It's respectful. I want to illustrate with a short true story that was moving and meaningful to me.

In the spring of 2005 I suffered a heart attack. I was hospitalized and had an angioplasty. Someone from the workplace bought one of those huge get-well cards that everyone signs along with a personal message. Receiving that card with all those signatures and messages in and of itself meant a lot to me. I'm a sucker for sentimental gestures like that. But one comment stood out from all the others. It came from a Chinese scientist whom I barely knew and whose English was rudimentary. But somehow his limited English expressed a sentiment that brought tears to my eyes[186]. It said:

"You care people. People care you."

Imagine how I felt when I read that. That was pretty much my most treasured memory of the workplace.

---

[186] It still does.

Take yourself off probation

In the "Apply some detachment…" section in the first chapter of Part II, I mentioned the CEO who preached "performance is the only reality." This rather unpleasant individual had another related principle that fell under that larger umbrella. He told us that we all (the senior product division managers) should consider ourselves to be on probation every day. If we had a good month or a good week, that was great…for that month or that week. But we were never to consider ourselves to be successful because of some past accomplishment, no matter how recent. We were to ask ourselves what we could do for the business that day, and as part of that philosophy we needed to prove our value to the company each day. As such, were we all on probation, every day and for every day into the future.

As a young man with a young wife and two small children who had just moved to Montreal because of my promotion, this business philosophy was not pleasant for me to hear. I had not uprooted and moved the family to a place where we had no roots and a language deficiency, so that I could be on probation. I had been successful in my previous position back in Alberta, which was why I had been offered the promotion. But none of that mattered anymore. Now I was on probation, with dependants and no hope of alternate employment because of French language deficiency. My High School French was not even close to being adequate.

Naturally I confided to Bev my uneasiness with this "you're all on permanent probation" situation. I can't remember exactly what she said, but in effect it was something like, "That's nonsense. Take yourself off probation." Bless her little cotton socks. That's just what I needed to hear. Only someone from a working class neighborhood north of the Assiniboine in Winnipeg could come up with something like that so casually.

From that evening forward, I took myself off probation. Bev bought me a little whimsical wooden toy that was a monkey doing flips and tricks on a gymnastic high bar. When you turned the crank, the monkey did his thing. Bev said I should keep it on my desk at work and whenever I felt some pressure about being on probation I could give the monkey a spin. Doing that would remind me that I wasn't a trained monkey who could be manipulated into fear by a nasty tyrant.

That was 1986. When we moved back to Alberta in 1987 the monkey made the trip back with us and took up his place on my new desk. He stayed on my desks for 22 years until I retired in 2009. I gave him many a therapeutic spin since 1986. I still have him. Now he's in my Max Guitar Care shop, but I don't need to spin him anymore.

Do your absolute best at your work. In fact, make your work an art form whenever possible. But do not be manipulated by fear tactics. Take yourself off probation. As my father-in-law Ernie Harris used to say, "Biff![187]"

Work – concentrate on your job

I said earlier that the two big reasons why people don't succeed in the workplace are that they don't manage their interpersonal relationships well and they don't apply themselves to their work. In the previous section I provided some principles that apply to the former reason. In this section, I'll provide some principles that apply to the latter reason. When you go to work, go there to work.

Woody Allen said that "80% of success is just showing up". When he said that, I don't think his intended meaning was that you could be successful in the workplace 80% just by showing up with the remaining 20% of your time and effort devoted to surfing the net, exchanging pleasantries with your Facebook friends, gassing and gossiping with colleagues, and sending and receiving e-mails. That's not what you trained for and that's not what you agreed to with your employer when he decided to hire you. When you're at work, make sure your priority is getting your work done. I can think of five good reasons for that.

First, as a conscious person, making your actual work your #1 priority in the workplace is the ethical thing to do. When you agreed to the terms of employment, you made certain promises, both explicit and implied. The basic idea was that you would work to the benefit of your employer's organization and in return your employer would compensate you. With some people, as time passes they seem to forget their part of the bargain. Once the bloom is off a new job, many employees evolve a sense of entitlement about their salary. I am amazed how some people develop the idea that they have a right to their pay and maybe they'll get around to doing some work when they feel like it. This mistaken way of thinking is not for you. Accepting pay without making your best effort to earn it is

---

[187] Ernie told me years ago about getting the strap at school when he was a little boy. Corporal punishment was common in those days, especially for boys. Each time the teacher would hit little Ernie's outstretched hand with the strap, Ernie would respond "Biff!" And he would not cry. I love that story.

contrary to the Yama of *Asteya*[188]. To my way of thinking, to behave that way is unethical.

Make your work an art form. Take pleasure in doing what you do for the sake of the task itself, rather than for the sake of recognition, approval, or reward. The Bhagavad-Gita[189] says, "You have the right to the action itself, but not to the fruits." Do the best job you can without expecting someone to tell you how wonderful you are.

What if someone were to ask me something like, "If you publish a book are you not entitled to the royalties?"? I would answer with something like this. Yes, you betcha I am entitled to royalties. I hope some eventually arrive in the mail. But if that were my major motivation for writing the book, I would be missing most of the value from the project, which is inherent in the actions of completing the project in and of itself. The bigger value to me in a project like writing this book comes from the back and forth interactions with my editors, the thoughts I've had to work through and refine, and hopefully also to hear from some of my readers. The true value lies in the work itself, not in the rewards that may or may not follow.

You may find from time to time that your colleagues may want to interrupt you while you are trying to work. They may interrupt you with some question, clarification or request for opinion that will help them complete their work properly. When that happens, help out. You need to be a good team player. But when you're done, you need to return to what you were doing. I have a magical statement you can use at times like this. It is:

"I've got to get back to work."

You may also find from time to time that your colleagues may want to interrupt you while you are trying to work with a distraction that is not work-related, like talk of sports, kids, or office politics or gossip. In that sort of case, you have no obligation to accept the distraction. You may decide to allow a 1-2 minute interruption to be polite or minimize ruffled feelings. If a colleague wants to boast about how their smart kid just won

---

[188] Asteya is non-stealing. There are many subtle ways to appropriate what does not belong to us. If you convince yourself that someone else "has so much and won't miss this if I take it", you are giving yourself permission to steal. This behavior may help you feel better in the short run, but in the long run is still a violation of this Yama. See: http://yoga108.org/pages/show/98-asteya-non-stealing-one-of-the-ethical-precepts-of-yoga.

[189] The Bhagavad-Gita is an allegoric and sacred Hindu text.

a spelling bee, you perhaps want to show a polite but mild interest. But as before, you need to get back to work. I have a magical statement you can use at times like this too. It is:

"I've got to get back to work."

If the interrupter persists as though he is hard of hearing or has selective hearing, or maybe because he figures hearing his own voice is more important than you getting your work done, you might say something like:

"Fred, I've enjoyed this break, but I've got to get back to work."

Believe it or not, you actually can say that. It's honest and assertive. I know you can say that without adverse consequences, because I have said it many times in the workplace myself. Develop a reputation as a person who is dedicated to getting his work done, and has little interest in gossip or office politics.

Second, when you make getting your work done your top priority in the workplace, you make a reasonable work/life balance eminently possible. We all have seen people who come in a 7 AM, race around breathlessly all day with a 15 minute break to cram a sandwich down their throat, and then leave the office at 7 PM or later. Maybe these people have seen *"How to Succeed in Business without Really Trying"*, which lampooned superficial manipulative behaviour. A big difference exists between being busy and being effective. Those are two very different things. But more on that later.

I firmly believe that you don't need to put in breathless 12 hour workdays[190] to be effective and successful in the workplace. Once more, I know this to be true from personal experience. The keys are good time management and most importantly, focusing on getting your work done. I think if we followed one of those 12 hour workday people around and tracked what they actually did with their time, we might find that they devote much less than those 12 hours to doing their actual work.

I remember early in my work life learning a lesson from a colleague named Bill. Bill was a few years older than I, he'd been with the company longer, and he was a real achiever. Bill had just been promoted to a job with a lot of responsibility. Since we lived close to each other in the same

---

[190] I suspect people who behave this way at work do so to satisfy some offbeat or self-nullifying psychological need. You don't want to go down that road yourself.

suburb, sometimes we commuted to and from the job together. I worked in the Chem Lab, which was basically a 7:00-3:30 job, with the need to work later only arising very occasionally. But Bill's new job was as a line Divisional Supervisor in production, in charge of several departments, each managed by a foreman. Bill never seemed ruffled and he was always ready to leave for home at the same time as I. Once I asked him how he was able to manage his work that way. Bill's answer was something like, "Mike, I can get done in half a day what takes other people a full day and I can get done in 8 hours what takes other people 12. I don't need to work more than 8 hours a day."

Well that floored me. Bill's answer may sound a bit arrogant but it was true. And his statement has stuck with me for more than 30 years. Bill was a smart guy with good assertive communication skills. But I figured that I was also a smart guy with good assertive communication skills. Bill was a few years older and more experienced but I figured if Bill could do it, so could I. When I was in my most responsible position, when I led a R&D business unit, I made it a habit to work diligently[191] for 8 hours a day, then say good night. I reckoned that I could get done in 8 hours what took other people 12. And I also understood that most activities that kept other people busy banging around for 12 hours a day had little or no impact on results. Those activities were nothing but a waste of time and effort so I made it a practice to avoid them.

Keeping my workday to 8 hours allowed me to have other interests outside work, like my family, yoga, music, and many other things. And I did that while meeting my performance objectives. Good old Bill.

One caveat here: If you happen to be in management like I was, your work includes being available to your staff. If you're responsible for the work and results of other employees and they request your time and attention to help them technically, to help them clarify a priority, or for whatever reason, that's legitimate. To be a good leader you must help them when they need it. You may have your own projects to work on and when you're busy attending to them, you may sometimes find the needs of your staff to be a frustrating interruption. When you feel that way, discipline yourself. Remember that you need the contributions from your staff to be successful.

If you need to finish a task you might set up a time with your employee

---

[191] If I haven't made this point clear enough, I'm going to state it explicitly here – the key is to <u>work</u> for 8 hours a day, not just show up and blow away your time in activities that are not your work.

for later in the day. But don't be one of those managers who says he'll meet you for 15 minutes a week from next Tuesday. That's B.S. Make yourself available. In his Seven Habits book, Stephen Covey says you manage resources but you lead people. Your leadership relationship with your staff is a sacred one, so hold up your end. If your people need your time, give them your time.

When these circumstances arise, sometimes you won't be able to keep to your 8 hour workday. When that happens, go with it and don't resist. Also, the nature of some jobs demands the occasional 12 hour workday. For example, if you're working as a scientist or technologist working in the biological or agricultural sciences, sometimes you'll need to monitor or sample a biological process which doesn't necessarily follow an 8 hour day. In a job like that, 12 hour workdays may be relatively commonplace. In cases like that, I recommend you take compensating time off to maintain your work-life balance.

Either way, the point remains. If you concentrate on getting your work done, you make a work-life balance possible.

Third, when you make getting your work done your top priority in the workplace, you will experience much less stress from your work and all its responsibilities. If you have a big workload you may feel some anxiety about the sheer volume of it. And your workload may include some tasks that either you don't enjoy doing very much or you're not so sure that you even have the chops to complete the task successfully. Let's look at those three situations separately.

If it's a huge amount of work that's causing you to feel stressed, what do you think might be the best way to apply yourself to that situation? By complaining to your colleagues about your workload, perhaps interrupting them from their work when you do that? By checking Facebook or rattling off some personal e-mail correspondence to clear your mind for work? I think you know the answer. The answer is to get to work on your work. If it's a huge task facing you[192], try breaking down the whole job into manageable sized components that you can handle in a day's work. And remember, you can accomplish in 8 hours what would take most people 12 hours. But if you fritter away valuable work time by doing non-productive things, you will feel more stress not less.

If you're feeling some stress because your workload includes some tasks that you don't enjoy, what do you think might be the best way to apply

---

[192] Like writing this book is for me. What - you think this is easy? I've never written a book before and I've been at this for more than a year now. Sheesh.

yourself to that situation? By delaying those tasks until you feel more like doing them? Maybe by avoiding them altogether and hoping someone else might do them or that they'll be fine going undone? I think you know the answer. The answer is schedule those tasks into your workday for the time that's best suited to your bio-rhythm and get them done. Every job includes some tasks that the job-holder doesn't enjoy doing. When I ran into this situation in the workplace with a subordinate or colleague who was whining about having to complete a task he didn't enjoy, I would quote Mark Twain. This is a great quote which is public domain now, so you can use it as you like. I prefer to credit Mark Twain for this one, but that's up to you. The quote is:

"When you have to swallow a frog, don't look at it too long."

Perhaps you're feeling some stress because your workload includes some tasks for which you're not sure of your competence to complete it to an acceptable level. If you're feeling a little stressed because of this situation, please feel comforted in the fact that you have a good reason for feeling that way. So what do you think might be the best way to apply yourself to that situation? Once more, by putting it off or avoiding it? If you do either of those, the situation will only get worse, you'll feel more stressed not less, and you'll have good reason for it. The answer is to increase your competence.

Competence is the meeting of skill and confidence. Competence is task specific. No person is either fully competent or fully incompetent. I consider myself to be a competent guitar tech. I have trained for it and received two certificates which testify to my having learned the skills one would expect from a guitar tech. And my clients are happy with the work I do for them. Sometimes they even give me tips when paying their invoices. I have developed skills and as I have applied them over a period of time I have become confident that I can solve guitar tech problems.

I've been going to the same dentist, Andy, for about 30 years. I've already retired from professional work and Andy has been winding down his practice for the last few years. He's due to retire fully next summer. Andy is eminently skilled as a dental surgeon. And since he's practiced for well over 30 years, he's also confident in his skills. Andy is competent as a dental surgeon. But do you think I would trust Andy to work on one of my guitars? No way. He's not competent as a guitar tech. And if Andy has the flu, do you think he would call me up to perform a root canal on one of his patients? Nope. I'm not competent as a dental surgeon.

The guitar tech/dentist story illustrates the task-specific nature of competence. I want you to understand that if you are not competent to do a good job on a task in the workplace, you don't need to beat yourself up over it, or lose your overall self confidence. When it comes to this issue of task specific competence in the workplace, I have worked with two categories of people. One category is the generally confident, assertive type who appreciates that no one expects them to be good at everything. These folks ask for help when they need it. They are clear on what they're good at and what they aren't, and they recognize that others in the workplace possess skills that complement theirs. The other category is the sort that can't bear to ask anyone for help. I would hazard a guess that these guys and gals haven't done their work to control their egos. These guys do the best they can to hide their task-specific shortcomings. The reality is that they might as well walk around with a big scarlet letter on their foreheads because everyone in the workplace can recognize what they're trying to conceal. This situation is especially damaging to the organization if the person happens to be senior in responsibility. Unfortunately, most organizations are imperfect enough to have people in positions of high responsibility that are in this second category. They try to conceal their task specific incompetencies with smoke, mirrors, and slight of hand.

When I was coming up, I had the good fortune of working several years with a senior executive who was from the first category. Our skills complemented each other and he wasn't the least shy about acknowledging when he needed to defer to me on some tasks. And I never forgot that he was the boss and recognized his authority to make decisions within his responsibility area. When he delegated to me I was happy to do a good job on a task to which both of us knew that my skills were better suited than his. Our division performed better than some of others because of this smart allocation of resources.

But what does this have to do with your stress over having tasks in your workload for which you don't feel competent? The answer lies in recognizing when the situation arises and telling yourself the truth about it. If you don't feel competent, you have the responsibility to speak up to your boss about it. Maybe you lack some technical skills. Maybe you just lack confidence because your technical skills are newly acquired and haven't yet been seasoned with enough experience. Either way, you have nothing to be ashamed of. If you're a competent guitar tech, you probably aren't competent at root canals. And I wouldn't trust my dentist to do a fret job. The point is, you can't be good at everything, and no one realistically expects you to be good at everything. Remind your ego of that. Ask for help or training when you need it. You'll experience less stress and you'll be a better employee at the same time.

Fourth, when you make getting your work done your top priority in the workplace, the workplace will be a much more pleasant place for you and the people around you. All your interpersonal relationships in the workplace will flow more smoothly. You will build for yourself a solid reputation. Your boss, your colleagues, and your subordinates will find you easy to like and pleasant to work with. While no one person can define the culture of the workplace, you can make a solid and positive contribution. I believe that the most pleasant and satisfaction producing workplaces are the ones that include mutual respect, teamwork, and a good work ethic that concentrates on results. I was always amazed at the teamwork on the TV show CSI New York. Those people work long hours under high pressure. But they all pitch in and do their parts. The members of that team demonstrate the values of mutual respect and good work ethic to which I refer. Ever see Danny Messer slacking off or complaining about Mac Taylor? I don't think so. Danny's too busy doing his work. When they're working a case, the members of the team are all too bust doing their work to get involved in interpersonal issues or office/lab politics.

Finally, when you make getting your work done well your top priority in the workplace, you will be much more likely to work your way into the best job for you in that organization, by promotion or otherwise. You will be in the flow. The previous point and this last one are a little more subtle than the earlier ones. The only way you'll be in the flow in the workplace is when you are immersed in your work and you are making your honest best effort. And when you're in the flow, almost by definition things fall into place for you. I'm not trying to say that if you work hard, you'll become the CEO. But if you stay with the same organization for a while, the tasks for which you are best suited will tend more to come your way than the tasks for which you are less suited. Your position in the organization will evolve organically like a well fitting pair of jeans. You will end up in the place that's best for the organization and also is the best fit for you. But I must stress that for this to happen, you need to be in the flow. And for you to be in the flow at the workplace, you need to make getting your work done your top priority.

Stay fit – do your own heavy lifting

This recommendation is similar to the one above about concentrating on your work. But it's different too. I refer here more to the quality or flavour of your work than the quantity. In the next section of this chapter when I examine time management and the notion of using your time effectively, we'll introduce the idea of "high-leverage" tasks. These are the tasks that require your special expertise and the ones that you plan your day around so you can complete them successfully when you're at your best.

This is especially important for those of you who rise to positions of responsibility and influence in their workplaces. I have noticed a disappointing tendency among some senior staff to stop doing the hard brain-work that is actually at the heart of their responsibility area. I believe this tendency is more common in the public sector than it is in the private sector. In the private sector, executives have a direct financial stake in the outcome and are naturally incented to create positive results. In the public sector, the culture and definitions of success are different than in the private sector. Senior public sector staff are more likely to keep their heads down and avoid difficult decisions and controversy.

I can best illustrate what I'm getting at with an example from the research sector. Imagine two vice-presidents, Larry and Fred[193], each in charge of his own division, consisting of several research business units. Fred is one of these guys to which I refer. Once he got into the role of VP, he pretty much gave up on doing his own hard thinking and planning. He preferred to coordinate the work of others. When the CEO asked for strategic plans, Fred really had no vision of his own for the division and hence no idea how to proceed with a strategic plan. So he delegated this key project to one of his captains. As you might expect, the resulting product was mediocre; it lacked vision and purpose. The CEO was unimpressed.

Larry on the other hand was a young VP with drive, vision, enthusiasm, and a good work ethic. He understood the importance of taking responsibility for the strategic direction of his division. Larry didn't mind the heavy lifting of thinking hard and long about the best and creative resolution to strategic issues. Larry was out front. He worked on tasks that were future oriented rather than having tasks pile up on him. When the call came for a strategic plan, Larry charted the vision and direction of his new division then requested input from his captains that

---

[193] I could have chosen a female name here for gender neutrality – but this example is based on a real life experience and in this case both Larry and Fred were men.

was consistent with their own responsibility levels and content expertise. Larry's plan was bold, clear and concise. His division went on to become successful. Fred's did not. Within a couple of years, Larry's division grew to include Fred's.

Fred and Larry both left the company but in different ways. Fred was pushed out when his division was folded into Larry's. Larry left to take on an entrepreneurial role outside the company because the company moved too slowly for his taste.

For a few years, I had the pleasure of working as a direct report of a senior executive with qualities like Larry's. He never developed the laziness to slough off the heavy lifting. He always did his own brain work. He planned for the future and worked through senior strategic issues before passing on work packages to us, his captains. It was an exciting time and I think we did some good work.

This principle is not restricted only to senior executives. I have some friends that work in the public and non-profit sectors. From my perspective of looking in from the outside, and from what they tell me, it seems to me as though many people in those sectors seem to prefer to review and coordinate the work of others over doing the actual heavy lifting themselves. People who actually prefer to put themselves out there and do the hard-thinking work are in the minority.

But I recommend that if you want your work to be fulfilling, be in that minority. Any chance you get to contribute to the actual creative process, grab it. Whatever level you are in your workplace, don't be afraid of using your noodle. If you have a thinking job, do some thinking, even if it's hard work. That's why you get the big bucks.

Manage your Time Effectively

Have you ever noticed how some people in the workplace always seem calm while others often seem frantic? Have you ever noticed how some colleagues always turn in their in their monthly reports and program plan drafts on time while others are chronically late? Those chronically late colleagues are the same ones that put in the breathless 12-hour days that I mentioned earlier. Do statements like this have a familiar ring to you?

> *"Oh! There just aren't enough hours in the day…"*
>
> *"I'll get to it as soon as I find the time…"*
>
> *"I'm just so overloaded…I can't make that deadline…"*

"I've always got some much to do. I can't even make progress on my own projects..."

"I'm always putting out fires! I just can't seem to catch up and get on top of it all. It's just the nature of my job..."

We all know that we live a world that's much faster-paced than it used to be. We all know that we're bombarded with more information than we need and demands from every direction that exceed our abilities to meet. As Brad Paisley would say, "Welcome to the future[194]". How do we cope with all that in today's workplace? The answer is the same as it was 35 years ago[195], only now the answer has become even more important than it used to be. The answer lies in learning how to manage your time effectively. In this section, we'll examine that set of skills.

The reality is that everyone has exactly 24 hours in a day. The folks who always get their work done on time and leave for home and family after an 8-hour workday have the same 24 hours as the folks who frantically bounce from crisis to crisis and put in a 12-hour workday without accomplishing much. So what's the difference, you ask. Entire books have been dedicated to time management. Sections in famous self-help books cover the issue in deep detail[196]. But in this little book we don't go into anything in deep detail[197]. I figure my readers don't need or want that.

I first learned about time management in a one-day seminar. That was about 25 years ago so the content is public domain. Once you "get it" it actually seems fairly simple. The more difficult part is putting the principles into your daily practice. If you're one of those people who runs around stamping out fires for 12 hours every day, your colleagues will expect you to continue in that role. Everyone else benefits from your fire-fighting efforts. Once you start behaving differently, other people may need to adjust their expectations. But stick with it.

I believe I can boil down the complex issue of effective time management

---

[194] "Welcome to the Future" (DuBois and Paisley) form the album "American Saturday Night" 2009.
[195] Take a look at "WKRP in Cincinnati", one of my favorite shows from around the time I started working full-time. The characters didn't even have computers on their desks. In those days we communicated face to face, by telephone, and written correspondence with ink on paper.
[196] Stephen Covey, Brian Tracy, and many others have written on this subject. Dr. Covey's "7 Habits..." has a good section on time management.
[197] Of course that doesn't mean we're superficial – just economical with language, right?

into an essence of four principles. If you comprehend the principles and apply them, you will be successful at managing your time. Imagine the issue of time management as a big three dimensional edifice, like an obelisk with four faces. Each time management principle is like a face on that object. It is one whole, but it has four faces. The four principles regard the object from a different perspective, and cover the 360 degrees it takes to regard the object from all perspectives.

The Time Management Obelisk

<u>Organize around your priorities</u>. The first principle of effective time management is to organize around your priorities. As I said in an earlier chapter, when I walked into that time management seminar many years ago, I expected to learn some behavioural based techniques for how to be more efficient with time, i.e. how to get more output from a given length of time. Instead, the seminar leader asked each of us to write down privately what were the five most important things to us. As I said in the earlier chapter, he was asking us to examine our values. Hopefully our priorities will be in harmony with our values.

So, when you're organizing your work and how you will allocate your precious time, I encourage you to allocate time to the tasks that hold the highest priorities for you. This principle can apply to how you organize your life in the broadest sense. Hopefully you devote your precious time to your highest priorities. But we're examining your work life here, so let's restrict the discussion hereafter to effective time management in the workplace.

In almost every workplace these days, employees have goals and objectives. You set your performance objectives at the beginning of the fiscal year, review progress periodically during the year, and measure performance as results obtained against the objectives at the end of the fiscal year. If reasonable common sense is present in the workplace, an individual's performance objectives will be consistent with the objectives of his work unit, his supervisor, and the strategic priorities of the organization[198].

Therefore when I say organize around your priorities, in general I mean devote your time and attention to meeting your objectives. If you're planning for the month ahead, set priorities based on what you plan to achieve that month and allocate time resources accordingly. Seem obvious? Yes absolutely! Do people actually do that? Nope…not all the time or consciously anyway. I used to have a 3 by 5 card ahead of me hanging from my bookshelf just above my computer terminal. It said something like,

> *"Is what I am doing, or what I plan to do, really leading me closer to my objectives?"*

I got that phrase from the time management section of the 7 Habits learning tapes I listened to when commuting. The point is that as long as your objectives are in harmony with the organization's larger-scope objectives, then pursuing the realization of your objectives is doing your job. The corollary is also true, if you devote your time to activities that do not take you along the path to meeting your objectives, you're not doing your job; you're jacking around. I hung that little card where I could see it as reminder not to lose sight of the importance of organizing around my priorities.

We've been talking about fairly big-picture planning and time resource allocation here, and I stand by everything I have said. But some reasonable exceptions exist at the smaller scale also. Sometimes an individual's personal priorities my not align perfectly with organizational objectives. Let's say you've just returned from an international business trip where you've run up over $3,000 in expenses, including air fares, ground transportation, lodging, meals and so forth. You will have a personal priority of filing your expense claim so that you can get reimbursed more quickly than if you delay. It's going to take you 30 minutes to complete that expense claim whether you do it now or wait until later to do it. Your spending 30 minutes completing an expense claim is not consistent with meeting company objectives. Horsefeathers! While your timely reimbursement is not necessarily a top priority of your employer, it is a reasonable and legitimate priority of yours. Get that expense claim into the system then get on with your work. You don't need to wait until the end of the workday

---

[198] If an individual's performance objectives are not in harmony with the larger objectives of the organization, chances are that person is in store for an unhappy work experience.

and then do it on your own time. Your being away on the business trip was a legitimate use of company time. So is completing your expense claim for timely reimbursement.

But the basic first principle applies. If you want to manage your time effectively, organize around your priorities.

Urgency and importance. The second principle of effective time management is to understand and apply the differences between urgency and importance. Urgency and importance are not the same thing. If you want to achieve and meet your objectives in the workplace you need to spend your time on things that are important and not just urgent. Important activities have an outcome that leads to the achievement of your goals. Urgent activities demand immediate attention, have immediate consequence, and are often associated with the achievement of someone else's goals. If you manage your time effectively, your own important items will not become urgent. More on that to follow.

Former US President Eisenhower said, "What is important is seldom urgent and what is urgent is seldom important." In the workplace we often concentrate on urgent activities because they are the "squeaky wheels that get the grease." They demand immediate attention because the consequences of not dealing with them are also immediate[199].

Both Eisenhower and Covey have illustrated the distinction between urgency and importance with a four quadrant matrix:

---

[199] See: http://www.mindtools.com/pages/article/newHTE_91.htm

Figure 1: Urgent/Important Matrix

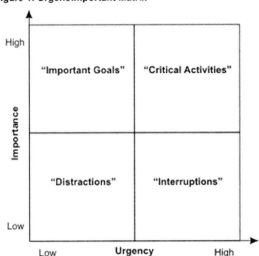

You can categorize any task or activity that comes your way as either high or low urgency and high or low importance. If you want to meet your objectives, you need to devote your time and attention to the important tasks. And work on important items before they become urgent. If you plan and allocate your time well, you can do that. If you have this flexibility, you need to set aside some time each day, preferably at the time of day when you are at your best[200], to devote to the high-priority tasks in your important/ not urgent category before they become urgent. The point is that if you are always responding to urgencies, you won't have time to work on the impactful tasks that are most important to your meeting your objectives. That's a situation you don't want for your workplace.

You will remember the illustration of that fire-stomper person who buzzes around like a horsefly in a jam jar putting in a 12 hour day and complaining that he never has enough time. Now you can recognize this person as someone who always responds to the urgent and ignores his own important tasks until they become urgent too. It's relatively easy to respond to the urgent, especially if you enjoy the adrenaline rush of moving from one pressing task to the next. But it's a trap you don't want to fall into. Once you get used to responding to the urgent, everyone else will get used

---

[200] Everyone has a bio-rhythm. My best time of day was 10 AM – noon. That was the slot I allocated to my big important tasks so I would stay on top of them before they became urgent.

to it too and they will expect it from you. That makes it difficult to change once you have developed this habit.

Learn to distinguish between the urgent and the important. A phone ringing is urgent. It may or may not be important. The ding on your computer that indicates that an e-mail has just come in is similar. When you hear that ding, it's tempting to see who has what to say. But chances are, unless you are waiting for an important contribution from a colleague on a mutually important team-task, the e-mail is nothing more than a distraction: not urgent and not important. When you are working on an important task, ignore distractions[201]. If you work in an environment that includes teamwork, sometimes to be a good team player you may want to bend this rule and respond to a colleague's urgent request for help. But make that the exception not the rule. Of course when your boss tell you to drop what you're doing and switch to something else, that's different. In that case, you'd be well advised to do as he says. One of the prerogatives of management is to set priorities and allocate resources.

Defending your distinction between what's urgent and important to you in your workplace is your personal responsibility. Don't expect anyone else to do this for you or even necessarily respect your distinction. Your distinction may not be to their advantage. After all, if you respond to an urgent request from a colleague to have you do some of his work for him because his project is due tomorrow, and that's the case because of his own poor time management, your response may be more in his interest than yours. If you decide to help out in a situation like that, do it consciously and for the right reasons. For the most part, you're on your own in making the distinction between urgent and important. But doing so is an important discipline. And remember the old Dilbertesque[202] expression,

> *"Your lack of planning does not create an urgency for me."*

Making the distinction between urgency and importance helps you to meet your objectives. And if your objectives are aligned with those of the organization, then doing so is in your interest and also in the interest of the organization. Anyone competent in managing time will recognize the difference between urgency and importance. And he will devote his

---

[201] I like e-mails as much as the next guy. But right now when I'm working on this book, I have my e-mail account turned off. I don't want the distraction. When I take a break from writing, I check my e-mails.

[202] I don't know for sure if this quote actually came from Dilbert, but it's the kind of thing he would say.

time and effort to the important tasks before they become urgent. Watch a senior executive for a day and see how much urgency they respond to – not much.

So don't fall into the urgency trap. Once you do, it's a hard climb back out.

Efficiency and effectiveness. The third principle of effective time management is to understand and apply the differences between efficiency and effectiveness. As Stephen Covey succinctly put it, efficiency is doing things right while effectiveness is doing the right things. The workplace demands performance in both efficiency and effectiveness. 100 years ago when we had a production based economy, factory owners would engage so-called "efficiency experts" to squeeze the last bit of efficiency out of a factory production process with their stop-watches and clipboards. In present day, with energy costs and environmental concerns being as important as they are, process engineers work to achieve every energy and by-product efficiency possible.

Once you know that a task needs to be done by all means look for the best way to do it. By the "best way", that might mean the fastest or cheapest, with the least use of resources, minimum waste, and conforming to quality standards. That's efficiency. But what if the job doesn't need to be done at all? What if doing it has no impact on the overall result we're trying to achieve? That's a question of effectiveness. As I stated in the beginning of this chapter, I started my professional working life with Canada Packers. I worked in Quality Assurance. We performed chemical, microbiological, and physical analyses to monitor production processes. But the central business of the company was a packing house. Ours was an old fashioned fully integrated plant, with several storeys, where cattle and hogs went in the top and prime cuts and processed products like wieners and bacon came out the bottom. Every production department was measured against a battery of production efficiency measures weekly. The foremen were responsible for maintaining and improving efficiency standards.

Although all the production departments did their best to maximize efficiency, overall the plant was doomed to failure, which was more a question of effectiveness than efficiency. A multi-storey fully integrated plant was the way to go in the early part of the 20th century when energy and labour were cheap and the markets were local. But all those fully integrated plants have closed in favour of modern streamlined and specialized plants which are far more cost-effective. A 1950s-design fully integrated plant could not compete in prime cuts with a modern large scale boxed beef plant located strategically close to several cattle feedlots. Similarly, it couldn't compete with a specialized processed meat products plant either. Maximizing efficiency of the production departments had no effect on the ultimate outcome because the basic concept of the plant was outmoded and ineffective.

Stephen Covey provides a great illustration of efficiency and effectiveness in his 7 Habits book. In the story, a group of workers are clearing a jungle[203]. As they work at it, they become better and better and eventually quite efficient at it. They're making great progress, when one day the leader decides to make an effectiveness check by climbing up a tall ladder to check out the bigger picture. From his tall ladder he's above the green canopy and can see for miles in every direction. The people down on the ground can only see the jungle around them. The leader calls down from his ladder, "Wait! Stop! Wrong jungle!"

If your work group is clearing the wrong jungle, it doesn't matter how efficiently you're doing it.

This question of efficiency and effectiveness can be scaled down to your job in your workplace too. It's not just for huge projects and issues like production plant design and jungle clearing. Your job will include several tasks and efforts. Some of them will be impactful toward your meeting your big objectives and being successful. Some will not. You need to be able to distinguish between whether your best efforts are contributing to your effectiveness or your efficiency.

This may sound a lot like the distinction between urgency and importance. The difference may be subtle but it's not the same aspect of time management. With urgent and not important things, you likely want to be efficient because you want to get those items out of your way quickly. Or maybe you want to ignore them altogether because they aren't important. So let's say we're restricting this discussion to items that are important.

You can still make an effectiveness distinction between those important items because some of them will be more impactful, i.e. success on them will have a bigger impact on meeting your objectives than will the other important but less impactful tasks. Some time management authors call this sort of distinction the "high leverage" distinction.

---

[203] Ignore the environmental distaste of this story. It's just an illustration.

When you're planning your year, month, week, or day[204], you will be ignoring the unimportant tasks and concentrating only on the important ones – the ones that move you along the path toward the achievement of your objectives. But those important tasks will not all have the same impact. Select the most impactful, the highest leverage of the important tasks, and assign them the highest priority. Put your time and effort resources there. Assign lower priority to the tasks that have lower potential impact, in your judgement, on moving toward the realization of your objectives. Be discriminating in where you put your precious time and effort. Concentrate on the tasks that will make the most difference, i.e. provide the biggest return on your investment[205]. Ask yourself, what's the most important, most impactful thing I can do today? If you do that, you're being effective.

A closely related analogous distinction is the one between results and effort. A competent effective person will produce results. He knows how to select the high leverage important tasks and he has the technical competence to deliver on them. Results follow. A result is an outcome from an effort. In the workplace, we set objectives in the form of desired results. Let's say I set the objective of reducing my weight from 215 to 200 by June 30. I've set the objective in terms of a measurable result and I've put it on a timeline. I will choose some strategies and tactics to meet my objective, like swimming twice a week and cutting back on cheeseburgers and beer. June 30 comes, I weigh myself, and the scale says 205. Did I achieve my objective? The answer is partially but not completely. The result was 205 and the desired result I set in my objective was 200. What about effort? I swam for 30 minutes twice a week, cut cheeseburgers to zero and reduced beers from 15/week to 4/week.

Was I successful? That's a different question. In terms of effort, yes I was because I put in the effort that I had planned to make. But in terms of results, no I wasn't successful because the desired result was 200 and the obtained result was 205. If I were to analyse results against effort I'd conclude that the planned effort wasn't sufficient to obtain the desired result. Where's the time management principle you ask. I'm coming to that.

It's great to see an employee giving his or her best in the workplace, but the fact is that effort doesn't matter much if they aren't getting the

---

[204] Do this. Actually plan your year, month, week, and day. Don't just walk in and start working on the thing closest to your thumb.
[205] The biggest "bang for the buck" as it were, old chap.

right results. The notion of effort is confusing to many people — how can they be faulted if they didn't get the results that were expected of them when they put in a 100% effort? In the results oriented workplace, effort is all well and good, but what matters on your performance review is the results you obtained[206].

Where this boils down to a time management principle is that achieving results is all about effectiveness. I am sure that achieving results has much more to do with doing the right things than it does from doing things right. Let's say we have two employees, Fred and Alison. Fred has superior technical skills to Alison. Alison has superior savvy to Fred in recognizing which tasks are important and high leverage. Given a specific same task to perform, Fred will complete it faster and better than Alison. But in the hurly-burly real world of the modern workplace, where there's always more to do than there is time to do it, and no one has a full time overseer to assign repetitive specific tasks, Alison will produce superior results to Fred year after year. Alison understands effectiveness. She knows that to achieve results, she has to choose the high leverage tasks.

The corollary is the fire-stomper person who makes a big show of all the effort he's making, how busy he is all the time, how he never has any time and so forth. This is the guy who is ineffective. He knows all about effort but he doesn't know where to focus his efforts. If you're wondering whether it's possible for you to outperform this hard-working, well-meaning colleague by working smarter not harder, the answer is an unequivocal yes. I know this is true because I did it myself for years, putting in an effective 8 hours while others put in a partially ineffective 10 or 12 hours.

Put your effort where it matters and don't spend time on activities that don't matter.

<u>The Pareto Principle</u>. The final principle of effective time management is perfection and the Pareto Principle. I remember visiting a dentist's office years ago and being taken by a poster on the wall that said something like "Perfection is important in parachute manufacturing and dental surgery." The implication was that perfection isn't necessary in other pursuits. As it turns out, that is true and very important to understand when you're working toward managing your time effectively.

If you haven't heard of the Pareto Principle, buckle up. This could change the way you look at things. Here's the deal. The Pareto principle

---

[206] See http://www.wisebread.com/effort-vs-results-the-difference-between-trying-and-getting-it-done

(also known as the 80–20 rule) states that, for many events, roughly 80% of the effects come from 20% of the causes. An Italian economist Vilfredo Pareto observed in 1906 that 80% of the land in Italy was owned by 20% of the population. Then he developed the principle by observing that 20% of the pea pods in his garden contained 80% of the peas[207]. Business scholars began to see the broader applications of the Pareto principle. For example, if you're a salesperson, 80% of your sales revenue will come from 20% of your clients. Now that we know about efficiency and effectiveness, where do you figure successful people put their attention? On that 20% that produces 80% of the revenue of course.

In your work, if you have a complex and big task to complete, apply the Pareto principle. Imagine a theoretically perfectly completed task. You can get it 80% perfect in 20% of the time it would take you to make it perfect. If it's a task that would take a technically competent person 10 hours to complete to 100% perfection, you can do an 80% perfect job in two hours. How much of your time is that final 20% worth. That depends on how important it is for that task to be 100% perfect and it depends on how high up you are in the organization.

Let me share with you a radical opinion. In the workplace, unless you're into parachute manufacturing or dental surgery, most jobs don't need to be 100% perfect to be perfectly effective. If you're a lawyer preparing a legal brief, you may need to be letter perfect in word choice and grammar. But let's say you're preparing a briefing for your boss, e-mailing him about a situation or concern, or composing a memo with a new policy. That sort of correspondence flies around regularly these days. How perfect do they have to be? I would guess to be completely effective, those pieces would need to be 80%-90% perfect. But I know from experience that people spend an hour or more polishing a one-pager that they first-drafted in 20 minutes. Was that final 20% worth the extra 40-60 minutes? Likely not.

And if you happen to be fairly high up in the organization, here's something for you to think about. You're probably paid too much to do a perfect job on anything. At your pay rate, if you get 80% value from 20% of the time on any task, move on to another high leverage task that demands your expert contribution. If 100% perfection is required, you need to delegate that final 20% to someone else. That final 20% is too expensive to the organization if you do it. If you're in the final 10 years of your career, in a well paid senior position, all your time must be devoted to high leverage tasks.

---

[207] See: http://www.80-20presentationrule.com/whatisrule.html

I used to baffle my direct reports when I applied this principle in the workplace. But when I explained, they got it. And I encouraged them to do the same in their workgroups. That final 20% is not for you. For most jobs (other than parachute manufacturing or dental surgery) 80% or 90% perfect is perfectly good enough anyway. There's plenty to do. Move along. Go get 80% of the value from another high-leverage task.

Keep your effort within your circle of influence

I introduced the concept of Covey's circle of influence at the beginning of Part II, in the Master your Inner World chapter. The circle of influence is definitely an inner world discipline but it's an inner world discipline that has important application to your success in and enjoyment of the workplace. The workplace is a great place for you to keep your thoughts and energies focused within your circle of influence.

Is your boss a lightweight with no backbone? Is the CEO a narcissistic ego-driven freak with no feelings or regard for the people who actually do the work? Are those IT service guys slow to respond and not customer-focused? Maybe those things are true; maybe they aren't. But either way, your role in the workplace is not to improve the character of your boss, the human touch of the CEO, or the responsiveness of the IT service group. Your role is to do your work and just possibly, make your work an art-form. Never mind about the shortcomings of the nincompoops around you, or the stupid matrix organization where you have two bosses, or the senseless bureaucracy that slows decisions and progress to a grind.

Are you frustrated with the size of your circle of influence? Do you think you'll enlarge it by complaining about it as often as you can to anyone who will listen? If you read about circle of influence in the earlier chapter, you'll know that sort of behaviour has the opposite effect. Spending your time, thoughts, and energies outside your circle of influence will shrink it not enlarge it. The quality and quantity of your work will suffer, as will your reputation as a team player and your energetic attractiveness for the sort of influence you crave.

As you know from the beginning of Part II, the way to enlarge your circle of influence is to concentrate your thoughts, energies, efforts, and power within the circle. As a former CEO said, "Keep your ass up, your head down, and get your work done[208]." That quote may be a little crude,

[208] Dr. George Miller, Acting CEO, Alberta Research Council Inc., 1996.

and I don't care much for the "ass up" image, but I must find something worthwhile in that quote because I still remember it from when I heard it in 1996. I believe what George meant to emphasize was not the ass up part but the dedication to concentrating on what you can affect directly, which is working within your circle of influence. If you concentrate your energies within your circle of influence, you will be productive and you will develop a well-deserved reputation for being a no-nonsense, trustworthy, team-playing, go-to colleague. Keep your energies and efforts within your circle as a long-term discipline, and with that reputation people will start to come to you for advice and opinions on issues larger and outside your circle. When that starts to happen, just watch your circle grow in size. Formal increases in the size of your circle in the form of promotions will follow.

I know this approach is successful because it worked for me. I never asked for a promotion or "promoted" myself by skylarking around. In fact for me it was more the opposite. I remembered what George had said and kept to my work. Nonetheless, in each of the three jobs I held over 34 years, I was always promoted. I avoided evening schmoozing events and I didn't do breakfast meetings because I wanted a work-life balance and I didn't consider them to be priority high-leverage activities, at least for me. I worked hard for 8 hours then I went home to my family. The company never owned me. I exchanged a hard day's work for good pay. My relationships with my employer or clients were simple and clean.

The way to enlarge your circle is not to go politicking around, gossiping, power-exchanging, trying to select the best butts to kiss, pathetically making yourself as visible and promotable as possible. That's the small-minded, mean-spirited, ego-centric, manipulative, insincere, and all too common way to go about it. The problem with that sort of approach is that it drains your energies away from your actual work, interferes with the trust you're trying to build, and builds a large gap of incongruity between what you project and what you really are. We already know about the psychic cost of that sort of non-genuine shenanigans. That is not for you.

The genuine, value-driven, from the inside-out way to enlarge your circle of influence is to focus with discipline your thoughts, energies, time, and efforts within the circle. When you go home to your family at the end of the day, you can feel good about yourself. You won't need to release negative energy, which was pent up from maintaining your incongruity gap all day, by drinking a stiff one or lashing out unkindly at your loved ones.

That doesn't mean you don't care about the things that bug you. If you are actively engaged in the organization, of course you'll want to improve it. But work toward improving it the right way, which is from within your circle of influence.

Make your work and art form

I mentioned this phrase above but I thought it was worth a brief explanation here. We're nearing the end of this chapter on Working for a *Living*. Since you spend so much time and effort at it, why not make your work an art form? Stay within your circle of influence but don't be bounded by your position description and do much more than the minimum. Always be on the watch for small opportunities when you can make your work a form of personal expression. When you make your contributions in the workplace, find ways of making your work product show up as uniquely you...so your colleagues and customers will think to themselves, "That was Alison!"

Anyone who has watched 30 Rock knows Kenneth Parcell.[209] Kenneth is totally self-actualized as an NBC page. Kenneth makes his work an art form. There's simply no page like Kenneth.

I'm not suggesting in any way that you attempt to pattern yourself after Kenneth. If you've been reading this book, you'll know that I wouldn't want you to pattern yourself after anyone – only that you know yourself and be true to yourself. When I ask you to consider making your work an art form, remember, this is your life and you spend a lot of time in your workplace. Since it's your life, when you're there, be there, not somewhere else. Put your personal stamp on your work. Make it an art form with you as the artist.

Follow "The Consultant's Creed"

I'm going to close this chapter and Part II with some lighter material that I'm calling "The Consultant's Creed." I would footnote the source if I could recall it. It's from a publication I read back in the 90s when I was doing some consulting and teaching on the side. The creed consists of four rules that the author believed every consultant should follow if he wanted to

---

[209] See: http://www.youtube.com/watch?v=Uaiv0xzRLaY

satisfy and keep his clients. Like a lot of good stuff, once you apprehend it, it stays with you. I'm pulling this material from my memory[210]. I believe these rules are for anyone working for a living, whether you're a consultant, a contract professional like I was, or a salaried and pensioned employee. Here is The Consultant's Creed:

Show up on time. If your workplace or your job has a start time, show up on time every day. Being punctual is good manners. It demonstrates your organization, your maturity, and your dependability. This rule applies to more than showing up on time at the beginning of the work day. If you have a scheduled meeting, show up on time for that too. It's respectful to the chairperson. Some people are so habitually late for meetings that I used to wonder if they did it on purpose, as if to demonstrate how busy or important they were. Of course, that behaviour is not for you. If you're the one who has scheduled the meeting, start on time even if some participants aren't there. That's one of the lessons we learned in Dale Carnegie training. Starting on time is respectful to the people who made the effort to show up on time, and it demonstrates that you're serious about a scheduled start time. And when your stragglers show up 5 minutes late, don't stop the meeting to catch them up. That rewards their slack tardiness.

Say please and thank you. It's not difficult to maintain a standard of politeness in the workplace. When someone turns in their report, say thank you. If you have an assistant, and you ask them to do something for you, say please, even if that task is part of their normal duties. When you're speaking to a colleague to ask for an opinion or some assistance, say please. When they do what you have asked, say thank you. And by all means, when someone has done an especially good job on a task and that has helped you toward meeting your objectives, recognize that good effort with a sincere thank you.

Do what you say you're going to do. We've already covered this point when we examined being trustworthy, but it's worth mentioning here as well. In the workplace you need to build a reputation of being a straight-shooting responsible person who follows through and does what he said he was going to do. This rule applies to the not so pleasant consequences as much as it does to the more regular and pleasant routine of keeping your

---

[210] Like most of this book.

promises to colleagues about turning in a completed contribution on time and so forth.

Let's say you're a manager and you have an employee whose performance is good in every respect except for one: he doesn't turn in his reports on time. His lack of reliability in meeting deadlines limits your group and your personal performance. You need to address this situation and improve it. You tell this employee that his tardiness with reports is a performance issue and will come up at performance review time. When performance time comes around, you absolutely must raise this issue with the employee and be serious about applying whatever consequences you indicated would apply.

Whether its fun or not, you need to do what you say you're going to do. That way your colleagues, subordinates, and supervisors will take your word seriously. Make it happen.

<u>Finish what you start</u>. Karl Malone had a long and distinguished career as a power forward for the Utah Jazz of the NBA. He played 18 seasons and retired in 2003. During his playing days, Malone had the nick-name "The Mailman" because he delivered. Need a layup to win the game at the buzzer? It was John Stockton to The Mailman for the two points. Having a reputation as someone who delivers is a great reputation to have. In the workplace you need to deliver too. I've worked with lots of people who liked to start things but few people who had the character to see things through to the end. They'd say things like, "I'm more of starter than a finisher. I love new things but once it gets going, I get bored and prefer to move on to start something else." Sure - starting things is lots of fun. It's creative and enjoyable. Finishing things is lots of work.

We have a small Nazarene community church in our neighbourhood. It's on a well travelled thoroughfare. The Pastor is well known for posting interesting thoughts on his marquee sign for people to read and think about as they drive by the church. Last week his sign said "We get judged by what we finish not by what we start". As I drove by, I thought, "Wow! I need to put that in my book".

I've included that statement here because I agree with it. This is coming from someone who has started a lot of new initiatives. A couple of the positions I held were specifically to do that, i.e. to explore new businesses and new applications. When no template existed, people would look to me to come up with a way to get things started and reduce it to practice.

Once I became in charge of a large group of creative, intelligent, hardworking people, I came to realise that the workplace has lots of starters.

But if you want to be effective in the workplace and appreciated by your boss and colleagues, develop the discipline to see your projects through to completion. Of course this must be true for consultants because they can only invoice once they finish the report.

Be like Karl Malone, deliver.

Part III:
The Dessert Tray – A selection to please your palate

Part II was the meat of the book. Part II covered my opinions on the collection of important topics and principles that I believe might help any of us lead a happier and more fulfilled life. Part III is a short collection of miscellany that I want to include in the book that doesn't belong in either Part I or Part II. Part III also includes my methods for making bread and soup, which I also recommend for a happier and more fulfilling[211] life, and my closing comments. Here comes our server with the dessert cart. Loosen your belt, lean back, and read.

---

[211] And maybe a more rotund and bodacious life also.

Home Maintenance and Neighbourliness

Avoid noisy, polluting gas powered suburban guy-toys

Just because you live in the suburbs and all your neighbours have an F-150, a RAM 1500, or a Chevy Silverado, that doesn't mean you need to own a big truck too. And just because the guy across the street has a chain saw that doesn't mean you need one of those either. In our neighbourhood, almost any time from 10 AM to 10 PM, any day from spring to fall, you can always hear at least one motorized suburban guy toy. It will be droning, growling, sputtering, or screaming in the distance or right next door. If it has an electric motor or gasoline powered engine, guys will buy it. If it has a gas-powered engine, even better, because they're noisier than electric motors. We're not just talking lawnmowers here. We're talking chain saws, weed whackers, edgers, roto-tillers, hedge trimmers, leaf blowers, table saws, and snow blowers for the winter. If it has a motor, the guys will be off to Canadian Tire to buy one. And don't forget your gas-powered electric generators – gotta have one of them too. The noisier the machines are, the more thrilling the masculine charge they provide. Mmmmm…power!

You don't need a chain saw. Realistically, how often will a suburban homeowner need to fire up a chain saw to do a little trimming? Not more than once or twice every five years, you figure. Nope. Nothing like the destructive power of a chainsaw chugging and vibrating in your strong masculine arms. And isn't that screaming roaring engine noise exciting to the male psyche? Never mind that you could do the job silently with your strong masculine hands holding an old fashioned hand saw. Or maybe use an old fashioned pair of hedge clippers.

Whatever happened to the respect for peace and quiet? How about enjoying the quiet and gentle sounds of birds singing or leaves rustling in the trees? Instead of chirping birds or leaves rustling, we have a suburban male generated, gas-powered small engine cacophony. With all the power tools and motorcycles roaring around, the only quiet months around here are in the winter. And even in the winter, it seems like the guys can't wait to go out there and fire up their snow blowers. That snow's not going to get the best of you! Truth is, you probably don't need a snow blower either. I clear my snow with a shovel. It's quieter and doesn't pollute the air.

If it weren't so ridiculous, it would be funny. I shake my old grey head. Come on guys, could you please dial back the macho just a little? This year don't buy any more powered suburban guy toys. Canadian Tire is doing fine. Please think twice about what time of day it is before hauling out and starting up the equipment you already own. And while you're considering that, ask yourself whether you actually need to break the peace at all with that noisy polluting item of affluent affectation. Quiet is nice.

No gas powered lawn mowers before 11 AM

I use a push mower to cut my grass almost all the time. I'll use my power mower at the beginning of the season and sometimes during June when we need to cut the grass every five days or so. Occasionally I'll use the gas mower during if we've been away for a couple of weeks in the summer and the grass has grown up some. At times like that, collecting the clippings for the compost heap in the grass catcher behind the power mower is the way to go because the clippings are too long to leave on the lawn. Otherwise, I use my push mower. It's effective, nearly silent, and easy to push. I leave the clippings behind to decompose on my lawn, supplying nutrients, and helping to hold moisture. Mowing the lawn with my push mower is actually less effort than with my power mower and it's a lot more enjoyable too.

I understand it's not realistic to expect everyone to switch to non-powered push mowers just because I recommend it. It's just too much fun for the boys to crank up that loud and heavily polluting 6 hp Briggs &

Stratton. Brmmmmmm!! So let me suggest a reasonable guideline here. Let's keep those beautiful summer mornings and evenings peaceful. Don't use your power mower before 11 AM and make sure you're done by 8 PM. Now that I'm retired, I fully expect to hear at least one powered lawnmower and weed trimmer, maybe more, droning, moaning, and groaning away at any time during the day. But let's agree to keep the mornings and evenings quiet and peaceful.

No tree stumps on the front lawn

When a tree gets old, damaged in a storm, or simply too big, sometimes you have to have them cut down. Whether you hire an arborist[212] or do it yourself, don't leave behind a tree stump. That's tacky and trashy. An arborist will grind the stump down below the surface for you. Yes, yes, we all know that they charge extra for that service. The other side of the story is that when you leave an ugly tree stump in your front yard, everyone who walks or drives by your home knows that you were too cheap to pay that extra fee.

And please believe me; you're not fooling anyone if you try to make some sort of whimsical yard decoration out of your stump. Turning it into a planter or flower pot support doesn't cut it. It just looks sad. You may as well leave a rusting old pickup truck or a pile of rotting lumber in your yard. You may as well hang a hand-painted sign on your stump that says,

> *"A redneck lives here. I'm too lazy or too cheap to have this stump removed."*

If you must remove a tree, do it properly and do it completely. Remove the stump too.

No need to shovel snow after the first day of spring

We can get snow for 6 of the 12 months in a year. By the time spring rolls around most of us are ready for it. And the novelty and romance of shovelling snow has pretty much worn thin by then too. So why not let yourself off the hook and say no more snow shovelling after the first day of spring. If you really want to be nice and neighbourly to your newspaper delivery person and letter carrier go ahead and shovel your walk to the

---

[212] An arborist or arboriculturist is a professional in the practice of arboriculture, which is the cultivation, management, and study of individual trees.

front door. But when we get snow in April or May, honestly, you don't need to shovel your driveway. It's not that unusual for us to get a big snowfall in May, when the days have been longer than nights for 6 weeks and temperatures can reach 20 degrees. Yet I see my neighbours out there with their shovels and snow blowers under the warm sun clearing snow from their driveways. Wouldn't want the car tires to rest on snow right? Come on man, that snow will be gone by tomorrow or the day after.

Even when a cold-snap follows the spring snowfall, I say leave the snow where it lays. It will soon be gone if you just leave it alone. The good Lord giveth and the good Lord taketh away. That applies to snow too. Please – let me take you off the hook – let me lift you from that meaningless hamster wheel you're on. Park your snow blower and hang up your snow shovel March 21. Have some dignity for goodness sake.

Say hello to your neighbours and help them out when you can.

When new neighbours move in next door, I like to treat that event the old fashioned way. I knock on the door, introduce myself, and say welcome to the neighbourhood. I make a point of learning their names and calling them by name when I see them. I don't gossip over the fence with them or ask them any personal questions but when I see them I say hello and call them by name. My neighbour on one side has the same philosophy. He always smiles and greets me by name too. Sometimes we do little neighbourly favours for each other. I know his wife and kids by name and say hello to them too. They're a nice polite friendly family.

My neighbour on the other side is less friendly. I figure he forgot my name about 2 minutes after I introduced myself when he moved in. In ten years he's never called me by name. He doesn't smile and usually doesn't say hello. Maybe I'll get a curt nod if he can't avoid it. What, saying hello and smiling costs you $10 or what? Never mind. I can only control my part. I say hello to him and call him by name.

Pick up after your dog

This little responsibility should go without saying, so I'll be brief. If you have a dog, for goodness sake clean up after it. My dog eats a healthy diet rich in fibre. And she's a big dog, so she's a prodigious producer, if you get my drift. When I take her for a walk, she pretty much always rewards me with a nice fresh dump.

When we go out, I always have a plastic bag in my hip pocket. When she assumes "the position" I am ready to do my part. And I do, even if I have to walk through 20 yards of snow to get to the site. It's a public park. Kids play there. We all have a right to expect a park that's free of doggie doo-doo. Same goes for the back yard. Always pick up dog droppings before cutting your lawn. If you do it every day or two, even better.

Miscellaneous

Don't gamble

I'm going to suggest here that if you don't gamble, don't start. And if you do gamble, then stop. Nothing good can come from gambling. When you gamble nobody really wins. Let's say five guys sit down to play poker. Four of them lose $100 and one of them wins $400. How do you figure the guys that lost $100 feel about it? Was it good clean fun and good fellowship? I kind of doubt it. I expect they're going to feel kind of chapped about it. With that $100 he lost, one guy could have taken his family of four out for a nice lunch. A second guy could have a bought a bag of groceries. A third could have bought his wife a nice gift and so forth. Losing $100 in a poker game kind of bites and that's obvious.

But what about the big winner who now has $400 bulging in his jeans that he didn't have before? He must feel pretty good, right? Well I guess he might, depending on his level of consciousness. But if he contemplates what has just happened he's going to have some difficulties feeling good about it. What he's done is taken $100 from the pockets of each of the other guys and put it into his own pocket. What's to feel good about? He hasn't added any value. He hasn't created any net prosperity. In fact I would argue that the combined losses of the other players far outweigh the gain by the one winner. Each of those players has lost the opportunity to animate and do something good for his family or himself with that $100.

Its potential is simply gone to them. If you can accept that, then clearly the net outcome is negative.

Don't play poker with your pals. Don't play poker with strangers either. The winning and losing part of gambling serves to separate rather than connect us. As vibrating life forces our natural state is to be connected in vibration. Don't play Video Lottery Terminals (VLTs) or casinos either. Doing either of those is contrary to common sense. We all know that casinos and VLTs generate winnings for their owners. That's why they're there. A casino isn't there as a public service. It's there to capitalize on the gullibility, greed, weakness, and desperation of the people who go there and on net, lose money. Bar owners don't install VLTs to give their customers something harmless and fun to do. They install them because they make money for the house.

Let's introduce the concept of expected value, which is a fundamental for anyone working in probabilities and statistics. The American Heritage Dictionary defines expected value as the sum of all possible values for a random variable, each value multiplied by its probability of occurrence[213]. If you and I each put up ten dollars on the flip of a coin, that makes twenty dollars in the pot. I bet you I can throw heads. The odds of my throwing either heads or tails is 50%. If I throw heads I get $20 but if I throw tails I get $0. My expected value is ($20 X 0.5) + ($0 X 0.5) = $10. When the expected value is the same as what I bet, a probability expert would say by definition, it's a "fair game". If five guys sit down to play poker, and we assume they all have equal skill and that the cards fall randomly, then that's a fair game too. Of course to the extent that in reality skills are not the same and that cards my fall more favourably to one or more players and less favourably to the others, it becomes less of a fair game.

But that's definitely not the case with casinos and VLTs. We all know that the house wins. For that reason alone it's blatantly obvious that gambling at a VLT terminal or casino has an expected value ratio of less than one. When you do that, you are not playing in a fair game. Over time, you're going to lose and you can absolutely count on it. It's a mystery to me why anyone would gamble in a game when they know their expected value ratio is less than one. That's the case every time you lay down a bet at a casino or a VLT.

When I say it's a mystery to me, that's after asking people about it to try to understand why they do it. People love to go to Las Vegas and lose

---

[213] See: http://www.answers.com/topic/expected-value

money in the casinos. When I ask about it, they say something like, "*It's fun. It's exciting. I set aside how much I'm willing to lose each day. Once that money's gone, I stop playing for the day.*" Huh?!? I'm not kidding. People actually say things like that. It's fun for them to lose their money in casinos. Go figure.

One time years ago we were visiting the home town on a summer vacation. Steve was invited to go to the local casino. He was about 18 at the time. It won't be a big surprise that Steve knows how I feel about gambling. I was greatly relieved when he turned down the invitation. We got to talking about it and I wondered out loud about people's motivation for wanting to gamble in casinos, knowing full well that the odds are stacked against them. Steve speculated "Maybe they're just trying to win a life." Wow! Out of the mouths of young dudes.

Before we leave the topic of gambling, on which I am unashamedly judgemental, I have to say a couple of things about lotteries. When I said above don't play poker with friends or strangers, don't play VLTs or casinos, I now want to add, don't play lotteries either. Some people say playing lotteries isn't gambling. Well, lotteries are indeed gambling and your expected value when you buy a lottery ticket is much lower than it is playing VLT or casino. In fact that's the basis of a rather curious argument people sometimes make when they rationalize buying lottery tickets. Since they know their chances of winning are remote, and since they know that a good portion of lottery ticket revenue flows to government coffers, they say they're participating in a form of voluntary taxation. "*The money goes to a good cause…*". Really. I'm not kidding. That's what they say.

Let's put some numbers to this. In this case, I did a little on-line research. In a Canadian Lotto 6/49, to get all 6 numbers, your odds are one in 14 million. Let's say the jackpot for getting all 6 numbers is $10 million and a ticket costs $2. To put up $2 to win $10 million may seem like a good investment. And you can double your odds if you buy two tickets for $4. If your odds of winning are one in 14 million, then doubling your odds to two in 14 million is statistically insignificant. Yet that's what people do. When the jackpot is big they buy several tickets to increase their odds.

Theoretically, the lotto guys would have to sell 14 million tickets at $2 each to ensure statistically that somebody won. That would make their take $28 million and their payout $10 million. How does your investment look now? I guess if you're the one who gets the $10 million, it looks pretty good. But for the 13,999,999 who didn't, not so much.

It saddens me to see long queues of people waiting their turn to lay down their money on a 6/49 ticket when the pot gets big. First, the reason the pot gets big is that's it's so unlikely to hit. Second, the people in the queue look grim and down on their luck. They look to me like the folks least in a position to give their money away to the government and to the eventual winner. They dream that their problems would be over as soon as they win the lottery. As Steve said, perhaps they're trying to win a life.

And remember, when you think about how wonderful it would be to win the lottery, you're not catching money in your hat that floats down from the sky, made especially for you. Just like in the poker game, your winnings come from all the other people who have lost. In a poker game, it's a little more personal, when you can see the other's faces, feel their fear and smell their sweat. But when you win the lottery, you have taken money from that grim looking 65 year-old woman in the worn coat with the grey face and unhappy affect. She's the one you saw a few days ago, waiting 8th in line to buy her three 6/49 tickets. The government takes half or more of ticket sale proceeds, some administrative costs are deducted, and you get the rest. Just remember where your winnings come from. If that doesn't bother you, fine, fortunate for you. But as the Rabbi said, include me out.

I fully recognize that this anti-gambling opinion I have may be off-putting and unpopular with my readers. People just love to gamble. They love the thrill of laying it on the line. As our Grade 7 Phys-Ed teacher said, "Tough". This is a book about my opinions. You don't have to like my opinion on gambling and you don't have to agree with me[214]. But I'm not going to change my mind. Nothing good can come from gambling. But lots of misery, disappointment, broken families, and desperation can. Don't gamble. If you have the habit, kick it.

Walk your dog

Walk your dog every day, whether you feel like it or not. The exercise and fresh air are good for you as well as good for Fido. Your dog will enjoy the fresh air and exercise too. Equally important is how much your dog values the camaraderie of being out with you. It's absolutely the high point of your dog's day. They don't ask for much in return for what they give us. Give them this.

---

[214] Not to sound a little defensive or anything like that.

Imagine the thing you like to do most. Maybe it's going to a ball game on a beautiful summer afternoon or evening. Maybe it's sitting by the campfire with a loved one and a cold one in your hand as the sun goes down. Maybe it's perusing an art gallery, attending the ballet or the opera[215]. Well, your dog values that walk in the outdoors about that much.

If your circumstances allow, take your dog to a designated off-leash area, so he can really open up and get those large muscles moving. He/she will run around like crazy. Also, at an off-leash area, your dog will get to socialize with other dogs. That's important to them also. Don't be alarmed by the snarling, snapping, or growling sounds. Dogs need to establish dominance or submissiveness in their interpersonal relationships. Some people are like that too. Dogs just do it differently than we do. They won't hurt each other. Only an emotionally unstable dog will hurt another dog for sniffing its butt.

And one last reason for taking your dog for a walk whether you feel like it or not: doing so is good discipline for your ego. If that little voice inside starts whispering that you're too tired to walk the dog or it's too cold out, that's precisely the time to get the leash, the poop bag, a few milk bones for your pocket and head out with your best pal.

Make bread and soup

We have long dark winters here at latitude 53. I think making simple comfort foods like homemade soup and bread during the dark and cold months are nourishing for the spirit as well as the body. I recommend it.

I'm not going to offer recipes here. I don't cook from recipes anyway. If I did, I imagine it would stultify my creativity. I really like that tall long-haired chef Michael Smith[216] on the Food Channel. He cooks simple food on his show, with a lot of joy and enthusiasm. He never seems to measure anything. And everything comes out perfectly. If I were younger and wanted to be a chef, I'd want to be like Michael Smith. I wouldn't mind being 6 foot nine either. Although maybe I'd shave off the stubble.

My Bread Baking Method: I started making bread when our son Steve was a baby. Baby Steve liked to get up at 5:30 AM, seven days a week. I realized one day that if I were going to get up that early anyway, I may as well do something useful with those early morning hours. I used to take

[215] Ha ha – just kidding.
[216] See: http://www.foodnetwork.ca/ontv/hosts/Michael-Smith/host.html?hostid=23495

some pride in having my dough in for the first rise at 7:30 AM and being done by noon.

Once Steve, and later Robert too, got to be 2 or 3 years old, they'd work with me on baking bread Saturday mornings. Bev got them little rolling pins and aprons. I'd give them each a ball of dough to work with at the loaf forming stage. They'd roll out their dough and form it into a little ball. They would let it rise and bake it in a temperature tolerant tea cup. At the end of the process each of the boys would have his own bun. It was precious.

People used to encourage me to publish my bread-making method. I'm more or less doing that here.

1. <u>Make your dough and first rise</u>. This is the most complicated part, although it's not complicated if you take it one step at a time. First turn on your iPod.[217] If you want to be organized, gather your tools and ingredients. You'll need a big bowl in which to mix your dough and let it rise. I use a big stainless steel one. You'll need a smaller bowl to proof your yeast, a melting pan for your shortening, a wooden spoon to mix your dough, a plastic spatula/scraper, some measuring spoons and a measuring cup, and a big sharp knife to divide your risen dough. To form the loaves later you'll need a rolling pin. For ingredients you'll need some dried yeast, milk powder, shortening, salt, sugar and/or honey, white flour, whole wheat flour, and any fancy ingredients like wheat germ, cracked wheat, multi-grain, that sort of thing, and tap water.

    Start by proofing your yeast and melting your shortening. Put a cup of warm (body-temperature[218]) water into your small bowl. Stir in a teaspoon of sugar to dissolve. Then measure in your yeast, roughly about one teaspoon per loaf. My batch makes 5 loaves, so for me, I put in a couple of tablespoons (that's 2 envelopes) of yeast. Stir and set aside. Now measure your shortening, about ¼ cup, into a small melting pan and let it melt on low while you turn to starting your dough.

    Put 1 cup of warm water per loaf into your big bowl. For

---

[217] I suggest you have your iPod in a dock, playing through speakers, a few feet away from the action. You don't really want your earphone wires flopping around. And your hands are going to get covered with flour.
[218] Yeast likes to metabolize at 37 deg C just like us.

me that's 4 cups, since I have the yeast softening in 1 cup. Stir in 1 ½ cups milk powder. Then add your salt and sugar. I use about 1 teaspoon of salt per loaf. For sugar, I use about ¼ cup each of melted or liquid honey and brown sugar. If you think that might make your bread too sweet, you can cut back to ¼ or 1/3 cup total. Stir all your ingredients to dissolve. Now stir in 4 cups of white flour one cup at a time. Once you have a smooth batter, beat 100 times with your wooden spoon.

Now add your melted shortening, fancy ingredients like 7-grain, cracked wheat, maximum one cup, the softened yeast in its one cup of water, and 2 or 3 cups of whole wheat flour, one cup at a time. Your dough will start to come away from the sides of the bowl. Now add more white flour, a half cup or so at a time, until the dough ball is ready to turn out onto your counter. Put a layer of flour on your counter and turn your dough out onto it. Now scrape the dough that's stuck to the sides of the bowl with your spatula on top of your dough ball. Put your bowl into the sink and let it fill with warm water while you begin to knead your dough.

Knead your dough for 10 minutes, adding small amounts of flour when necessary so it doesn't stick to the counter or your hands. You'll know when the dough is ready because it will become elastic and not sticky. Cover your dough ball with a clean dish towel while you quickly clean out your bowl that you so wisely soaked while you were kneading. It will clean out easily. Dry it with another towel and rub some shortening to coat the inside surface of the bowl. The bowl should be comfortably warm from having soaked in the warm water.

Now drop your dough ball into the greased bowl, shake it around a little, then turn it over so the new upper surface has a thin film of shortening on it that it picked up from the bowl. That will stop it from drying out during rising. Cover the bowl with the slightly damp towel you used to dry it after you cleaned it. For rising your dough, you want your oven to be slightly warmer than room temperature. To achieve that, I turn the light on inside the oven and turn on the oven element for about 30 seconds. No more. With a satisfied smile on your face, slide the bowl into your oven to let your dough rise for 1 ½ hours.

Now clean up and come back in 1 ½ hours. A good baker cleans up as he goes.

2. <u>Punch down and second rise</u>. Here is the most fun part of the whole process. Your dough should be nicely risen now, starting to smell good, and about twice the size it was when you put it in to rise. Remove the towel and give it a good vertical punch. Take the dough out and form it into a nice ball again, return it to the bowl like you did before. Cover and put the bowl back into the oven. Turn the oven on for another 30 seconds if it has cooled off. Now let your dough rise a second time, 1 to 1 ½ hours.

3. <u>Form your loaves and third rise</u>. Remove the bowl and punch down again. With a big sharp knife, divide the dough and form separate balls, one for each loaf. In my case, that means five smaller balls of dough. Cover the dough balls with your tea towel while you lightly grease your loaf pans. Now comes the artistic part.

    Take one ball of dough onto the counter, leaving the others covered, and roll it out into a rectangle. The width of the rectangle should be roughly the length of your loaf pan. Now lift up the rectangle of dough and flip it over so the smooth side is down. Don't worry; it won't stick. Now roll the rectangle toward yourself, pushing the sides in with your palms as necessary. You'll have a cylinder shaped piece of dough. That will be your loaf. The smooth rolled side will be on the outside, making your loaf as pretty as pie.

    Carefully place the formed loaf into the pan, tucking the ends under as necessary. Complete the same process with each ball of dough and place your loaves, covered, into the oven to rise a third time. Give the oven another 30 second warming if required. Let the loaves rise for 1 – 1 ½ hours until they nicely rise out of the pan. Since you left the light on in the oven, you can check on the rising of your loaves without opening the oven and cooling it off.

Now clean up your big bowl and anything else that needs cleaning.

4. <u>Bake and cool</u>. When your loaves have risen, carefully remove them from the oven. Let them rest, covered, on the counter, while you heat the oven to 375F219. When the oven is hot, carefully but quickly slide the loaf pans into the oven. Bake for 30 minutes. While the loaves are baking, arrange your cooling racks on the counter and have your oven mitts ready for action. After the loaves are baked, with your oven mitts on, remove them and place them on the racks. Immediately remove the baked loaves from the pans by turning them over in one hand and catching the loaf top-down in the other. Now place the hot loaves, out of their pans, onto the racks to cool. Put aside the hot pans so they can cool too. Don't let the loaves cool in the pans.

Let the loaves cool for about 30 minutes before you sample them. Feign modesty when your loved ones rave about your bread.

<u>My Soup Making Method</u>. When I was a lad I used to watch my mother making soup with chicken and turkey carcasses and bones. Every time we had a chicken or turkey, a batch of soup followed. Her soup tasted much different than anything from Campbell or Lipton. It wasn't bright yellow in color and the flavour was real, rather than a mixture of salt and chemicals. My mom used her pressure cooker, which made stock much faster than possible with a regular open stock pot. But the batch size was limited by the size of the pressure cooker. It was just about the right size for the bones from one bird.

When I became a young man on my own, one cold winter night I decided I wanted to make soup too. My first few batches weren't spectacular but making soup isn't difficult and I soon got the hang of it. I started off using a pressure cooker but soon decided I wanted to switch to a larger batch, on the logic that making a larger batch is not much more work than

---

[219] If you want to be extra sophisticated, you can heat the oven to 400F, put the loaves in to bake and then immediately cut the heat to 375. That approach covers off the fact that the hot oven will lose some temperature when you open it up to put the loaves in.

making a smaller batch. So now I use my mom's old canning kettle for a stock pot. It's one of those big, blue enamel jobs. It probably holds 15 to 20 litres, which is a man-size batch. Now every time we have a chicken or a turkey, I collect the bones and put them in a freezer bag and toss them in the freezer for a time when I want to make soup. No fuss, no muss, and no pressure about making up your soup right after having eaten the bird. Save all the bones in that freezer bag, including the neck, wings, and so forth. I don't save the giblets[220] because I think they're borderline revolting. But if you want to save the giblets and include them in your stock, go for it.

When I make a batch of soup I take 3 or 4 frozen carcasses from the freezer and away we go. Since your batch size may be smaller than mine, I'm not going to supply a recipe here, with measured amounts of ingredients. I'll just explain how I do it and you can adapt the method and measures to your own batch size. The method has three stages. First you make stock, then you separate all the spent ingredients from the stock, then you cook with the final ingredients.

1. <u>Make stock</u>. This step is simple and fun. First, put on your apron and chef's hat. Turn on your iPod and put a kettle on water on to boil. Sharpen your knives. Now empty your frozen chicken or turkey bones into the stock pot. If they're coated with ice, you can rinse that off under the tap before you toss the bones into the stock pot. As soon as your kettle boils, pour the boiling water onto the bones and turn the element on under the stock pot. Fill the kettle again and put it back on to boil. You're going to add boiling to the stock pot water one kettle at a time until the stock pot is full.

   Now start cutting up your vegetables. You can add pretty much anything green to the stock pot, but only add fresh ingredients. Your stock is sacred – you don't add wilting brown vegetables that are past their time. Those go into your compost not your stock pot. For sure you're going to want an onion, a few carrots, a few stalks of celery, and a couple of cloves of garlic. You don't have to cut the vegetables attractively here. They're going to be separated out later when the stock is done.

---

[220] The giblets are those mysterious biological looking things that are in that little bag in the body cavity before you cook the bird. They are the heart, gizzard, and liver. Sometimes the neck is in that little bag too, if it isn't still attached to the bird.

So go ahead and hack them up boldly into fairly big pieces. For example, an onion (peel way the skin first) can be just cut into quarters or sixths and tossed in.

Toss in all your cut up vegetables and keep adding boiling water. Now you add salt. This is important. You add salt not just for flavour but also to increase the solubility of proteins from the bits of meat stuck to the bones. All you biochemists out there will recognize that I refer to the principle of "salting in[221]". I make a fairly big batch so I need a lot of salt. For me it's 1/3 – ½ cup. You might use less salt if your batch is smaller. Either way, don't be shy about adding salt. You need it to dissolve proteins. Along with the salt, I add a dozen or so peppercorns and a couple of bay leaves. Some people add herbs and spices to their stock pots. I don't. I add them at the final stage.

If you plan on including legumes in your finished product and you have them in dry form, this is the time to measure them into a bowl and rinse with cold water. Then drain and cover them with boiling water. You're going to soak them while your stock is cooking. Sometimes I add legumes and sometimes I don't. When I do, I'll measure out a cup or a half cup each of white navy beans, red kidney beans, pinto beans, soybeans, green or red lentils, yellow split peas, that sort of thing.

Now that you have all your ingredients in the stock pot and it's full and boiling, and you're soaking your legumes, turn the heat down under the stock pot to the point where it's simmering rather than boiling. Cover the stock pot and let it simmer for about four hours. During that time, check on it every now and then to make sure it's still simmering, giving it a good stir with your wooden spoon. And make sure your legumes are still covered with water. As they soak, they absorb a lot of water. You may have to add some.

---

[221] Proteins are big molecules, polymers of amino acids with complex structures caused by the nature and proximity of the amino acids to each other, the interactions among them, and the environment. Some amino acids are polar and some are non-polar/hydrophobic. By hydrophobic I don't mean they have rabies; I mean they are "water hating". Their nature is more oily than ionic. When the environment is more ionic – like it becomes when we add salt – the proteins become more soluble because their polar parts like the ionic environment.

2. <u>Separate stock from spent ingredients</u>. This step is much less fun but it's gotta be done. Put your apron back on. You need to get all those spent bones and veggies out of the stock. I arrange four big bowls and pour the stock through a coarse colander into the bowls. After each pass, I discard the spent ingredients into my compost container. When the stock pot is empty I wash the inside in the sink. Then I pour the stock from the bowls through a fine strainer back into the stock pot to catch any more disgusting solids. I wash out the inside of the bowls and repeat the process with the fine strainer, rinsing out the strainer after each pass. That way the stock goes once through the course colander once and three times through the fine strainer. After that, I'm left with a clean stock pot with nicely filtered stock and four bowls, a colander, and a strainer to wash. The stock pot won't be full anymore because of all the spent ingredients you've separated out. But that's fine. We're going to add our final ingredients at the next stage.

3. <u>Cook with final ingredients</u>. Now we enter the home stretch. Keep your apron on. Here you do need to make a nice job of cutting up your vegetables because this stage produces the finished product. I use about the same quantities of onion, carrot, and celery as for the first stage, only now I cut them up nicely and evenly into smaller pieces. Throw in another bay leaf or two if you're inclined. And add your soaked legumes. Add your secret herbs and spices now. I use parsley, sage, and oregano. Don't measure...that's not for you. Add what you think will be a tasteful amount. You don't need to add any salt because you used lots when you were making the stock. Bring your soup back to boil then cover and reduce temperature to simmer.

   If you have included legumes you need to cook for another four hours. We don't want undercooked legumes. If you haven't added legumes, cook for a minimum of another two hours. Either way, when you have about another hour's cooking time to go, add your pasta. You don't add your pasta at the beginning of the final stage because if you overcook your pasta it gets mushy. I use about 500 gm of fettuccini or linguini pasta, broken by hand into 1 – 2" lengths.

When your soup is done, you can enjoy a bowl with some of your delicious home-baked bread. I divide my finished soup into a number of Tupperware-type containers and let them cool overnight. Remember, we make soup in the cold months. Next morning, I put one container into the fridge and the others into the freezer.

This method was for chicken or turkey soup. You can use a similar approach to make beef barley soup with beef bones or to make French Canadian pea soup with a ham bone and split peas.

In Closing

Apply some basic yoga principles to your everyday life

I have referred a few times in this book to my yoga practice. Now that we're near the end, I'm going to leave you with some fairly bare outlines of a couple of the fundamental topics. I'm not qualified to write to any depth on this material so I'm keeping it brief. But my yoga practice is an important part of my life and like everything else, I have opinions on it. Since I think about this material every day, I wanted to include some mention of it here. These principles may seem like common sense to you. I hope that's the case. If you want to look into this material more deeply, I encourage you to do so. I'm going to introduce you to the Purusharthas, the Yamas and Niyamas.

The Purusharthas[222] are like four pillars holding up your life. If you want a meaningful fulfilled life, you need all four pillars. And you need to have some balance among the Purusharthas. Each is an aspect or facet of a human life. If you ignore any of them, you're going to have big difficulties. The four Purusharthas are:

1. Artha (prosperity) involves taking care of our basic physical needs. For most of us, this means having money to provide the essentials. Even the most spiritual among us need to fill their rice bowl. Monks must pay attention to Artha just like

---

[222] See: http://swamij.com/purusharthas.htm

    you and I do. We all need to attend to providing for ourselves and others.

2. <u>Kama</u> (pleasure) involves enjoying yourself, with some mindfulness and discipline. If you love ice cream, make sure your life includes some. But Kama includes mindfulness too, to guard against our falling into the ego trap of a continuous cycle of fulfilling and craving. Life is a miraculous gift. Enjoy!

3. <u>Dharma</u> (duty) is the inherent nature of things, the natural law. To live in dharma is to fulfill ourselves in the flow, in harmony with the universe. Dharma includes your humble response to your situation in life.

4. <u>Moksha</u> (freedom) is the direct experience of truth and reality. It is the liberation from false identities and conditioning, and apprehension of our true nature as consciousness.

Living the Purusharthas every day is not an easy discipline. Awareness of them as principles and fundamental guidelines however is possible for all of us.

<u>The Yamas and Niyamas</u>[223] are the first and second of the so-called eight limbs of yoga. The Yamas and Niyamas are restraints and observances, sort of "stay away from this" and "do this" guidelines for a happy and successful life. They make up the foundation of our practice. The Asanas, or the physical postures and exercises are another limb of yoga. Some people think of yoga practice as only the Asanas, and participate for the physical benefits of the Asanas. To benefit in a more holistic way from yoga practice includes grounding ourselves with a fundamental basis for ethical living. The Yamas and Niyamas provide that basis.

I will list the Yamas and Niyamas, and add a few words about what the restraints and observations mean to me.

The Yamas, or restraints, are as follows:

1. <u>Ahimsa</u>: non-harming, non-violence. This means not harming others, oneself, other sentient beings[224], the environment and so forth.

---

[223] See: http://www.bradpriddy.com/yoga/yamani.htm
[224] Some people base their commitment to vegetarianism on Ahimsa.

2. <u>Satya:</u> truthfulness. Not intending to deceive others with our words or actions, or even in our thoughts.
3. <u>Asteya:</u> non-stealing. Not taking something that doesn't belong to you. Making business transactions that are fair to both sides. Paying your taxes.
4. <u>Brachmacharya:</u> The conservation of energy for spiritual practice. Sexual maturity in the sense of regarding others as human rather than as sexual objects. Moderation and non-excess in general.
5. <u>Aparigraha:</u> non-grasping, non-possessiveness. Avoidance of greed and the acquisition and hoarding of objects.

The Niyamas, or observances, are as follows:

1. <u>Saucha:</u> purity and cleanliness inside and out. Treating the body as a temple. Keep yourself clean on the outside and uncorrupted on the inside.
2. <u>Santosha:</u> contentment. Acceptance of our life situations. Think of the Christian convert St. Paul who found contentment in all circumstances, including physical ailments and unjust imprisonment.
3. <u>Tapas:</u> right effort, self-discipline. Doing the right thing whether it's expedient or not. Maintaining our commitment to simplicity and our spiritual practice.
4. <u>Svadhyaya:</u> Study, contemplation, and application of sacred texts and spiritual writings of the learned and gifted.
5. <u>Ishvara pranidhana:</u> Dedication to the highest. Surrender to the truth of higher power and order in the Universe beyond the small self. Humility in the face of the vastness.

One Final Word

Looking back, writing this book really hasn't been too difficult. It's mainly a collection of my opinions on things. Since it's merely my opinions, I haven't had to undertake extensive research to build a case or prove my points. Either you agree with my opinions or you don't. But I hope you have found them interesting. From my own perspective, putting down these thoughts has been a fascinating experience. I've had to think a few things through and check my own views for clarity and consistency. Mostly, the process of writing this book has reminded me if what I believe in. For the last year and a bit, I've been examining my beliefs and values. This subject material has been on my mind almost all the time.

Some of the thoughts and feelings I have expressed are personal. They aren't things I go around talking about to the general public. Yet here I am, baring my soul and deeply held personal convictions in a book for anyone to read. That's the nature of the project I guess.

On that note, I want to share what I believe is a relevant personal experience. In the writing of the first draft of this book and in the editing and re-writing process that followed, I have had to apply the principles I've described in this book and take my own advice many times. It's been a great lesson in humility. And I continue to apply the lessons and principles every day in my own life. I never wanted to create the impression that I have all this stuff down-pat. As I said earlier in the book, personal development is an on-going life-long process. To coin a brand new phrase, it's a journey not a destination.

Here's a real-life story that illustrates how I have had to apply the principles I've described in this book. The Universe being what it is, I have been put to the test in recent days. This story is current. At the time of writing, it's still going on, although I can see an end in sight. Last Friday I was working on the book, nearing the end of final edits and re-writes, when I heard a little beep and my computer crashed. This wasn't a little fender-bender, this was a major crash. When I was able to restart the computer, everything was gone. The screen's appearance was what you see with a brand new computer with no programs and no data.

I knew that the manuscript was safe because I had backed it up on a thumb-drive at the end of the session the day before. But everything else was gone. My supporting files for the publisher with text for the covers, and so forth plus all my electronic communication with the publisher were gone. All the records from my home based guitar tech business were gone. All my photographs, recorded music and sheet music, and all my e-mail records were all gone too. I was perturbed. I took the computer to our local shop to see what could be done. This was not a good situation for an author close to submitting his first book for publication.

I found out today that the damage was caused by a computer virus. All the data was recovered but all the operating programs are gone. The virus just hid the files and produced the appearance that the hard-drive was wiped. I will need to buy a new computer, obtain new operating programs, re-load all my data and rebuild from there.

I tell you this story because of how I've had to apply some of my own principles to stay as calm and grounded as possible.

Naturally I have experienced several emotions since the computer crashed, and none of them has been pleasant. Certainly I have felt anger, frustration and resentment, along with some bewilderment...like, just how catastrophic will this be? Regarding the application of the principles, first I had to accept 100% responsibility. I know that a space exists between the event and my response. I know that I made the right choice in not providing my name, address, e-mail address, and credit card number to "update my license" as the virus asked me to do. I didn't cause the virus but I guess I could have been more diligent in upgrading my anti-virus software. I let it slip after I retired. And maybe I opened one too many pop-up windows. So I'm responsible for that and I'm responsible for what I do to recover from the incident.

To cope with my emotional state and worry, I've had to apply some detachment, to make sure that the pesky guys who infected my computer with their virus do not have the power to control my emotional state. I know well that anger bites the angry, and I'm fully aware that the virus perpetrators are not suffering because of my anger. I don't want to suffer from it either. So I'm going to maintain some detachment and manage my own emotional state.

Finally, I decided to offer no resistance. This situation stinks. It has occurred at an extremely inconvenient time. But as Burton Cummings sang in an old Guess Who song[225], it's here and it's real. If you read the section on "Offer No Resistance", you know that it does no good to obsess that the present situation is not as you think it should be. That goes for me too. Everyone's life is filled with little speed-bumps and big frustrations and disappointments. That's part of the human condition. With the principles offered in this book, I have tried to provide some tools to make it a little easier for any of us to cope with some of life's complications. But I want to

---

[225] "Hang Onto Your Life" from The Guess Who album "Share the Land" (1970)

be clear on this fact: I need to apply those principles also. We never know what challenge awaits us around the corner.

Right now I'm typing on Bev's laptop, which she graciously offered me to use, updating the manuscript file that I had backed up on my thumb-drive. In a few minutes I'm going to an evening yoga class. Tomorrow morning I'm going to work on a client's guitar, and then I'm going out to buy a new computer.

My editors offered me perspectives across ranges of experience and differences in gender. I realize that different parts of this book might resonate more with some people and not with others. To me that's not a surprise. The concept was to share what I've learned, from the mundane to the metaphysical. I didn't go into any one topic to exhaustive depth because I'm not a learned expert in any of those topics. Like I said earlier, I'm just a regular guy. But I have been motivated to watch what's going on and learn from my experiences as the years have passed.

In one of my footnotes I said that one of the purposes of the book was to provide the reader with some clues and insights on how they might get into the flow earlier, more often, and for longer periods of time. I don't claim to be in the flow all the time – far from it. After all, I am assaholic and prone to falling victim to my ego and similar conceits. Readers who are particularly astute may have picked up on what I intended to be an overarching metaphor. The same person who wrote about the important principles of Part II still gets annoyed by his neighbours' noisy lawnmowers and weed-trimmers. After participating in all those yoga classes where the teacher reminded us that distracting sounds are just vibrations passing over us, that sounds only become annoying noises when we attach a story and judgement to them, they still bug me.

So after writing this book, I am still aware of my chronic assaholism.

But getting back to being in the flow, I'm pleased to report that now I recognize what it feels like to be in the flow or out of the flow. And honestly, I am in the flow now much more than I used to be. The reason for that is the comprehension and disciplined application of the principles I have described in this book.

If you feel moved to contact me because of something you've read in this book, please do so. I'd like that. If we already know each other, just call or e-mail. If we don't know each other, you can contact me through my publisher. I will get back to you.

Here's a lovely thought to close this little book. This quote comes from one of my yoga teachers, named Carol. She led classes at our local studio during one summer a couple of years ago and then moved on. Carol used to close her yoga classes with this benediction[226], that we take our yoga off the mat into the outside world and our everyday lives by doing these four things:

- Live simply
- Speak kindly
- Care deeply
- Love generously.

May it be that way with you.

---

[226] I used to attend Lutheran services regularly. At the end of the service, our Pastor would send us out into the world with the benediction, "Go in peace and praise the Lord". The yoga teacher's blessing at the end of her class had a similar positive and loving feel to it.

Acknowledgements

Thanks to Gracie, with her irrepressible good spirits and enthusiasm, who's always up for a walk outdoors. That's where I do my best thinking and that's where I came up with a lot of the ideas and illustrations for this book. If it weren't for Gracie, I probably would have stayed indoors more, especially in the winter, and the quality of the book would have suffered for it.

Thanks to my editors for your hard work and insights. The book is better because of you. Thanks to those kind folks who agreed to read my first-draft manuscript and provide dust-jacket quotes. Thanks to Blue Flowing Water Woman for spiritual guidance at the beginning of the project.

Thanks to Uncle Walt, who did more than any pal could realistically be expected to do.

And a big thanks to Bev, for challenging my ideas and positions, and for all the support and encouragement during the difficult stages, and from start to finish. In particular, during the early stages of the editing and re-writing processes, when I struggled in an attempt to incorporate all the suggestions from the editors, Bev reminded me that the book needed to speak with my voice. That was an important reassurance, so thanks for that.

–Mike